THE CRIMINAL RECORD COMPLEX

The Complex. Illustration courtesy of Shana Agid.

The Criminal Record Complex

RISK, RACE, AND THE STRUGGLE
FOR WORK IN AMERICA

MELISSA BURCH

PRINCETON UNIVERSITY PRESS
PRINCETON *&* OXFORD

Published by Princeton University Press
41 William Street, Princeton, New Jersey 08540
99 Banbury Road, Oxford OX2 6JX

press.princeton.edu

GPSR Authorized Representative: Easy Access System Europe - Mustamäe tee 50, 10621 Tallinn, Estonia, gpsr.requests@easproject.com

All Rights Reserved

ISBN 9780691272108
ISBN (e-book) 9780691272115

Library of Congress Control Number: 2025939515

British Library Cataloging-in-Publication Data is available

Editorial: Fred Appel and James Collier
Production Editorial: Jaden Young
Jacket Design: Ben Higgins
Production: Erin Suydam
Publicity: William Pagdatoon
Copyeditor: Cindy Milstein

This book has been composed in Arno

Printed in the United States of America

10 9 8 7 6 5 4 3 2 1

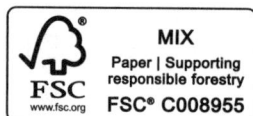

CONTENTS

PREFACE

THIS STUDY was born from a groundswell of organizing, policy, and legal advocacy that blossomed in the early 2000s across the United States to challenge the stigma and discrimination associated with having a criminal record. In California, the former prisoner-led formation All of Us or None conceived a campaign called "Ban the Box," which demanded the removal of the question "Have you ever been convicted?" from applications for employment, housing, higher education, and beyond. Rooted in a civil rights framework and based loosely on a foot-in-the-door logic similar to the American Disabilities Act, the reform aimed to allow people who had been criminalized to compete for opportunities on the basis of their skills and qualifications by delaying decision-makers' access to stigmatizing information.

In 2006, I joined the staff of A New Way of Life Reentry Project, a nonprofit organization dedicated to assisting women coming home from prison in South Los Angeles. Part of my work was to help establish a legal clinic in collaboration with the UCLA School of Law to advocate for people facing employment discrimination on the basis of criminal records.[1] Through the clinic, I began to learn firsthand about the many barriers people faced in the job market. A New Way of Life's founder and then executive director, Susan Burton, was an active member of All of Us or None, thus the organization became a leader in campaigns to advance the first Ban the Box ordinances in Los Angeles.

Though it's hard to fathom now, given Ban the Box's ultimate success in cities across the United States, at the time elected officials in Los Angeles were quite reluctant to enact this modest reform.[2] Their reluctance puzzled us. Ban the Box seemed like precisely the kind of symbolic policy they should jump at the chance to support. It didn't prevent employers from conducting background checks or ultimately refusing to hire a person because of their criminal record. It simply symbolized a commitment to "second chances." As we struggled with little success to persuade the County of Los Angeles Board of Supervisors and Los Angeles City Council to adopt this basic measure, I became ever more driven to understand, What was their reluctance—and by extension, employers' reluctance—really all about?

This book asks how and why we came to be in a situation in which the majority of employers cannot or will not hire people with felony convictions. In order to effectively challenge criminal record discrimination, I believe we need to better understand it, to more deeply comprehend the ideas and motivations that drive, animate, and sustain it.

THE CRIMINAL RECORD COMPLEX

Job seekers in line outside BGM Staffing. Illustration courtesy of Karson Schenk.

Introduction

IN A BUSY commercial plaza in Southern California's Inland Empire—the greater metropolitan region east of Los Angeles—six men and one woman who had recently been released from prison gathered around plastic folding tables for day one of "job-readiness orientation." The program was hosted by the Hub, an organization that since the 1970s, has been helping job seekers with recent felony convictions to find and maintain employment in cities across the United States.

I pulled into the parking lot matching the address I had been given, festively outlined by car-dealership-style red, white, and blue triangle streamers, but had difficulty finding a spot. I soon noted the reason: a long line of smartly dressed twenty- and thirty something-year-olds extending across the Western wear shop and Indian banquet hall to the entrance of "BGM Staffing." This agency, I would soon learn, was charged with hiring workers for a nearby twenty-two-acre retail distribution center that employs approximately one thousand people, and hundreds more during peak holiday periods. With few exceptions, the Hub's eager clients just a few doors down could not qualify for the jobs because of their recent felony convictions. Indeed, the Hub was founded precisely because not all people who need a job can get in a line like BGM's.

Pressing through the tinted glass doors made heavy by the air pressure difference between inside and out, I was greeted by two large posters suspended from the ceiling with long wires—one featuring a group of men working together on a landscaping crew, and the other, a woman embracing her mother. Beneath the posters, a white folding table displayed the day's newspapers, a few organizational brochures, and a freestanding easel for announcements. The space was expansive, approximately fifty by seventy-five feet, and sparsely furnished. Fluorescent lights lined the high ceilings and a tightly-woven forest-green Berber carpet covered the floor.

Glancing to the far end of the room, I spotted Janine, the Hub's regional director and my primary point of contact, seated behind her desk in the corner office, talking on the phone.[1] I took a seat in the most obvious place—a dirty beige sofa next to an artificial fern adjacent to the computer room. Laminated letters spelling "WALL OF FAME" were hung at the computer room's entrance to inspire the dozens of job seekers who would pass by it in the coming year on their way to fix résumés, check email, and run job searches on Craigslist. Glued beneath the letters was a seven-foot tree cut from construction paper from whose branches dangled the names of every "job seeker of the month" as well as the fifty-one men and women who had acquired permanent jobs in the first year of this location's opening. Approximately one hundred more names would be added in the coming year, reflecting the organization's then placement rate of approximately 58 percent.[2]

Before long, the Hub's mid-forties, Hispanic job coach, Jorge, invited me to join the new cohort in the conference room where he was leading the job-readiness orientation.[3] Taking a seat at the table, I asked lightly, "How was the commute?" The replies were sobering. Gary had taken three buses, having left his home in Colton at 5:00 a.m. in order to reliably arrive by 9:30 a.m., even though Colton was only a few miles away. Brian had ridden his bike four miles to reach a direct bus line. Roshaun, Courtney, and Jaime had each taken two buses. Ronaldo had driven all the way from Victorville—a journey that takes somewhere between ninety minutes and two hours depending on the time of day. Jamal stayed quiet. Having arrived in just forty minutes, door-to-door, in the comfort of my newly acquired Toyota Camry, I vowed never again to complain about traffic.

Gary, white and male with short white hair, was likely the eldest, somewhere in his sixties. He had been imprisoned for a little more than ten years. Gary's last work experience had involved leading teams to set up and tear down booths at convention centers and other event venues. Prior to this, he had worked in warehouses. He enjoyed the events trade, but as he explained, the work was physically demanding, and both the passage of time and toll of prison meant that he was now far from the physical condition he used to take for granted. The other obstacle to returning to events work was that the jobs are by definition irregular and the hours long, and Gary now had to be at mandatory drug and alcohol counseling every day at 5:00 p.m. as a condition of his parole. Additionally, he needed a pass from his parole officer, even for local travel. As a person with a sex-related conviction and on the sex offender registry, even after completing parole, Gary's movement would forever be monitored and restricted.[4] He would need to find a job with set hours and location. The nearby Ashley Furniture warehouse or the warehouse for Friendly Dollar the major bargain retail chain, he figured, would be ideal.

Brian, light-skinned, Latino, and in his mid-twenties, was the youngest of the group, and the only one in the cohort who had never really had a job. He had recently applied for a service job with a trucking company. The manager said he met the qualifications, but then asked if he had any convictions. When Brian replied that he was "fresh out of prison," the manager gave him a funny look and said he couldn't give him the job because it meant being behind the counter with the cash register, though Brian's conviction had nothing to do with money or dishonesty. On another occasion, Brian told the group, an employer had asked directly what exactly the conviction was for, to which Brian had simply replied, "A 192(a)." "The manager asked me what that was," Brian recounted. "I said, voluntary manslaughter and his eyes got real big and he was like, OH!!"

Jorge took the opportunity for a teaching moment. "Part of the training will be learning to talk about the conviction, without saying the penal code or the name of the conviction—these are off-putting."

Roshaun, an African American man in his mid-thirties, had come to the Hub when he became discouraged going it alone in the job market. Most recently, he told the group, he had interviewed at Pizza Hut and a regional chain by the name of Lucille's. At Pizza Hut, he had stumbled in his responses to the manager's performative prompt: "Show us how you would sell a pizza." Lucille's had been eager to interview him, he said, but wanted to do so at 7:00 a.m. in the city of Ontario, an impossibility by bus. Since his release from prison, Roshaun had been searching for jobs in the restaurant industry, but despite his experience as a cook with several major restaurant chains, he was not catching a break. The Hub, as he understood it, provided mentoring, training, and support to its job-seeking clients, and most important, would lend its reputation and connections in the business world.

Courtney, an African American single mother of two, had been pursuing her certified nurse aide license prior to imprisonment. On release, she had sent a letter along with her fingerprints to the California Board of Registered Nursing. It replied that her felony conviction, which had been classified as violent, prevented her from obtaining the license. After further communication, the board determined that because her conviction was not related to nursing, she could eventually nurse again, but not until completing her parole. She would have to look for something else in the meantime to support herself and her kids.

Jaime, a Latino in his early forties, had worked as a construction journey-man prior to imprisonment. He was accustomed to working and making good money, having begun his career in concrete construction during summer breaks back in high school. "I've never been on an interview," he told the group, somewhat boastfully. "For construction, you just show up and talk to the foreman.[5] Plus, I've always been working." On his release from prison a few months prior (having been incarcerated a little less than two years), Jaime had tried his usual job-seeking methodology: he'd headed straight to an active jobsite, talked to the foreman, and got himself hired. There was a euphoric sense of freedom to being back at work, he said, but after three days, the com-pany discovered he was on parole and asked him to leave. This was somewhat surprising given the construction industry's reputation as "felony friendly." The foreman encouraged Jaime to return to the job once he was off parole. The problem, it seemed, was not that they didn't trust him, and certainly not that they didn't like his work, but rather that a company policy prohibited hiring people on parole. The experience humiliated Jaime, and he worried that it might recur if he continued to go it alone in the job market. Setting aside his aversion to associating with a program for "ex-cons," he had swallowed his pride and enrolled at the Hub.[6]

Ronaldo, short, strong, brown-skinned, and by far the sharpest dresser, ar-rived each day at the Hub in freshly pressed khakis and a polo shirt, tucked in with a belt. While guys with a history in construction tended to feel uncom-fortable with the Hub's professional dress requirement, he didn't seem to mind. Ronaldo had more than a decade of fence installation experience—chain-link, wood, cast iron, you name it. If you needed a fence, Ronaldo was your guy. He also had general construction skills, but fencing was what he liked best. Ronaldo had spent thirteen years in prison. He was married to a woman who worked as a manager at a nearby company that made parts for military airplanes. His old boss had been giving him odd jobs since he got out of prison and would have been glad to take Ronaldo back, but most of the contracts he was getting were through the State of California, which required extensive background checks. "The crazy thing is," Ronaldo told the group, "I can actually pass the checks because I don't have a drug or sex-related con-viction." As he explained, however, the mere fact of having a conviction trig-gered a process so onerous and time-consuming that his boss, a small business owner with minimal administrative capacity, just couldn't do it.[7]

Finally, Jamal, dark-skinned, African American, and exceptionally quiet, was only in his late thirties, but had been incarcerated the longest—sixteen years. This sentence was meted out near the end of the 1990s, when the United States' reliance on imprisonment was marching vigorously toward its zenith. Black men in particular were disproportionately targeted for imprisonment, and the courts gave them longer sentences than their white counterparts.[8] Despite the long time in prison, Jamal's job history was fairly robust. As a young man, he had managed an Applebee's restaurant and also worked several years as a medical technician in a psychiatric hospital.

———

This book argues that decisions to hire or not hire people with criminal records have less to do with employers' personal attitudes or beliefs, and more to do with the contexts in which they make hiring decisions. One significant and underexamined part of that context is the emergence of a "criminal record complex," a set of public and private interests that encourages the exclusion of people with criminal records in the name of protecting businesses and organizations against risk. To develop this argument, *The Criminal Record Complex* chronicles daily interactions between employers, workforce development professionals, and job seekers with recent felony convictions in the Inland Empire, analyzing how, why, and under what circumstances discriminatory decisions based on criminal records get made.

When this research began in 2014, 80 percent of the Hub's clients were categorized as male. The majority were between the ages of twenty-six and forty-five. Twenty percent were under the age of twenty-six, and 15 percent over the age of forty-five. All participants had been convicted of felony offenses—45 percent with convictions classified as "violent," and 11 percent as sex related. Although these classifications do not necessarily accurately reflect (much less contextualize) actual events, they nonetheless sound alarming to the lay ear.[9] These people had come to the Hub in hopes that the organization could help them find work quickly. Most had been referred to the program by parole officers and case managers; others had asked permission to participate after having become discouraged by going it alone on the job market.

Jorge explained the basics of the Hub's four-pronged social enterprise program model. The next few days would be devoted to résumé preparation; Friday would involve training for the organization's transitional work crew. Next week, they would be employed three days per week for up to seventy-five days through a landscaping contract brokered between the Hub and a city government. This arrangement would allow them to earn an immediate income of ten dollars per hour and build recent work experience. On the off days, they would participate in job-readiness coaching, including online job search and interview training, and begin looking for permanent work. When deemed "job ready," Jorge would assign them to one of the Hub's "job developers"—professionals charged with cultivating and connecting people to job opportunities—who would feed them leads and support them in a range of ways to become and remain employed. Although the majority would ultimately succeed, all would struggle in various ways to find work. Many would graciously allow me to observe and document those struggles.

Criminal Record Employment Discrimination

People with criminal records who are looking for work in the United States face a stark reality: finding work is an urgent priority, but many employers cannot or will not hire them.[10] Although the precise percentage of US businesses conducting criminal background checks is difficult to quantify, since at least the mid-2000s, most have done so as a matter of routine and used the information in the process of selecting competitive candidates.[11]

This was not always the case. Prior to the 1970s, a prospective employer would not likely even have known about a past conviction. Records of arrest and prosecution were collected as well as consulted primarily by police for the purposes of policing and criminal justice. Criminal background checks were rare in employment contexts, reserved only for positions of significant public trust.[12] Within a span of just forty years, criminal background screening grew from a tool unique to law enforcement to a widespread practice in employment, rental housing, college admissions, volunteering, and personal life.

Today, even a minor criminal record such as an arrest or misdemeanor conviction can trigger significant consequences in the job market.[13] Most acutely impacted are the 610,000 people released from state and federal prisons each year, whose level of joblessness is about 60 percent, and the nearly 20 million people with convictions classified as felonies, whose average annual income is about $7,000 less than people with similar levels of education who lack criminal records.[14]

That 80 million US adults (1 in 3) have a record of prior arrests, convictions, dismissed charges, or charges pending is the result of the United States' unprecedented escalation of the use of surveillance, policing, and aggressive criminal prosecution that began in the 1970s.[15] Whereas throughout the 1900s until the early 1970s, the United States held less than 200,000 adults in prison or jail (approximately 96 people per 100,000), as of 2024, there were 1.9 million people imprisoned or jailed (approximately 531 per 100,000), and an additional 3.7 million on probation or parole.[16] These globally and historically unprecedented numbers led scholars as well as activists to decry an era of "mass incarceration," "mass conviction," "mass probation," and "mass supervision."[17]

Yet describing a phenomenon as "mass" can downplay its targeted nature.[18] As of 2022, the average rate of Black imprisonment was 911 per 100,000, nearly five times the rate of white imprisonment (911 per 100,000 versus 188 per 100,000). Data collected in 2011 showed that compared to 8 percent of the US population, 23 percent of African Americans have a felony conviction. When comparing only men, the disparity was that much starker: 33 percent of adult African American men have a conviction classified as a felony, versus 13 percent of all adult US men.[19] American Indians are imprisoned at a rate quadruple that of whites (801 per 100,000), and people of Latin descent at a rate double that of whites (426 per 100,000).[20] Women's imprisonment rates have grown at twice the pace of men's for at least the past two decades, and Black women are especially overrepresented.[21] As for socioeconomic status, the median annual incomes of people who get sent to prison are 41 percent lower than non-incarcerated people of similar ages at the time of their incarceration.[22] People who have been imprisoned are nearly twice as likely to have no high school credential and are eight times less likely to complete college.[23]

But it's not just that *rates* of imprisonment and felony conviction are unevenly distributed; it's that their impacts are unevenly felt. While having been incarcerated has a negative impact on unemployment for all groups, studies of employment outcomes since the early 2000s have shown that employers repeatedly choose white male applicants with criminal records over Black male applicants with criminal records.[24] Those parsing gender show that women with criminal records are generally more detrimentally affected in the job market than men, and that women who have been imprisoned tend to get hired at lower rates than men who have been imprisoned.[25] This is partly because concern about convictions is more pronounced in positions more often occupied by women, such as those involving customer contact or office work, and because women tend to dominate key industries in which criminal background checks are required by law, such as childcare, education, and health care.[26] As I will discuss shortly, however, it is also related to long-in-the-making gendered and racialized ideas about criminality.

Somewhat counterintuitively, then, in "absolute terms," the negative economic effects of imprisonment are most visible among white people with substantial preprison work histories.[27] However, as others have noted, to observe that groups with more advantage in the job market have the most to lose is not the same as reasoning that the effect of imprisonment on their job prospects is therefore greater.[28] At the end of the day, Black formerly incarcerated women experience the highest levels of unemployment (43.6 percent), while formerly incarcerated white men experience the lowest (18.4 percent).[29] It is a basic argument of this book that use of criminal records in employment decisions represents one of the most important contemporary processes exacerbating inequalities along lines of class, race, and gender in the United States.

This problem is not limited to the United States, however. Though the widespread public availability of criminal records in the United States is unmatched in other Western countries, and criminal record-based restrictions and disqualifications are more extensive, long-lasting, and severe, there are nuances to this exceptionalism as well as signs that it may be shifting.[30] For example, in Europe, where public access to government criminal record databases has been strictly limited, employment discrimination based on criminal records is still permitted, and the number and scope of state-sponsored limitations appears to be growing. Evidence also suggests that US-style commercial providers of criminal record data have begun to emerge, finding ways to work around privacy restrictions.[31]

In recent decades, public leaders in the United States have attempted to mitigate the systemic unemployment of people with criminal convictions in a variety of ways. Most significant, in 2012, the spotlight created by the Ban the Box movement prompted the federal Equal Employment Opportunity Commission (EEOC) to update its *Enforcement Guidance on the Consideration of Arrest and Conviction Records in Employment Decisions*.[32] The agency had long reasoned that because Black and Latino/a peoples are disproportionately represented in rates of arrest, conviction, and imprisonment, to deny jobs on the basis of criminal history may have a racially disparate impact.[33] The new policy sought to reduce these disparities by prohibiting blanket exclusions such as "no felonies," and instead required employers to conduct "individualized assessments" of applicant's criminal records, taking into consideration the nature and gravity of the conduct, time passed since the conduct, and/or completion of sentence as well as the "nexus" between the nature of the conviction and the job duties.[34] Initial difficulties with enforcement notwithstanding, a number of successful lawsuits directed at high-profile companies discriminating on the basis of criminal records drove home the possibility of being held accountable, causing many employers to revisit their policies.[35]

Ban the Box policies also proliferated across the country. In 2013, then California governor Jerry Brown directed all government employers to remove conviction questions from their applications and delay background checks until it was determined that an applicant had satisfied the "minimum employment qualifications" for the position. In 2015, US president Barak Obama followed suit, removing conviction questions from applications for federal employment. Many cities and counties also implemented far-reaching "Fair Chance" policies requiring more uniform as well as transparent processes and procedures, including delaying inquiries about criminal records and background checks until after conditional job offers have been made. In some places, these policies also apply to employers in the private sector. As of this writing, Ban the Box and Fair Chance initiatives have been implemented 37 states and over 150 cities and counties across the United States.[36]

Despite these successes, however, widespread and pernicious discrimination persists. While some evidence suggests that employment outcomes for people with criminal convictions have improved, research using a range of methods and in different parts of the United States has shown that many employers misunderstand as well as deliberately ignore Ban the Box and Fair Chance regulations, do not use the EEOC guidance criteria, and/or have implemented the most visible procedural requirements while leaving the substantive aspects of their hiring practices unchanged.[37] Even in California— home to the most sweeping legislation regulating the private sector use of criminal records ever enacted in the United States—a recent study of Inland Empire employers found that roughly 75 percent of hiring decision-makers were still unwilling to seriously consider an applicant with a drug, property, or conviction classified as violent. In direct violation of the Fair Chance act, nearly 80 percent continue to consider criminal history prior to a conditional offer of employment.[38]

You see, even if education and enforcement were undertaken and employers could somehow be made to comply with the letter—or even spirit—of the law, a great deal of discrimination would still be taking place. This is because nothing in the law ultimately prohibits employers from rejecting someone on the basis of a criminal record. In fact, many state and federal laws *require* exclusion.[39] The law thus maintains an uneasy straddling of the idea that criminal record discrimination is, on the one hand, incompatible with the goals of rehabilitation and reintegration, and on the other, sometimes warranted. This wishy-washy stance—allowing while simultaneously discouraging discrimination—not only generates on-the-ground confusion; it requires employers to hold two incompatible ideas side by side: discrimination based on criminal status may be unjust, yet is justified. Confusion is further compounded by procedural reforms that have not so much worked to eliminate discrimination as to make it more consistent and orderly.

From Sentiment to Systems

Common explanations of employers' aversion to hiring people with criminal records tend to focus on perceived risks: the idea that bringing people with criminal records into the workplace increases businesses' exposure to liability, reputational damage, financial loss, or worksite violence. Though little evidence supports the notion that criminalized people introduce increased risk to the workplace, studies have shown that employers fear being held legally responsible for the actions of their employees, feel obligated to minimize risk and discomfort for other employees, and are broadly concerned about public reputation and customer perception.[40] Despite a lack of correlation between the type of crime and likelihood of subsequent participation in criminal activity—even for crimes considered serious—evidence suggests that employers are especially concerned about bringing people with certain types of convictions into their organizations, particularly those classified as violent or sex related.[41] Some explanations of employer aversion emphasize the role of stigma: employers' negative perceptions of and attitudes toward people who have been criminalized.[42] Studies supporting a stigma thesis have found that employers view job candidates with criminal records as untrustworthy or unreliable, and may associate a criminal record with negative characteristics including tardiness, absenteeism, drug and alcohol problems, and inability to get along with coworkers.[43] Stigma theses have also explored the ways unfavorable ideas about criminality intersect with negative ideas about race to produce doubly negative employment outcomes for Black criminalized job seekers.[44]

The job market experiences elaborated in the coming chapters in many ways affirm these interpretations of employer behavior. We will see that there is no shortage of prejudice against people who have been criminalized, nor a shortage of racial bias, and the idea that it's risky to hire someone with a criminal record circulates widely. As I made my way further into the private sector world of work, however, it became ever more apparent that the problem of criminal record employment discrimination was not merely the outcome of individual employers' attitudes, perceptions, concerns, or beliefs. While the worldviews and personal backgrounds of business owners and hiring managers certainly informed how they related to the applicants they interviewed, sentiments and ideas simply weren't the main factor accounting for many of the hiring decisions I witnessed.

Rather than conceive of individual bias or racism as motivating hiring decisions, this study draws attention to the underlying systems, structures, and vested interests that shape employer's ideas and practices. Sociologist Lori Freedman's study of physicians' willingness to provide abortion care provides a useful parallel. Just as Freedman found that decisions to provide or not provide abortion have more to do with constraints resulting from the financial restructuring of medicine than with personal attitudes regarding abortion, I found the distinction between employers who hired people with criminal records and those who did not derived more from structural conditions than from "unwillingness" or "aversion." To adapt Freedman's helpful phrasing, while openness to hiring people with criminal records may be a necessary precondition for inclusive hiring, it is alone insufficient.[45]

Watching job seekers interact with employers revealed dozens of scenarios in which hiring managers and business owners *wanted* to hire or promote the Hub's clients, but did not do so because someone with more authority in their human resources (HR) department or legal team would not approve it, their company had agreed to a general liability policy that precluded it, or a legal statute prohibited people with convictions from the role. Though it is important to note that such policies are not always as fixed as employers perceive or portray, busy employers without a particular investment in hiring people with convictions often simply accept restrictions at face value, without taking time to further investigate or negotiate.[46]

For example, Ronaldo's old boss in the fencing business absolutely would have rehired him but for the State of California's Michelle Montoya School Safety Act, which requires school districts to obtain criminal background checks on all employees prior to hiring, including the employees of businesses that contract with school districts for janitorial, administrative, landscape, transportation, and food related services, and prohibits any person who has ever been convicted of a "serious" or "violent" felony from being employed by a school district in any capacity.[47] Likewise, Courtney was rejected not by her home health employer or its clients but instead by the California Board of Registered Nursing, which reserves the right to disqualify any applicant with a criminal conviction within the past seven years as well as any applicant with a "serious felony" (regardless of timing) from obtaining a nursing license.

Recall too that Jaime's foreman wanted him on the construction site, but company policies beyond his immediate control prevailed. A concern with criminal records, I noticed, did not often seem to derive from employers' own reasoning or experiences.

A focus on individual employer's perspectives is reasonable given the tremendous discretionary power afforded them in the United States. But an overemphasis on personal viewpoint can reinforce the problematic idea that actions are the unfettered manifestation of the stuff in people's heads, or that people discriminate only or primarily *because* they harbor biased ideas.[48] Not only is the correlation between thoughts and behavior less strong than we may imagine, as sociolegal scholar Amanda M. Petersen underscores, an individual-level, psychologically based approach focused on "single decision points" tends to downplay the institutional, historical, and systemic factors shaping those decisions.[49] While researchers and advocates continually default to the ideas of employer "unwillingness" and "bias," I believe we need to shift the lens beyond this bad actor framing to the external risk policies, practices, and logics that play a huge role in shaping employers' ideas and decisions. Observing daily interactions between hiring managers, criminalized job seekers, and workforce development professionals in the Inland Empire taught me that hiring is much more than an individual-to-individual exchange.

The Racial Risk Economics of Criminal Records

There was a glaring irony in the Hub's location, a stone's throw from a busy staffing center where the vast majority of its job-seeking clients could not get hired.[50] Although a handful of Hub clients succeeded in getting jobs at the warehouse, they were hired through a different staffing agency that handled the janitorial services and did not have a felony conviction barrier.[51] It was not lost on anyone at the Hub that the jobs at BGM Staffing next door began at eleven dollars per hour, while the cleaning jobs paid nine (California's then minimum wage). This proximate juxtaposition of people doing comparable work for different rates of pay provided a constant reminder of two job markets: one for first-tier candidates and another for the disparaged second. Equally telling, however, was that the so-called first-tier jobs paid only eleven dollars per hour.[52] Indeed, people with criminal records join labor markets long stratified by differentially valued labor; their criminalization merely intensifies this stratification.

Criminalization produces people willing to work for the lowest wage—simultaneously justifying jobs that pay nine dollars per hour and naturalizing the idea that a good job pays eleven. This tiered labor market with criminalized and racialized people at the bottom can be traced to capitalism's larger history of making risk profitable and criminalizing populations seen as lacking value, posing a danger, or otherwise getting in the way.

———

Histories of capitalism reveal how the astonishing generation of wealth in the nineteenth-century United States was a product of not only human labor but also commercial risk taking and the commodification of those risks. Indeed risk itself became a capital.[53] Whether the commodity was fish, timber, rum, indigo, rice, cotton, European indentured servants, or enslaved Africans, protection against potential losses (insurance) played a key role in global trade— so much so, writes historian Jonathan Levy, that the Atlantic slave trade "would have been impractical without [it]."[54] Just as the construction of racial difference became central to capitalism's development, in this context of maritime sea voyaging, slavery and plantation economies, race generally and Blackness in particular became foundational to risk management's logic.[55] Throughout the twentieth century, racialized notions of risk permeated a range of social structures serving capitalist development, becoming a key variable in actuarial assessment criteria for health and life insurance, property value assessment, banking and lending, credit scoring, and government programs.[56]

Notions of *criminal risk* and the treatment of particular people, activities, and communities as criminal have played key roles in the pursuit of profit. Since the earliest days of conquest and colonization, criminalizing systems have been deployed to contain, control, and disappear populations deemed unwanted, unneeded, or threatening to pursuits of wealth and power. For example, during the United States' westward expansion, criminalization and incarceration served as central strategies for the elimination of Indigenous people along with the containment of poor white itinerant men, Chinese immigrants, and Mexican radicals seen as threatening to the colony.[57] Newly emancipated Black people were actively constructed as criminal and treated as especially threatening.[58] In the US South, the practice of hanging was used as a tool to maintain the racial economic order, by primarily targeting upwardly mobile Black people who were acquiring wealth and property, while the chain gang system reinforced gendered and racialized ideas about who should do what kinds of work.[59] During and after Reconstruction, a range of laws restricting the rights and privileges of people with convictions served to control free Black peoples' movement, coerce their labor, and prevent their participation in elections.[60]

This targeted criminalization both relied on and reinforced the idea that Black people had a special propensity toward crime. Historians have detailed how, in the context following emancipation, social scientists leveraged statistical data and Darwinian evolutionary theory to raise questions about Black humanity as well as appropriateness for citizenship, touting high Black arrest and imprisonment rates as proof of cultural deficiency and inherent criminality.[61] Prominent criminal anthropologists such as Cesare Lombroso conducted pseudoscientific bodily measurements, germinating the idea that criminals were an inferior biological "type" who could be identified and monitored.[62] Despite the efforts of trailblazing activist-scholars like W. E. B. Du Bois, Franz Boas, and Ida B. Wells to refute this logic with empirical evidence, the idea took hold that African American crime was rooted in biology, in contrast to an understanding of crime committed by European immigrants and working-class whites as rooted in environment and condition.[63] These ideas were also gendered. Whereas white women were generally viewed as pure, submissive, domestic, and therefore incapable of serious criminality, Black and Indigenous women were constructed as defiant, undomestic, immoral, and unfeminine, rendering them unrecognizable as true "victims," and heightening their vulnerability to both interpersonal and state-based male violence.[64]

In the 1970s, methods aiming to *predict* criminal risk began to grow in popularity, along with a broader shift in philosophies of criminal management away from treatment and reintegration, and toward punishment and incapacitation. Control techniques became animated less by desires to observe, evaluate, or rehabilitate individuals, and more by efforts to classify, categorize, and manage according to the perceived likelihood of "reoffending."[65] Through this "actuarial turn," statistical and other probability methods were increasingly used to determine surveillance and policing priorities, set bail policies, specify sentence length, and consider eligibility for release from prison.[66] In these statistical calculations, a prior criminal record came to serve as the principal proxy for the prediction of future crime.[67] By recoding the fact of having been convicted as the key indicator of future threat, actuarial tools folded systemic vulnerabilities into seemingly value-neutral criteria, marking people as permanently criminal and justifying the perpetual management of their "riskiness."[68] When background checks emerged as gatekeeping mechanisms in the economy, they singled out workers with criminal records as less desirable, allowing for greater exploitation and control.

The Criminal Record Complex

Sometimes the things that strike us in the field are the least spectacular. A few months into the field research, one of the Hub's job developers, Sasha, invited me to ride along with her to a rural part of San Bernardino County. Without a particular destination in mind, Sasha sometimes liked to search for job leads by just driving around and stopping at busy-looking establishments that matched the skills or interests of her current caseload to ask whether they were hiring. Entering the commercial strip of a small town named Yucaipa, we stopped to inquire about possible job openings at several establishments, including a small welding shop (several Hub clients were enrolled in a welding class through a community college), and with Roshaun in mind, a restaurant. Winding along a back road off the main drag, we spotted a help wanted sign outside a bakery. Encouraged, we stepped inside the storefront, filled with the pleasant aroma of fresh pastries. I hung back while Sasha approached the woman at the front counter. "Good morning! We noticed you're hiring," she began. "Could you tell us a little bit about what you're looking for?" The clerk was friendly. "Right now we need another baker, someone with kitchen experience who doesn't mind the early shifts." Sasha continued to chat her up, asking questions like, How long have you been in business? Family owned? Do you bake for supermarkets or is it mostly walk-ins? How should someone apply?

Then as she was so good at doing somewhere in the flow of the conversation, Sasha slipped in the crucial question: "By the way, do you guys do background checks?"

"Funny you ask," the woman replied. "We've never bothered, but I guess we're about to start because the new payroll company we just hired includes it as part of the package."

Having internalized the individual-level and attitude-focused frameworks described earlier, my initial foray into the business community was, in hindsight, something of a search for individual "excluders"—employers denying applicants out of deeply held biases about crime and race—and "includers"—employers hiring out of progressive beliefs or goodwill. Yet in this moment at the bakery, I witnessed how, through the banal administrative practice of payroll, the managers of this small business on a country road—heretofore unconvinced of the need for criminal background screening—would soon be conducting checks on all new hires as a matter of routine.[69] Through interactions like these, I came to see how a narrow focus on employers as individuals detracts from our understanding of the broader processes, institutions, and practices that structure employment. In this story that I had presumed would be about two actors—employers and job seekers—a third always seemed to be in the room.

As I elaborate fully in chapter 2, the shift in the bakery's hiring processes can be traced to the creation of systems of criminal identification by private police agencies in the late 1800s as part of their efforts to protect mines, factories, railways, warehouses, banks, and other capitalist enterprises.[70] During the early 1900s, the use of these records grew among judges, wardens, doctors, and other professionals working inside prisons and other parts of the legal system, while during the Cold War and McCarthy periods in the 1940s and 1950s, governments and large organizations turned to background checks as a way of demonstrating loyalty and legitimacy.[71] In response to radical political organizing in the 1960s and 1970s, police expanded the scope and volume of the intelligence and investigative data they were collecting, while emerging technologies facilitated the digital integration and automation of new databases, and improved systems for sharing criminalization data among law enforcement agencies.[72]

At the same time, legislatures were laying the foundation for discrimination by enacting an increasing number of statutes excluding people with convictions from accessing public benefits such as student loans, subsidized housing, and food stamps; removing voting, parental, and other civic participation rights; and restricting criminalized people from working for public agencies, under government contract, and in particular industries and professions.[73] They did so both through direct statute and by preventing access to occupational and professional licenses, business permits, and other credentials.[74] "Moral panics," defined by cultural studies pioneer Stuart Hall and collaborators as situations wherein "the official reaction to a person, groups of persons or series of events is *out of all proportion* to the actual threat offered," also ratcheted up the perceived need for background checks.[75] In particular, moral panics around child protection in the 1980s and 1990s grew the number of occupations in which checks were not only allowed but often *required* and tethered to a stunning number of state-mandated restrictions.[76] Legislatures granted access to more and more users outside the criminal legal system, and more of the data were becoming available online.[77] Courts had been slowly expanding the scope of employers' liability for the actions of their employees, and in the late 1990s, when a handful of dramatic incidences of workplace violence resulted in multimillion dollar lawsuits, employers began to fear that failing to conduct background checks might expose them to undue financial risk.[78]

In this already intense climate of blame and litigiousness, the terrorist attacks of September 11, 2001, unleashed a tidal wave of racialized fear, shifting the lens of criminal risk toward Muslims, Arabs, and others perceived as such, and heightening the perceived need for tools to guard against potential threats.[79] Building on the foundations laid by policy and law, a commercial background screening industry blossomed to meet—and stoke—the newfound demand for background checks. Private firms flooded the market, working to turn criminal record data into a product for sale that could move quickly into the hands of end users.[80] With the support of professional experts in employment law and HR management to provide advice, information, and support, private screening firms took the practice to scale, making it possible for anyone who wanted to conduct criminal background checks to do so easily, cheaply, and efficiently. With racialized risk management as an animating force, the idea that harm could be prevented through background screening was aggressively promoted—a notion that was hugely useful and profitable for some.

I name this convergence of public and private interests that initially motivated, and now drives and sustains, the use of criminal background checks "the criminal record complex." These interests include state institutions such as police, courts, legislatures, government agencies, and regulatory boards; risk industries such as insurance, risk modeling, and background screening; and fields of expertise such as HR management, employment law, and workplace security. Through the creation of policies, laws, practices, and products promising to buffer businesses and organizations against risk, this assemblage of actors, institutions, and industries reinforces the idea that people with criminal records are inherently risky. In various ways, these entities stand to gain from the inaccurate assessment that people with criminal records are dangerous to employ.

My development of this concept draws its analytics explicitly from the well-known (though often misconstrued) concept "prison industrial complex." Popularized at the historic 1998 Critical Resistance conference in Berkeley, California, in the face of the United States' globally unprecedented prison boom, the term aimed to illuminate and critique the overlapping private and public interests driving police, surveillance, and prison expansion.[81] Activists and scholars highlighted how this reliance was propelled not by rising crime but instead an ensemble of actors whose motivations ranged from the concrete and obvious—prison guard unions seeking job security—to the more abstract—states' seeking to maintain legitimacy by appearing to provide security.[82] Naming a criminal record complex as a key node of a broader prison industrial complex, makes an argument that criminal background screening has little to do with creating safe workplaces or communities, and rather exists for the sake of those invested in the practice.[83] It is a strategy, to borrow sociologist David Garland's phrasing, that has been adopted not because it is known to solve problems but instead because it can "characterize problems and identify solutions in ways that fit with the dominant culture and the power structure upon which it rests."[84] This framing also joins the struggle over criminal records to the political vision and social movement to end the reliance on surveillance, policing, and imprisonment, and create lasting alternatives to punishment and control.[85] Given their wide availability, digital permanence, and state-sanctioned discriminatory power, criminal records are a linchpin of this reliance.

The Criminal Record Complex reveals how in a business climate characterized by fear and litigation, hiring decisions are increasingly shaped by the logics of preventative risk management that employers did not invent, and do not necessarily share. By unsettling common understandings of discrimination as mainly a problem of individual prejudice, and attending to the ways actuarial risk structures become embedded in everyday practices and organizations, this book furthers an understanding of how social marginalization gets reproduced through practices that appear necessary, rational, and value neutral.

An emphasis on the political and economic does not discount the role of discretion, or imply that employers' personal beliefs and values are not important; the two are of course interconnected and mutually reinforcing. My argument is simply that too much weight has been placed on the role of individual employer's subjectivity, and not enough on the broader forces shaping their ideas and constraining their choices.

It was my observation that most employers who conducted background checks did so out of a knee-jerk assumption that they are a good thing to do. By asking how criminal background screening became a mainstream and routine practice—a common feature on the menu of payroll packages—I interrogate rather than take this common sense for granted. *The Criminal Record Complex* casts doubt on the underlying assumption that criminal records provide a useful sorting mechanism. It questions their ability to sort suitable from unsuitable workers, to reflect people's essential character, or to accurately divide the world into good people and bad.[86]

Activist Research and the Politics of Method

I never wanted to write a book that would simply document how hard it is to find work with a criminal record. While there is value in putting to words the challenges people are experiencing, as a political intervention, I felt this kind of approach would rely on the liberal logic of "caring" that my data were demonstrating to be somewhat irrelevant. Rather than aim to change hearts and minds, I endeavored—with all the idealism of an organizer turned grad student (smile)—to discover something new that could be useful for challenging criminal record discrimination. I believed ethnography—with its power to illuminate how big systems work in daily practice, the details of how policies are enacted, and how practices are understood and felt by those experiencing them—could help.

The idea that anthropology could, and even *ought to*, serve as a tool of liberation was cultivated and taught to me by activist anthropologists at the University of Texas at Austin.[87] In that spirit and tradition, this study aimed to translate the most basic strategic question at the core of the social movement—What will it take to change this reality?—into the kinds of questions that could be answered through social scientific research. Like other scholars working at the intersection of employment and criminal records, I too began from a willingness framework: Why are so many employers unwilling to hire someone with a criminal record? Why, in the face of pervasive discrimination, are some willing? Over time, my engagements in the business community helped me recast these questions to the more pertinent: What makes exclusion and exploitation possible, and likely?[88]

Several important conversations helped me to develop these questions and design the research methodology. An early conversation with King Davis, then director of the Institute for Urban Policy at the University of Texas at Austin helped build my confidence in the importance of the distinction between employers who hire and don't hire people with conviction records. Identifying just one or two factors differentiating the two groups, he suggested, could be a crucial contribution. A conversation with one of the Hub's regional directors confirmed that even workforce development organizations know little about what differentiates employers who hire from those that don't. This director stressed that in his experience, however, most employers fall into neither of these camps; they are much more malleable than the hire / not hire binary portrays. He believed nuancing this monolithic picture could be enormously significant. Other leaders at the Hub were particularly interested to know more about who and what influences employers. They believed liability insurance to be a major driver of adverse decisions, especially for large corporations, but the details, such as what exactly increases or is believed to increase an employer's exposure, were less clear. They also wondered about the sources of employer's information about exposure to liability—how and with whom employers think through what they hear.

Not everyone embraced my research questions. For example, while job seekers at the Hub were generally receptive to my agenda, which they perceived as sympathetic to their challenges, they did not necessarily understand or agree with the basic premises of the research. Rather than share my concern with discrimination, they tended to emphasize their own responsibility to represent themselves well and prove to employers that they were truly trying to make a change in their lives. They self-criticized, remarking, "advocates can't be out there trying to persuade employers to take a chance on us if we're not doing what we need to do," and blamed the problem of discrimination on "a few bad apples ruining it for the rest of us." For some, discrimination seemed so commonsensical, so thoroughly justified, they did not even understand the need for investigation. "But Melissa, don't some employers not want to hire us because we're felons?"

Similarly, some reentry and workforce development professionals found my framing overly focused on employers. For example, when I explained to Jerome Smith, the African American leader of a local youth organization, that the ultimate goal of my research was to contribute to a change in how people with criminal records are viewed and considered by employers (a goal I assumed he would share), he almost yelled, "Have you run a logic model on this? You can't force employers to hire them, they have to figure it out! We need to get offenders to quit going to jail. Reform jails, not employers."

From Smith's perspective, the problem was crime and the socioeconomic conditions that produce it, not discrimination on the basis of criminal status. Energy would be better directed toward preventing people from going to prison in the first place through economic development and community investment—a focus of his organization. Smith and others rejected liberal approaches seeking to persuade power holders to "care" about the issue of reentry or see criminalized people in a different light. They made blunt comments like, "People think you don't have to reoffend. They don't understand or believe in social inequality." These and other rejections of my research lens were welcome, if uncomfortable, provocations that provided opportunities to push my thinking.

There were a number of reasons to locate the research in the Inland Empire as opposed to Los Angeles, where I was more familiar with the context and better connected. The first had to do with an observation shared by sociologist Katherine Beckett, based on her experience studying employers' and landlords' use of criminal records in Seattle.[89] Beckett explained how Seattle's politically correct and legally aware environment had encumbered her ability to collect meaningful data. At the end of the day, she said, "employers don't want to tell you what they are thinking or doing unless it's perfect, and then it's boring." As a region known for political and social conservatism, I hoped the Inland Empire would be a place where people would more freely express and enact racially bigoted, illegal, and otherwise unpolitically correct views, thus making discrimination easier to observe.[90] This presumption was based in part on Janine's recounting of how difficult it had been for the Hub to find somewhere to rent in the area. In multiple phone calls, she had plainly stated, "We provide employment services and transitional work for people coming home from prison." To this, landlords freely replied, "Sorry, we don't want people like that around," or, "We don't want to have you as occupants." After months of searching, Janine had finally encountered a landlord who supported the mission, acquiring this spacious suite that had been recently vacated by a low-end retail clothing store, and before that, a church. Job ads in the Inland Empire were equally blatant; "no felonies" and "must be able to pass a background check" were boldly displayed, with no regard for—or perhaps even awareness of—the illegality of blanket exclusions under federal law. Employers in the Inland Empire also regularly asked other kinds of discriminatory questions such as, "How old is the applicant?"

There were additional reasons the Inland Empire was an "ideal" site for this project. While rates of arrest and incarceration are slightly lower than the state average, as a region, the Inland Empire hosts a significantly higher percentage of adults released on parole compared to all other areas in California. The region also suffers from rates of poverty significantly higher than the national or state averages, and directs relatively fewer resources toward crime prevention, reentry assistance, and other social supports.[91] At the same time, from 2011 to 2016, the Inland Empire gained more than two hundred thousand jobs, 60 percent of those in moderately paid technical and blue-collar sectors, and the remaining 40 percent in low-wage sectors—a ratio of moderate to low-wage positions far better than the California average, but notably lacking in the number of management and professional positions available in other parts of the state.[92] In other words, the Inland Empire is a region in which there are (theoretically at least) lots of jobs for which people returning home from prison might qualify.

As the only entity in the region singularly dedicated to the mission of connecting people with felony convictions to employment, the Hub provided an excellent post from which to observe these dynamics. After formally introducing myself to incoming cohorts, I spent three to four days per week at the office, participating in classes, attending meetings, and chatting informally with the staff and program participants. A great deal of my time was spent in the computer lab, working with job seekers to prepare résumés and cover letters, submit online applications, make telephone calls, and communicate with employers by email. I especially came to love assisting with résumés and job applications. Crucially, it allowed me to get to know people as well as learn the details of their skills, past labor market experiences, and professional goals and interests—essential context for following their job market ventures. But more than this, coproducing a document that captured and promoted a person's best qualities built trust and camaraderie, and produced an immediate sense of satisfaction. Actually working on something tangible together also helped to cut through awkward class and race differences, and concretize the professional nature of the relationship.

Methodologically, the computer lab also provided one of the most effective ways to talk to people, which given the program structure, was somewhat difficult to do. Recall that after the first week of orientation, participants were hired on a transitional work crew for three days of the week.[93] This meant they headed out at 6:30 a.m. and didn't come back to the office until 2:30 p.m. to return equipment, often leaving quickly thereafter. Another obstacle to engagement was the layout of the physical space. But for the conference room, computer lab, and individual staff offices at the back, the space was wide open, and other than a singular sofa, lacked infrastructure around which to informally congregate. To address this, I set up a tiny standing desk (more of a podium really) conspicuously smack in the middle of the main suite—the opposite of anthropology's so-called fly-on-the-wall approach. I mostly prefer standing to sitting for desk work, but given that in the common area job seekers were also standing, I hoped that doing so made me seem more approachable. Whenever I wasn't in the lab, and always at 2:30 p.m. when the crew came in to collect paychecks and attend appointments with Hub staff, I stationed myself at my podium desk in hopes of striking up conversation as participants came and went. Though I'm sure I looked (and certainly often felt) a bit ridiculous standing there in the middle of the room, the technique was effective.

In addition to directly following job seekers, I closely followed the activities of job coaches and developers as they identified and nurtured potential work opportunities and helped job seekers prepare for and go after those opportunities. Whenever possible, I shadowed job developers directly as they circulated in the business community, talking to potential employers and working to establish relationships. I did this both at the Hub and less intensively at neighboring nonprofit organizations and local government-run programs as a point of comparison. I also sat in on meetings between job developers and job seekers at various sites, in which job seekers were trained and mentored to present themselves effectively to employers.

I did not begin with preestablished relationships with business owners or hiring managers, yet answering the research questions depended on close engagement with them, and ideally, the opportunity to observe hiring processes firsthand. With these goals in mind, I began to immerse myself in the Inland Empire business community as best I could, stitching together an eclectic methodology that allowed me to observe and interact with hiring managers and business owners in different locations, including HR conferences and trainings, informational seminars, and networking events. Hosted by a range of business, nonprofit, and government organizations, including the Inland Empire Economic Partnership, Employment Development Department, Society for Human Resource Management, and various chambers of commerce, participating in these kinds of meetings helped me to get a sense of the broader workforce landscape and talk to people in the business world about hiring in ways that did not require them to reflect directly on their own practices. I also made a point to be present at any forum directed at an employer audience that specifically addressed the topic of background screening—attending many seminars, webinars, and workshops in which employment law, HR, and/or screening industry experts advised employers on how, when, and why to use background checks.

Overall, I was pleasantly surprised by how generously I was welcomed and taken seriously by such a wide range of research informants in the business community. While some were more enthusiastic and willing to give of their time than others, most seemed to genuinely appreciate the opportunity to discuss, analyze, and reflect on their hiring experiences and practices.

My interactions in these business settings led to countless informal conversations along with approximately thirty-five formal interviews with small and midsize business owners, hiring managers, and HR professionals working for businesses and staffing agencies across many industries and sectors. Although I learned a great deal from these conversations and interviews, a simple comment made by one of my University of Texas at Austin mentors, Charlie Hale, kept coming to mind: "Ethnography requires more than just going around talking to people." I knew that in order to go beyond the reasons for decisions that employers may state or the views they freely express, I needed to see firsthand what it is like to run a business, how decisions about hiring get made, and how criminal records figure in those decisions. To my luck (which ethnography always requires), members of a regional Workforce Investment Board introduced me to the owners of a midsize trucking firm. As I detail in chapter 4, these owner-managers generously allowed me to repeatedly visit their workplace, and eventually, observe their hiring and personnel management practices in real time.

Generally speaking, I felt my appearance as a youngish, light-skinned Black woman as well as identity as a PhD student helped me to access people across business, government, and nonprofit settings, where I was generally perceived as nonthreatening, and my research project was viewed as of mutual interest or at least worthy of support. Still, as for all ethnographers, how I am perceived, understood, and positioned in the world both enabled and limited my "standpoint": what I could see and know in different environments.[94]

At the Hub, job seekers were by and large quick to trust my intentions and eager to participate in the research. My obviously empathetic stance, mixed-race phenotype, ability to properly pronounce Spanish names, and a gendered association of women with "helping" made it easy to connect across many differences. At the same time, I was sensitive to the power dynamics inherent in requesting consent from people whose needs and position as recipients in a social service program could cause them to feel pressured to participate in research. This led me to go beyond standard protocols to find ways to ensure that those participating fully understood that participation.

I was also cognizant of the troubling way stories about criminalization and redemption get used as cultural tropes of personal responsibility and meritocracy, and oversimplified so as to pull out and lift up what's useful for the writer. Moreover, given the constant comings and goings at the Hub along with the necessarily sporadic nature of my engagements with most job seekers, I knew I would not be able to tell fully contextualized stories. My more modest goal was thus to stay close to the emotion that seemed most important to the person about whom I was writing, and whenever possible, share my writing along the way.

Despite the Hub's overall organizational endorsement, it was easier to establish rapport with some staff members than others. There were some staffers with whom differences in viewpoint precluded easy trust about the analysis I would develop or how their work practices would be represented in writing. Sometimes this lack of trust caused them to withhold details about particular job seekers' experiences and employers' behaviors.

There were also limits to my engagement imposed by business and professional norms that constrained my interactions to business hours and settings. I especially would have liked to have joined job seekers on their early morning or evening commutes, visited with them in the places they lived or worked, and texted with them from my personal phone. However, this kind of interaction would have seemed inappropriate, may have put them or me at risk, and would have violated the norms of professional conduct expected between Hub staff and clients. In all, this nine-to-five style of ethnography felt suitable for my topic (and worked for my schedule as a mother of two young kids), but there were times when I wondered whether these parameters prevented a deeper understanding of some of the dynamics I was observing.

It is also a common problem for female researchers that their interest in men's lives be perceived as romantic, and like most female anthropologists working among men, I had to navigate situations in both business and non-profit settings in which my intellectual interest or apparent solo presence in the field was interpreted as a sign of availability.[95] For Black women and other women of color, these dynamics are further charged by the pressure to accommodate that stems from the politics of racial loyalty.[96] And for those who share political solidarities, the risk of unwanted sexual advance in ethnographic fieldwork is further heightened.[97]

By far the biggest methodological challenge had to do with accessing powerful people, organizations, and institutions that were less aligned with my research agenda, or what anthropologist Laura Nader first called "studying up."[98] In particular, there were many instances in which job seekers' applications were denied or offers of employment were rescinded, and they did not know exactly what had happened. This obscurity—exactly how, when, or why the adverse decision had been made—was precisely what I was attempting to demystify, but sometimes I could not get close enough to power holders to discern why or how adverse decisions were made. In some cases, HR departments refused to speak with me, or more often, politely evaded my calls. In other instances, I could not broach a conversation out of fear of damaging the Hub's relationship with the employer and other job seekers' prospects.

When I *was* able to speak with powerful people, the interactions sometimes felt uneasy because of my stance as an advocate for workers with records. Although I approached corporate professionals, including those in the screening industry, with a genuine, open curiosity about their motivations, perspectives, and stakes, and was always honest about my research agenda, there was some discomfort in knowing that they would probably not "like" the meaning that I would make of the data, or agree with the study's overall arguments and interventions. As Nader succinctly put it, "Anthropologists value studying what they like and liking what they study and, in general, we prefer the underdog."[99]

Finally, a word on field notes and anonymity. It would have been inappropriate and raised suspicion had I attempted to tape-record my observations. Instead, I took copious handwritten notes, often in the moment or as quickly as possible after an encounter. Wherever it seemed I could do so without making people feel uncomfortable, I took notes on my laptop, which allowed me to more accurately capture dialogue and save time. Once, a job seeker at the Hub expressed curious discomfort at the speed of my handwritten note-taking during a meeting between himself and a job developer. What on earth, he asked me afterward, had I been writing down? His observation led me to realize that I could capture dialogue verbatim, even when writing by hand, and needed to be more mindful of the somewhat shaky distinction I had made between digital recording and note-taking.

Every individual, organization, and company depicted here has been anonymized to the best of my ability. While some individuals and groups in professional and business sectors did not request or necessarily want anonymity, others did, and it was my decision to impose a uniform standard.[100] Except in instances where I am writing about a publicly known institution or association in a general way, names, places, and personal details have been changed enough to make informants unrecognizable to one another as well as the general reader. That said, there are undoubtedly some cases where local knowledge might allow a reader to discern the individual or organization being described. I have been most careful to protect the identity of research informants for whom anonymity was important.

———

If as a friend once suggested, "A book is an album," which is to say, more than the sum of its tracks, *The Criminal Record Complex* encourages readers to think deeply about where we are, how we got here, and what it will take to move forward.[101] We begin at the Hub, from the vantage point of people with recent felony convictions. Chapter 1, "Looking for Work with a Criminal Record," documents the devastating impact of the criminal record complex on the lives of people with conviction records who are entering the job market. Through differently situated job seekers, it highlights the reality that while all people with criminal records experience stigma and discrimination, the experience lands in distinct ways. Demonstrating the great lengths to which criminalized people go to get hired and maintain employment in the face of nearly insurmountable barriers, the chapter exposes the baselessness of the presumption that people with criminal records are somehow unfit or unsuitable for the workforce.

As an anthropologist, I was interested in the political salience of criminal records—how and why people came to think of them as a useful sorting mechanism. Chapter 2, "The Making of Common Sense," traces the historical evolutions of the criminal record complex to show how and why criminal background checks became nearly ubiquitous in employment contexts. While at first I thought I might write a historical chapter detailing the rise of criminal background screening in employment, and another about the vested interests and relationships that maintain and propel criminal record discrimination in the present, as I tried to figure out where to draw a line between the things that got the ball rolling and the things that drive and maintain it now, it became ever more clear that there is no clean break between past and present, nor always a tidy chronology. Drawing from primary policy and legal documents, HR, workplace security, and legal literatures, and observations and interviews with risk industry, employment law, and HR professionals, this chapter constructs an integrated (though necessarily incomplete) account of key actors and institutions whose combined efforts made routine employment screening possible, effectual, and attractive.[102]

Chapter 3, "Criminal Stigma and the Politics of Helping," explores the ways that job seekers and professional employment advocates navigate the stigma produced by the criminal record complex. It shows how, given the strong tendency in the United States to blame marginalized people for their conditions, the narratives that are taken up in job market encounters often reinscribe notions of personal responsibility.[103] By critically examining these challenging and politically fraught dynamics, this chapter strives to think along with people doing the work of brokering between employers and criminalized job seekers about how to do it in more liberatory ways.

Despite background check's near ubiquity, not all employers find them particularly useful for identifying reliable employees. In fact, many have found that people with criminal records (or otherwise imperfect credentials) make dedicated and capable employees. Chapter 4, "Good Sense Hiring in Small and Midsize Business," looks at the hiring approaches of business owners and managers in the Inland Empire whose ideas about what makes an ideal employee differ sharply from those proscribed by the criminal record complex. Exclusion may be in the interests of risk industries, but in my observation, it was not necessarily in the interests of individuals running businesses.

Finally, the purpose of this book is not only to enhance knowledge of criminalizing systems but to think with others about what it would take to change them. The conclusion, "Limits and Possibilities in the Struggle to End Criminal Record Discrimination," invites the reader, and especially those readers actively engaged in on-the-ground organizing, activism, and policy advocacy, to think about deep and lasting interventions. It argues for steps that not only make exclusion and exploitation less severe but also chip away at the core assumptions, values, and discourses upholding the discriminatory use of criminal records, to make room to build economies and workplaces that support true safety.

1

Looking for Work
with a Criminal Record

They were fully ready to hire me as assistant manager. And they said, "As soon as background comes back, we'll let you know." When my background came back, they said, "Well, we can't extend the job to you. . . . Something in your background is against our company policy."

There's a huge hiring right now for warehouse positions, loading and unloading, but they specifically state you cannot have a criminal background to unload and load trucks. It's basic manual labor. . . . I mean, I understand it can be a high-volume/high-priced product, but just to unload and load a truck?

I had an interview. It went well, but I received one of those letters. . . . When I called, they said that it [the conviction] has to be seven years or older, which is hard . . . because you need a job right now. I really feel like I've lost so many years. When do I get to have my life back? I did my time. I do all the requirements. I don't get in trouble. How much more time do I have to do?"

—INLAND EMPIRE JOB SEEKERS

STEPPING OUT OF my car into the Hub parking lot, I noticed Jaime, the concrete construction guy, approaching from the bus stop across the street. It was 9:00 a.m., and I could see he was sharply dressed for his first job-readiness assessment in tan slacks, white button-down shirt, and tie.

As we greeted one another, he smiled, running his hand along the length of his chest and remarking, "I had to watch YouTube in order to figure out how to tie this thing." Jaime was used to working and making good money, but was

29

less comfortable with the idea of "job seeking," particularly the kind pro-scribed by social service organizations like the Hub, whose emphasis on pro-fessional dress, procedures, and etiquette chafed what a long tradition in social science would call his "habitus": his general way of interacting with the world.[1] "I feel silly dressed this way," he said. "This just isn't me."

The more we talked, the more it became clear that it wasn't just the outfit that wasn't sitting right. He repeated the story he had shared with the group on the first day, about being asked by a foreman to leave the jobsite and how deeply shaken he was by the confrontation with his new status as an "ex-con." He had always believed this status was reserved for "bad people," he explained—people who are part of gangs or organized crime, people who had been to prison mul-tiple times, people *other than him.* The application of criminalized status to his identity seemed to have damaged not just his pride but his very sense of self.

Jaime spoke often about how he deeply regretted the harm he had caused to his family and the losses they had suffered as a result of his imprisonment, but he could not reconcile what had happened with his identity. "I was a good husband, a good father, a good provider. . . . I just made a mistake." As de-scribed in the introduction, this disbelief that he could be classified as criminal can be traced to the late 1800s when Darwinian principles were used to shift popular thinking about criminality from "a person who has committed a crime" to the more essentialized as well as deliberately racialized concept, "the criminal." I wished I could help Jaime shake the shame, though not through the framework he employed that differentiated himself from the "real bad guys." More critical ways of thinking about crime are deliberately avoided in prisons and most reentry programs, however. Instead, simple frameworks of personal choice and redemption stymie the kind of reflection, political educa-tion, and healing that could actually help people make sense of the events that unfolded and move forward.[2]

The two of us headed inside, Jaime to his first job-readiness appointment, and I to the computer lab, which was proving to be the best place to get to know people and make myself useful.

———

Two things surprised me in those initial weeks at the Hub that shouldn't have. One had to do with the racial composition of the program, which during the most intensive period of research was categorized by the organization as 31 percent Black, 39 percent Latino/a, and 25 percent white. This program composition accurately reflected the gross overrepresentation of Black people, notable overrepresentation of Latino/a people, and significant underrepresentation of white people in rates of conviction and imprisonment in California as well as nationally.[3] Yet I had not anticipated the discord between percentages and numbers—the fact that racial disparities notwithstanding, to walk into a room of people with felony convictions in this region would be to encounter roughly equal *numbers* of Black, Latino/a, and white people as well as many people whose racial identities were not easily categorizable.

The second actuality I hadn't anticipated was the Hub participants' wide range of relationships to the job market. While the majority had spotty and little formal work experience, including some who had never held a job, a significant number had undertaken occupations prior to imprisonment with the kind of longevity and dedication that we call "career." Thus simultaneously enrolled at the Hub were people who felt alienated from the job market or even intimidated by the prospect of a job, alongside those who felt a sense of belonging in the labor market and were anxious to reclaim a place within it. In snapshots of the daily grind, this chapter explores these differences, arguing that they must be appreciated and attended to in order to support people effectively, build true solidarity, and create substantive change. At the same time, it exposes the devastating similarities facing all job seekers with criminal records: the great lengths to which they are expected to go to in order to secure low-wage work, the exploitation and disrespect they often experience on the job, and the frequency and casualness with which they are fired.

My surprise at the Hub's diversity stemmed from overly simplified notions of the nature and scope of the prison industrial complex along with who gets sent to prison and why.[4] Given the United States' reliance on systems of surveillance, policing, and imprisonment to squash and disappear rather than solve a broad range of social, political, and economic problems—from poverty, addiction, and mental illness, to interpersonal violence, sexual abuse, and political dissent—its borders are more porous than many realize. That antiblackness is an overarching principle backing systems of confinement and control does not mean that only Black or poor people are affected; it means they are more frequently, severely, and qualitatively distinctly affected.[5] Technologies originating in antiblack logics can bleed into everyday laws and practices that affect other groups, or society as a whole, while antiblackness remains constant.[6] Additionally, the targets of criminalization shift over space and time. Thus alongside persistent raced, classed, and geographic disparities, decades of economic restructuring declining work opportunities, and divestment from education and health have also drawn greater numbers of white people, economically privileged people of all races, and people from suburban and rural areas into the prison system.[7]

In California, dependence on defense monies led the state to be hit particularly hard by the end of the post post–World War II boom.[8] A combination of military spending cuts, international competition, automation, and managerial decisions to seek cheaper places for production caused industrial plants to downsize or close altogether. Between 1980 and 1983 alone, California lost more than nine hundred automobile, lumber and paper mills, as well as food-processing, steel, and other industrial manufacturing facilities.[9] The closure of several major air force bases in the early 1990s led to the loss of another thirty-two thousand jobs.[10] Wages fell significantly, as did the share of union households, while rents, property taxes, gas prices, and the overall cost of living steadily rose.[11] People couldn't afford housing, poverty intensified, and the already major gulf between the rich and poor grew to astounding proportions.[12] Making matters worse, a statewide ballot measure curbing property tax increases (Proposition 13) severely limited counties' ability to generate revenue. This loss of a local tax base took a major toll on the quality of public services and education. Funding for public schools was slashed, libraries closed, tuition for higher education dramatically decreased, and the poverty rate for California children and adolescents rose to alarming levels.[13]

The Inland Empire was particularly hard hit. Having long been a mecca for Los Angeles families in search of affordable housing, waves of postwar migration were driven primarily by lower housing costs and property taxes. When residential construction collapsed in 2006 and was followed by the entire housing market in 2007, however, foreclosure rates rose to the highest levels in the country.[14] By 2012, 140,000 construction jobs had been lost, pushing unemployment rates in the region above 10 percent.[15] Governments, economists, and planners tried to gain back jobs lost in construction and manufacturing at the other end of the supply chain by investing heavily in port infrastructure.[16] Given its proximity to the ports of Los Angeles and Long Beach along with the availability of large tracts of land, they reasoned, the Inland Empire was well positioned to become central to a growing "logistics" industry to channel mostly Asian imports from the ports of Los Angeles and Long Beach to massive distribution centers, then on to consumers across the United States. Though jobs were indeed generated, the wealth of the industry tended not to trickle down to its more than one hundred thousand predominantly Latino/a and immigrant warehouse workers—many of them employed by temporary staffing agencies, which in addition to keeping wages low and minimizing benefits, provided a legal and logistical buffer for employers that made it difficult for workers to organize.[17] Adding injury to insult, the movement of so many goods via trucks and trains produced some of the highest levels of air pollution in the United States.[18]

The very people and communities made marginal or redundant by these economic crises and political choices were targeted for imprisonment, a double whammy that Ruth Wilson Gilmore and Craig Gilmore have described as iron-fisted abandonment.[19] High interest rates and unemployment provided justification for the dismantling of the welfare state, while law and order gradually became enmeshed with social services until it eventually replaced the social safety net as the primary response to domestic security.[20] Within a ten-year period (from 1986 to 1996), California built nineteen prisons, compared to just two in the entire decade prior and in contrast to one state university. The number of people imprisoned in California quadrupled.[21]

That criminalization casts a wide net does not mean the process lands everybody in the same boat. As job seekers' lived experiences reveal (and Black feminists have long emphasized), each of us has a range of attachments, investments, privileges, and disadvantages that are generated by different elements of our social positioning. These different aspects of our identities intersect in unique ways, and may shift in different contexts and at different times in our lives.[22] Thus while criminalization creates a "distinct form of political membership" based on conviction status—what sociologists Reuben Jonathan Miller and Forrest Stuart have called "carceral citizenship—there are many nuances in the way a felony conviction is experienced.[23] The move from statistical estimates to real life at the Hub brought the concept of "intersectionality" vividly to life.

As described in the introduction, the economic effect of imprisonment on employment prospects varies substantially across subgroups defined by race, gender, and work history—with Black formerly incarcerated women experiencing the highest levels of postimprisonment unemployment. Within these broad categories however, and especially in hiring contexts where quick decisions are made based on limited information, phenotypical nuances such as size, age, skin color, physical build, and fitness gain salience, as do matters of style and demeanor such as hair, clothing, the nature and placement of tattoos, facial expressions, manner of speech, posture, and perceived confidence.[24] Also at play are prevailing beliefs about particular kinds of "crime" and assumptions about what kinds of bodies are suitable for what kinds of work.

These intersections help explain how Isaac (who we'll meet shortly), a Black man in his forties who was clean-cut, fit, energetic, and articulate, was hired much more quickly than Gary, the white man in his sixties we met in the introduction who used to do events work.

Finally, beyond derailing career trajectories and damaging long-term earning power, criminal labeling can affect people's sense of personhood.[25] Criminalization has been shown to blacken racial status, causing changes in both self-identification and interpellation by others.[26] It can produce crises emerging from gender norms by disrupting gendered work identities, or positions in families as primary wage earners and parents.[27] And it can force people to abandon professional identities and make major adjustments in comportment and style. As this chapter will show, each job seeker faces a unique constellation of intersecting challenges impacting their prospects for employment. Yet for the majority, looking for work with a criminal record requires swallowing pride, making oneself vulnerable, and embarking on a major hustle to get hired.

Computer Room Blues

It was week two for the new cohort, which meant lots of time would be devoted to résumé preparation and online job searching. Poking my head into the computer lab, I asked, "Anyone need help?"

Hands shot up and "yes pleases" sounded from all six stations.

"What's E-Verify?" blurted a white man named Don, with considerable stress in his voice.[28] Don was beginning to question whether or not he should proceed with an application on Monster.com for "crane operator" in the city of Ontario. The application had already raised his anxiety by stating in two different places that candidates must "pass" both a drug and criminal background check—a vague and therefore discouraging notion.

While passing is generally taken to mean not having been convicted of a felony within the past seven years, in accordance with the California version of the Fair Credit Reporting Act, there are discrepancies in how the seven years are calculated, and many job seekers as well as employers misunderstand the details.[29] Job seekers erring on the side of caution often thus simply assume that "passing" means one's record is free of felony convictions. Furthermore, though federal law requires "individualized assessments," blanket exclusions of people with felonies are common, and many so-called individual assessments amount to no more than the assignment of individuals to risk groups. What's more, to the extent that actual individualized assessments take place, they are conducted by individuals lacking any lived experience or training that might qualify them to make such assessments.[30]

I first took a seat next to Gary, whose less than nimble fingers I could see were struggling to operate the mouse. Not having worked in more than ten years, Gary couldn't remember the details of his past work experience. Some people came to the Hub with printed versions of résumés crafted at other places and times. These résumés were often terribly written, but at least helpful for generating bulleted lists of skills along with reconstructing the dates and locations of past work experience. But many people were starting from scratch.

Gary wondered if there was a way to obtain an official record of his employment history. At his request, I called Social Security on his behalf, but was informed the office does not keep this kind of record. Next, he suggested the Employment Development Department might have a record, but that department directed me to the Unemployment Office, which kept me on hold for almost an hour, only to find there was no way to speak to an actual person.

Sketching a work history as best he could from memory, Gary decided to attempt an application for the position of "associate" listed on the website for Friendly Dollar, a major bargain chain selling miscellaneous housewares and trinkets. The first step was to create an account, which requires an email address. I suggested we first log on to his email, just to be sure the account was working. He couldn't log on, and so we began the process of changing the password. Yahoo, however, wanted to send a verification to his phone number in order to allow the change, and the phone number he had provided was that of the landline at the group home where he was currently living, so he couldn't retrieve the verification code. We dialed Yahoo help from his phone and waited on hold until he mentioned he had only two hundred minutes, so I encouraged him to hang up and call back from my unlimited plan. Yahoo kept us on hold for ten minutes or so, at which point we were disconnected. I next suggested we create another account—on Gmail—just so we could move forward with the application. This step was thankfully quick and easy. The Friendly Dollar account was a little slower going as it required that your password contain a special character, which means you have to use the shift key. It was difficult, in terms of physical coordination, for Gary's fingers to hold down shift and then lightly tap another key. I recorded all the log-on and password information for him on a large pad of paper, clearly delineating Yahoo from Gmail from Friendly Dollar though we deliberately kept all the log-ons and passwords as consistent as possible, so there was lots of overlap. Security be damned, I hoped this strategy would increase his chances of being able to log on later.

To our dismay, the software next prompted Gary to upload a résumé. Glancing at his draft, I realized it needed updating. The one warehouse job he'd had a long time ago wasn't reflected and some other details needed tweaking. Next the system asked for a cover letter—overkill, it seemed to me, for a basic warehouse position.

Before long, a woman in her late thirties came into the lab with some instructions for how to apply to Friendly Dollar printed on a half sheet of paper. Word must have gotten out that the company was hiring. I quietly hoped that her possession of these instructions would mean I wouldn't have to lead the tedious process again, but almost immediately, she accidentally exited the application and then couldn't log back on because the system said the email-password combination was not found—a combination she had created not five minutes earlier. Miranda decided it would be easier to create a new account and start the application from scratch. But the system recognized her email address as already linked to an account and so she was forced to create a whole new email in order to be able to start a fresh application. About thirty minutes later she was up and running, but before long, stumped by the request for a cover letter and the realization that her résumé did not reflect her five years' previous experience in various warehouses. Luckily, one of the Hub's job developers offered a cover letter that could be adapted. Theoretically, through this process Gary and Miranda had learned to edit, save, and upload files to the desired locations, but truthfully, for all of our sanity, I was doing most of the input.

While we worked, Ronaldo, the fencing guy, popped into the lab, slipping a smartphone out of his back pocket. "My daughter insisted that I get a modern phone," he said, "but I'm struggling to make use of it." Then demonstrating otherwise, he lifted the device to his mouth and spoke expertly into the mic: "Chain-link companies hiring in San Bernardino." Siri answered with the names of two businesses. "One's union, the other isn't," Ronaldo reported. It was hard to say whether his phone had in fact identified active job leads, but everyone in the lab was amused, and when he dialed without hesitation to ask if they were hiring, impressed by both his aptitude and confidence.

Whereas for many, the minutiae of job market preparation felt overwhelming, people like Ronaldo found it infantilizing. He had been playing along with the Hub's process, but it was clear he hoped to bypass this whole business of résumés, applications, and mock interviews. "Tell me about yourself," he snickered. "At my age [thirty-eight], I never had to do all of that." Ronaldo was also feeling demoralized by his first week on the transitional work crew. He had hoped the work would be more involved, but they had done little more than pick up trash along the highway. "Of course I know how to use a weed whacker," he snapped. "I feel like my brain is going unused."

Jamal, in contrast, the Black man in his late thirties who had been incarcerated for sixteen years, was experiencing considerable distress. "This is ridiculous that everything has to be done on a computer nowadays," he blurted. "I get so frustrated!"

It was hard to fathom what it must be like to have rarely, if ever, used a computer, and then find oneself in a job placement program in which the expectation is that a minimum of two hours per week be spent looking for leads and responding to online job ads. Rolling my chair next to his, I offered to type while he talked. There was a lot to capture. In addition to his time managing an Applebee's restaurant and his position as a medical technician in a psychiatric hospital, during his sixteen years of imprisonment across five different institutions, he had performed a lot of kitchen work as well as grounds keeping, snow removal, and some mechanics. He was surprised that I wanted to include all of this in his résumé, going back this far in his history and mentioning his in-prison work experience. It told a story, I explained, of someone who was responsible for taking the deposit to the bank at the end of the day, supervised employees, administered medication, and cooked meals for large groups of people.

Just then Janine leaned through the doorway, motioning me to follow her to her office, where she informed me that the police, accompanied by a parole officer, were on their way to arrest Brian, the young Latino—and the only person on the upside of the digital divide—who had been quietly polishing his résumé next to Gary. Apparently, an incident the night prior had led to an immediate warrant for his arrest. Unsure what form this encounter would take, what kind of disruption the police or parole might make, or how Brian might respond, there was nothing to do but carry on.

———

Nearly every interaction I had in the computer lab during my year at the Hub involved some version of the above-described angst and chaos. With the exception of Brian (in his twenties), no one knew how to even change the size of a font. Those who had work history struggled to reconstruct it, and even using the résumé and cover letter templates the job developers had created, the process caused extreme aggravation. No one could input or retrieve their passwords. They didn't write passwords down, lost the tiny scraps of paper in their wallets, or wrote them down slightly incorrectly, forgetting caps and other punctuation, or conflating log-on with password. Within this morning's group of computer room users, not one person knew how to compose an email or save a document where it could later be found. Gasps of awe resounded as I demonstrated the keyboard strokes (commands C and V) for cutting and pasting text. Most didn't know how to capitalize the first word in a sentence by holding down the shift key; some were not aware that one *should* capitalize. This is why the instructions for how to respond to a Craigslist ad posted on the wall didn't work, since they included directions like, "Copy and paste the 'Reply' email into the 'To' field of your message." People didn't even know how to open a new tab for an email without losing the page they were on, much less how to copy and paste. Many also didn't understand how to use email itself, or in some cases, conceptually what email is. Whereas in the past, job seeking in many industries could be conducted mostly in person, and doing so was encouraged and expected, it was now commonplace for applications to be completed online, and the process to require significant writing and word processing skills. Having been forcibly denied access to technology in prison, people coming home are often unable to use the software and equipment that has developed since their incarceration. The learning curve can be steep, and for many, nearly insurmountable.

Needless to say, by the end of the day, each person had produced a workable résumé draft, and some had submitted applications for jobs online—including Brian, who had been escorted calmly out of the lab and through the front door, hands behind his back, with his head held high. Janine had come back into the computer lab to assure everyone that no one from the Hub had reported Brian to his parole officer or called the police; that this had never happened before, and she didn't have the power to prevent it from happening here and now. They seemed to appreciate her words, but had little to say, each turning back to their monitors.

Ready or Not

Defined narrowly, the concept "job readiness" refers to the material preparation required to effectively look for work, including proper identification, appropriate clothing and equipment, résumé and cover letter, access to transportation, and so on. In practice, marketing oneself in the job market also necessitates a minimum threshold of economic stability, including having somewhere to sleep and shower, the right clothes to wear, and just as important, a base level of psychoemotional well-being from which to generate the necessary confidence, optimism, and sense of self-worth to project hireability. These deeper aspects of readiness and the causes of their absence often exceed social service organizations' capacity to address them, yet people need jobs whether they are ready or not.

———

On a typically busy morning, the whiteboard schedules outside Sasha's and Kristen's offices were packed with back-to-back job-readiness assessment appointments. Relationships between job developers and job seekers begin with this assessment, which allows the job developer to gather basic information about skills, prior experience, and any work impediments as well as gauge the job seeker's readiness to talk to an actual employer.

Don came in for his initial job readiness assessment with Sasha. His appointment had been scheduled for 9:30 a.m., but on arrival, he was notified that it would be moved to 10:30 a.m.

Don's huge mustache and long reddish-blond hair tied at the base of his neck were starting to turn white. His skin was weathered with deep wrinkles, but his energy communicated that he was still in his working prime and anxious to pick up where he'd left off prior to imprisonment. "I'm a union man," he told me, a heavy equipment operator by trade who earned $41 per hour at his last job cutting trees. Don believed the union would probably take him back, but not before he had a reliable car, as the jobs are rarely local. Further complicating the problem of transportation, Don's conditions of parole didn't allow him to travel beyond a fifty-mile radius without permission, and the union's dispatching system didn't allow time to wait for permission to travel—a common problem for people on parole in construction and other travel-intensive trades. There was also a $2,100 reentrance fee to get back into the union, he noted, but he was hopeful the union would let him pay this off with his first check. Don's goal, then, was to quickly get hired somewhere in order to save up money for a car and try to get back into the union. None of the heavy equipment operation jobs he had identified, however, were near enough to reasonably get to without a car. Adding to the pressure, he had other debts to contend with, resulting from the economic effects of the 2008 recession six years prior. "I haven't worked since 2006–7," he said. "Everything went bad for me at that point, when the housing market crashed."

Don soon learned that Sasha had called in sick and he would be reassigned to Kristen. Both the delay and reassignment induced considerable anxiety for him, as he was already worried about his ability to perform during the job-readiness assessment. Don was particularly anxious about the preliminary mock interview that Sasha—and now Kristen—would facilitate, to see how smoothly he responded to questions like, "Why do you want to work for us? Why did you leave the job cutting trees?" and the question that would arise from having checked the dreaded box, "I see here you have a conviction?" Based on his performance during this interaction, Kristen would decide whether Don seemed ready to begin actively applying for jobs and going on interviews, or would benefit from another week of coaching.

Adding to Don's discomfort was the light-brown, slightly oversized suit he had acquired for the occasion. He was also self-conscious about smiling because he had forgotten his top teeth at home. As the appointment time approached, I attempted to calm him by advising that he try to forget he was in a costume, think of the interview as a casual conversation, and remember that employers just want to get a sense of who you are. But Don's anxiety could not be assuaged with a pep talk. During the next hour, he would ask three times to be reminded of Kristen's name, where her office was (a visible stone's throw), and whether when the appointment time came, he should leave his backpack in the main room or take it with him.

As Don set off to his appointment, a young man named Arturo strode across the lobby toward my desk wearing pleated slacks, a burgundy guaya-bera, and matching dress shoes, hair swept away from his face. His spirits were visibly (and unusually) high. "Do I look good?" he asked. "You do!" I answered honestly.

Arturo had been unhoused since his release from prison. Although he was skilled at living on the streets as a result of having left foster care at an early age, the situation was making it difficult to dress appropriately or show up on time for job development appointments. He had partially solved this problem by getting married, prompting his wife's parents to allow the newlyweds to fashion a place to live in their backyard and his parole agent to agree to the new address because of his now legal relationship to the family, but the situation was obviously still less than ideal.

The nice outfit, I learned, was not only meant to impress Arturo's job developer. He announced, "I'm going to meet my birth mother for lunch." During Arturo's imprisonment, his then girlfriend had sought out his birth mother on Facebook and confirmed the relationship by posting a baby photo with which both were familiar. Arturo had received a letter from his mother saying that she lived in New York City, and in later communication, that she would be traveling through Southern California and wanted to meet him. Though he avoided discussing the details of his past, the pain of it was apparent in the information he revealed about the present, along with the scattered way he talked about his history of childhood abandonment, foster care, and street living. He also hinted that something bad had happened during his imprisonment that turned his eighteen-month sentence into four and a half years, marked him with a strike, and cemented the custody loss of his new baby.[31]

Next to arrive was Isaiah, a wiry and energetic young Black man. He came prancing through the doors grinning widely with a tiny baby strapped to his chest in a kangaroo pack, looking exhausted but proud. Isaiah had been caring for his nephew on the days he didn't work on the Hub's transitional work crew, he explained, so that his sister could go back to work. In fact, he and his girlfriend were in the process of trying to gain custody. According to Isaiah, his sister was not fit to care for the baby. Complicating matters further, Isaiah was largely responsible for his two younger siblings, whom he had thankfully been able to leave with his girlfriend for a few hours on this day. These financial responsibilities and lack of childcare assistance were making it difficult for Isaiah to look for permanent work, or even participate fully in the Hub's transitional work program. In fact, during his coaching appointment with Jorge, Isaiah would be advised that although his willingness to take responsibility for his nephew was admirable, he could not continue to bring the baby to appointments. To help make ends meet, Isaiah had been working occasional nights as a stripper. This had led to his being reprimanded for falling asleep in the Hub's work van; crew leaders had panicked when they couldn't find his slim figure, hidden from sight behind the long bench seats.

Last to arrive was Clifford, a tall Black man so disheveled and tired looking that his age was difficult to discern. He came trudging into the lobby on the verge of tears, hours late for his appointment with Sasha, whom he would soon learn had already left for the day. Clifford was born and raised in Los Angeles, but had been paroled to the Inland Empire because people are generally paroled to the counties where they were convicted rather than those where they are from. He desperately wanted to have his parole transferred to Los Angeles, where his support network was much wider. Yet his four months of free sober-living housing had recently expired so he had been staying with a friend for the past few weeks. This made it difficult to access clothing out of his belongings, which were stuffed into trash bags in his friend's garage, causing him to miss both yesterday's appointment with Sasha and an appointment with his parole officer, who would now be even less likely to approve his desired transfer. Moreover, Clifford was blind in one eye (disturbingly, as were two other Black men in the one year I spent at the Hub), and the other eye wandered. A doctor had advised him to quit the welding class that had been arranged and paid for by the Hub at a nearby community college out of worry that the activity could damage his only remaining good eye. This advice had dampened Clifford's spirits considerably as the classes had been providing him with a sense of purpose and enjoyment.

Virtually all the Hub participants' efforts to join the job market were impeded by a gamut of personal challenges, ranging from a lack of immediate income and transportation, résumé gaps, diminished social networks, and outdated skills and training, to inadequate housing, debt, digital illiteracy, and health problems. But whereas for some, these challenges were contextual and provisional, for others, the challenges were rooted in longer trajectories of deprivation, marginalization, and trauma. Watching people like Arturo, Isaiah, and Clifford—without adequate housing, childcare, or basic security, and yet struggling to rise to the occasion of job seeking—exposed the misnomer of "job readiness" for many. It highlighted the absurdity of social policy insisting that people work with little regard for the conditions that allow a person to be successful in a job.[32] It also spoke volumes to their determination and resolve.

Conviction's Losses

Imprisonment is intended to deprive a person of liberty, time, agency, connection, comfort, safety, rights, and privileges. After release, conviction continues to take aim at status and sense of self. One way it does so is by preventing people from returning to careers they previously enjoyed, undermining the sense of self that comes from performing—and being known for performing—a particular line of work. This loss of social standing, identity, and purpose affected many people at the Hub, and particularly those whose preprison identities had been strongly shaped by work.

———

Caleb sauntered into the computer lab and plunked down in a swivel chair. "Did you get me back in at the casino yet?" he asked in his characteristic dry humor.

"I did not," I replied, adding cautiously, "I've been wondering, though, if it might make sense for you to go ahead and apply for a job there, and if you're denied the license, appeal . . . just follow the process and see what happens?"

In the two years preceding his imprisonment, Caleb worked as a public safety officer at the nearby Indian casino, checking IDs and warding off troublemakers. "I loved my job, never missed a day, even won employee of the month," he told me proudly. Caleb believed his supervisor would gladly take him back, except that in order to work there, he would need a gambling license granted by the Gaming Commission of California, and people with felony convictions (except for possession of cannabis) are automatically ineligible for this license.[33] Caleb couldn't stop wondering whether there might be a way in through the backdoor. But when he called his old boss to ask whether he could pull some strings with the commission, his boss had said, "Sorry, things don't work like that anymore."

Helping Caleb at the Hub, it was clear his heart wasn't in the job search. He was going through the motions, but struggling to muster the initiative needed to perform the kind of active job searching that is expected of the Hub clients, and needed to succeed in getting hired. Moreover, given Caleb's age, physical condition, and the kinds of jobs most readily available to men with recent felony convictions, it was unclear what type of work he should pursue.

So far, Caleb had landed only two interviews. He'd botched the first, at Sears, by mentioning the great things he'd been doing "since his release."

"Release?" they had replied in confusion, which quickly turned to horror when the Sears manager grasped the prison reference.

Ironically, in mentioning his release, Caleb only encouraged the contrary reality.

One of Caleb's specific challenges was that other than the casino, his recent work history included four years managing a collection agency, which explained why his résumé still featured skills like Microsoft Access and Excel. This didn't translate well for the mostly manual labor jobs for which he was now applying. Most recently, he'd applied for a position as a janitor, and grasping at straws, a roofing job.

"Really?" Kristen had commented. "Now you're going to get on a roof?"

The situation was beginning to feel a bit desperate as Caleb neared the end of the seventy-five days during which the Hub's funding permits it to support clients with paid transitional work and job development services. Both he and Kristen were holding out hope for the only remaining active job prospect: a commercial laundry facility where several other Hub participants had recently been hired. But since the interview, Caleb wasn't getting a callback, despite Kristen's carefully worded follow-up email to the hiring manager crafted to ward off the ageism she suspected was at play by emphasizing his "high levels of energy and productivity." Her wording was a stretch. Well into middle age, not in great health, and still grieving the death of his mother while he had been in prison, Caleb's affect was anything but energetic. In addition to the loss of his mother, he was mourning a loss of identity and purpose over the work to which he could no longer return.

It was clear Caleb was stuck, but less apparent how he might find release. I wondered whether from a psychological perspective, Caleb should apply for a job at the casino and when denied the gaming license, follow the process to submit an appeal. My logic grew not so much out of belief that he would prevail but rather a hope that by fully pursuing his old job, regardless the outcome, he would be able to find closure. This strategy that had worked for Courtney who had at first been similarly stuck on obtaining a job as a certified nurse aid until she had written to the licensing board with her fingerprints and received a reply stating that because her conviction had not been job related, she would eventually be allowed to nurse again. She had explained that knowing she could potentially go back to nursing after discharging from parole allowed her to lay it to rest. Kristen, though, worried that Caleb's fixation on the unrealistic possibility of returning to the casino was preventing him from actually finding work, and for this reason, had not appreciated my suggestion to Caleb that he continue to pursue a job at the casino.

Pounding the Pavement

I could have just as easily written a book about how transportation policy perpetuates inequality. Despite relatively good overall public transportation coverage, according to a report by the Brookings Institute, the Inland Empire cities of Riverside, San Bernardino, and Ontario rank second to worst nationally in terms of the share of jobs accessible within a ninety-minute public transport commute because so many jobs are sprawled outside the urban core.[34] In this vast region with limited public transportation, most job seekers connected to the Hub didn't have cars. While a few had family members or friends who offered occasional rides, most relied on buses and bicycles to follow constant streams of uncertain job leads. Indeed, if there was one thing

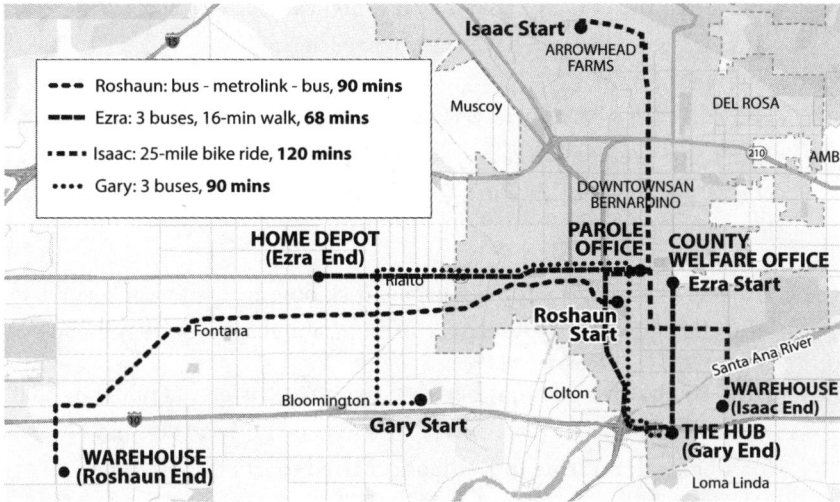

FIGURE 1.1 Typical commutes. Illustration courtesy of Karson Schenk.

all Hub job seekers had in common, it was an expectation—from parole officers, families, friends, nonprofit helpers, and themselves—to go to great lengths to get and keep almost any job.

The whiteboards outside Sasha's and Kristen's offices listed back-to-back appointments with clients already deemed "job ready." In these weekly meetings, job seekers discussed their progress with job developers, learned about new leads, and prepared for interviews. I stood at my podium desk to greet appointment goers, joining some in their appointments.

Courtney, the Black, single mother of two whose plans to obtain a certified nurse aide license had been derailed by conviction and imprisonment, was the first appointment on Sasha's docket. Rather than building a career in nursing, Courtney had been running all over town chasing random restaurant, clerical, and general labor vacancies.

COURTNEY: I went to that one company you told me about, but they said the work was too heavy. . . . They gave me another [affiliated] warehouse to try where the work is supposed to be lighter.

SASHA [looking at the paper Courtney has been given and recognizing the address]: Oh, OK, that's the address for Telehouse Staffing.

COURTNEY: The person I talked to also mentioned clerical work.

SASHA: Oh good, do you have clerical experience?

COURTNEY: Some . . .

SASHA: OK, I'll give a call to see what's required and get back to you. And I also need you to redo your application at Sophia's laundry and check "general pool"; we just found out that this is the pool they're hiring from.

Sasha also had a few new leads for Courtney, including an opening at Yoshinoya, a fast-food chain hiring at its Redlands location, about an hour away by bus.

SASHA: You have to go today between twelve and five. . . . I understand if you can't get there. I realize I'm giving you no notice. I also have a lead for a hair salon hiring in Redlands. I tried to call myself, but didn't get to talk to anyone. You should try calling. It just may be that your particular skills (braiding and some other styling) are what they need; you never know until you call.

Next door in Kristen's office, the expectation to pound the pavement had worn thin. Ezra, a white man in his mid-forties, had already been on the Hub's transitional work crew for seventy-five days and still hadn't found a permanent job.[35] Along with ten other Hub clients, he was on the list to start with a company called Precision Construction the following Wednesday, but yesterday, for the third time, the foreman had called Kristen to push back the start date for the five Hub participants he had agreed to bring on. Construction delays were to be expected in the industry, Kristen had explained over and over to the desperate candidates who wanted to remain hopeful about the sixteen dollars per hour possibility, but like Ezra, were running out of time. They felt frustrated and disrespected by the employer's repeatedly broken promises. In fact, it was not uncommon for companies expressing a willingness to hire Hub clients to not be fully forthright about job availability or the conditions, disregard job seekers' and developers' time and energy, and be downright unreliable—qualities that would never be tolerated in job seekers.

The primary purpose of Kristen's meeting with Ezra on this particular day was to make sure he was absolutely clear that he must be ready with a hard hat, safety vest, safety glasses, and steel-toed boots on his first day with Precision. Ezra said he thought he could borrow a vest and some glasses from a friend, and was planning to use the boots that had been provided by the Hub. He did not have a hard hat, however, and was flat broke. To solve this, Kristen encouraged him to go to Home Depot, request a printed invoice for the price of a hard hat, and then take this invoice to his parole officer to see if he would pay for it. "Others have had good luck with this," she added.

Ezra wasn't having it. He was edgy, impatient, and at this point, absolutely discouraged. "My PO [parole officer] is the worst of the worst!" he shouted. "He says no to requests for funds for anything at all . . . and anyway, his office isn't the one close to here." Kristen pushed back. Ezra had no income on the horizon before next Wednesday. This route seemed to be his best bet.

"Why not at least give it a try," she broached? "If it doesn't work, no big deal."

Ezra flew off the handle. "It *is* a big deal! I've been on the bus all morning and at the welfare office since 6:00 a.m. I was already near the Home Depot up there [near the parole office]. I'm worn-out, beat down, and I don't want to spend my entire day going to get an invoice and going to parole when I know it'll result in nothing!"

Seeing she had pushed a button, Kristen gingerly suggested Ezra check with Janine to see if he could borrow a hat, but Ezra wanted to close the conversation and have the last word.

"I guarantee you I'll have a hat by Wednesday, but I'm not going to waste my time trying to get it from parole."

At this moment, a younger white man named Ricky poked his head into Kristen's office, providing a welcome exit for Ezra. He had been working for nearly four weeks at Sophia's laundry—a 110-year-old commercial laundry chain serving hospitals and nursing homes—where Sasha had encouraged Courtney to also apply, and where several Hub clients had already been hired at $9 per hour. Not only did it require enormous effort on the part of job seekers to pursue job leads that did not always materialize, those that did often offered few and/or costly benefits, and were exceedingly low paid, physically demanding, supremely boring, and as Ricky would soon demonstrate, dangerous.

Ricky was chatty with the adrenaline that comes from the first weeks at a new job. Gently removing his right arm from the sleeve of his hoodie, he dramatically displayed a fresh six-by-three-inch burn.

"You should have a doctor look at that," Kristen advised with concern.

"Doctors are part of the government."

"Oh, I see," she smiled, amusedly. "A right-wing conspiracy."

"Left," he corrected.

The unveiling of Ricky's burned arm reminded me of how, on more than one occasion in the Hub's common areas, he had pulled up his shirt to display a huge white power tattoo covering most of his back, reminding onlookers that the region's history as a Klan stronghold was not merely historical.[36] I wondered how he was navigating the mostly Latino plant. Of the six Hub job seekers to be hired there, he was the only white person, and save Garth, a young Black man, the only non-Latino. It could be that his whiteness and the language barrier exempted him from the dynamics that caused Alvaro (one of the Hub's first clients to be hired there) to quit after three weeks when coworkers relentlessly criticized his inability to speak Spanish. "You're a disgrace to me," his coworkers had taunted. "What's wrong man, look at your last name and the color of your skin. Por qué no hablas español?"

Ricky explained that he was waiting for his second paycheck in order to be able to fortify his bike tires and thereby simplify the six-mile commute. Another Hub participant who worked there and had a car (Juan) had been able to change his shift times so they could carpool, but this would only work on Wednesdays, Saturdays, and Sundays because Juan was off Thursdays and Fridays, whereas Ricky was off Mondays and Tuesdays in the seven-day-a-week plant. For now, Ricky would walk on the days he couldn't ride with Juan, which he estimated would take him a little over two hours. He was young and energetic, he reasoned, and thanks to the constant heavy lifting at the job, increasingly fit.

"Makes the days go by," he said, in reference to the heavy lifting. "But the dryers stink and it's hot in there." The other bad news, he complained, was that they take $5 per month from each paycheck until you pay off the $50 union joining fee, in addition to contributions for medical and taxes. All of this amounted to $46 from his first paycheck, and as the manager had explained to Sasha and Kristen, turnover rates were high.

"But I don't want to seem ungrateful," said Ricky. "I'd rather be happy than mad. Just be blessed. Be satisfied to see another day. . . . Plus, I gotta stick around for six months so I can get a raise. I was putting out fires for a dollar-a-day in prison, I can do it for ten." Indeed, Ricky had built the grit and physical stamina required to succeed at Sophia's laundry, and internalized the idea that he should be grateful for a job that was demanding, dangerous, and low paid, in a prison-based program jointly operated by the California Department of Corrections and Rehabilitation and Cal Fire, the state's premier firefighting agency. In this program, imprisoned people whose behavior has been exemplary, and whose convictions are not considered overly serious, have been trained and deployed to help prevent and suppress wildfires alongside free-world firefighters since the 1950s. Pay rates have increased significantly since Ricky's time, but the program still saves the state millions of dollars per year.[37]

Invisible Hands

For Black job seekers at the Hub, antiblack racism worked as an additional force shaping their employment prospects. Their experiences suggested a more nuanced interplay between race and criminal records than the commonly circulated ideas that employers use criminal records as a proxy for race (as an excuse to avoid hiring Black people) or race as a proxy for criminal records (to avoid hiring people with criminal records).[38] Rather, they described an amalgamation of dynamics that made it hard for them to discern where racism ended and criminal record discrimination began, or which was being deployed when. Some tried to name a conflation, describing criminal record discrimination as a form of "pseudoracism," by which they meant that criminal records acted as a foil, standing in as a cover for racist sentiment. At other times, they seemed to feel that criminal record discrimination worked as a form of protoracism in which racism served as a precursor to or a trigger for criminal record discrimination.

—————

Roshaun pressed through the double doors, wet with perspiration and out of breath. The day's heat was motionless and all-consuming, having begun early in the morning and intensifying throughout the afternoon as the asphalt radiated back surplus Btus. A month had gone by, and he was still striking out in the restaurant industry and beyond. He'd had five recent interviews: Walmart, Red Robin, McDonald's, United Furniture, and a staffing agency for a local cement plant. The Walmart interview took place the morning after a friend's funeral, he explained, and the questions all sounded the same. Neither United Furniture nor the staffing agency had called him back. He wasn't entirely sure what had gone wrong at McDonald's, except that he was unprepared to explain the gaps in his work history and had stumbled in response to the question, "Why did you leave your last job?"

Roshaun's early years had been spent in the High Desert, on the air force base where his dad was stationed, which he described as "a perfect world where everything was easy." But when his parents divorced and his father moved back to Kentucky, Roshaun moved with his mother and three siblings to the rural Inland Empire town of Adelanto, which he portrayed, in contrast, as "a place where there was nothing but tumbleweed and trouble." After a couple of short stints in juvenile hall, Roshaun was convicted on drug trafficking and gun charges, and imprisoned for six years. Seven years after his release in 2004, he was again convicted and spent another three years in prison. He had been actively looking for work since his release in 2014, determined to never go back.

The only interview that had gone well, he told me, was the one with Red Robin, where he'd spoken with three different franchise managers (one white man and two Black women) over three days of interviews, developing a strong feeling that they liked him. He wasn't sure what had ultimately gone wrong, but suspected it had to do with the fact that the kitchen manager with whom he'd had a final interview and the entire kitchen staff were Mexican. This had also been the case at most of the other restaurants where he had applied in the past few months. "Mexicans are all over food here!" he remarked with surprise; this had not been the case in Kentucky, where he had gained most of his kitchen experience among Black and white workers. Roshaun wondered whether this was part of the reason he wasn't getting hired or he had simply become overly race conscious as a result of spending time in California prisons where race consciousness is deliberately fomented.[39] "Before [having gone to prison], I wouldn't have thought twice about that Mexican hiring manager," he reflected. "But you can't never be sure."

In fact, you could be sure, if not about that particular manager, at least about the persistent presence of antiblackness in low-wage and semiskilled job markets. This takes several forms. Talking with Roshaun reminded me of sociologist Deirdre Royster's masterful study *Race and the Invisible Hand*. Through long-term observation of a cohort of Black and white male students in Baltimore who had attended the same school, performed at comparable levels, and demonstrated similar strengths and weaknesses of character, Royster tested the color-blind assertion that differences in job market outcomes between Blacks and whites can be explained by "hard" factors, such as education and training, or differences in "soft skills" like initiative, attitude, ability to work with others, and reliability. She found that race was a key predictor of employment and earnings, not only because of individual hiring manager's racist sentiments, but because Black Americans were much less likely than their white counterparts to possess the necessary interpersonal, group, and institutional connections to get them jobs.[40]

Roshaun's situation also brought to mind sociologist Devah Pager's ground-breaking study of job seekers in Milwaukee, which found that the effect of a criminal record was 40 percent greater for Black men than for white men, and famously, that employers preferred white applicants with criminal records over Black applicants with no record.[41] In parsing the details, Pager found that when broken down by six major occupational categories, restaurant employers were the least likely to request criminal record information on their applications, but also least likely to call back Black applicants. In fact, the size of the race effect more than doubled for restaurant jobs compared to other occupational categories.[42] Unbeknownst to Roshaun, though the restaurant industry was known for openness to people with criminal records, it was an industry that hires few Black people as well.

Research continues to show the many ways that antiblack racism remains a powerful force in today's job market. Employers significantly prefer white and Latino/a job applicants, so much so that Black applicants have to search twice as long as equally qualified white applicants before receiving a callback or job offer from an employer.[43] People with white-sounding names receive 50 percent more callbacks for interviews than people with Black-sounding names, and Black candidates from elite universities only do as well as white candidates from less selective universities in the job market.[44] As the Economic Policy Institute notes, "African Americans have made considerable gains in high school and college completion over the last four-and-a-half decades—both in absolute terms as well as relative to whites—and those gains have had virtually no effect on equalizing employment outcomes."[45] While these disparities often continue to be explained in terms of differences in skills and preparation, the gap is better understood in relation to numerous forms of structural discrimination in the US job market—including Black Americans' historical exclusion from opportunities for upward mobility, ongoing relegation to low-wage and nonunionized occupations, and the general imbalance of power between employers and employees.[46]

The High Road

It first struck me as ironic that in the entire year I spent at the Hub, the only person to land a coveted position through the BGM Staffing agency next door was Isaac, a Black man in his early forties. Isaac had been arrested at age eighteen. He'd spent one year in jail, but almost as soon as he got out, was reimprisoned on felony charges that kept him in a cage until he was thirty-eight years old. On coming to the Hub, Issac had walked over to BGM Staffing, and with little fanfare, gotten himself hired.

Like several other Black men I came to know at the Hub, Isaac had been subject to the severe sentencing common to the late 1980s, during the United States' globally unprecedented and racially targeted prison boom. It was my observation that these men who had survived decades of imprisonment tended not only to get hired quickly but also to remain employed for longer periods of time than their younger counterparts and advance more quickly.

This ease was due in part to a legal particularity in the Investigative Consumer Reporting Agencies Act (the California version of the Fair Credit Reporting Act), which governs how background screening firms and other agencies collect as well as distribute information. Under this law, a credit reporting agency may not report arrests that don't lead to conviction, convictions that have been granted dismissal by the courts, or convictions older than "seven years." Though confusion has abounded as to how these seven years are calculated, in practice (somewhat counterintuitively), conviction for a crime considered serious and subjection to a long prison sentence makes it easier to "pass" a background check.[47] Even so, these men's easy entrance into the labor market cannot only be explained in terms of a legal particularity. The violence of prisons and jails along with the struggle to survive within them leads to the cultivation of qualities that are valuable to the workforce, including self-discipline, endurance, the ability to contain emotion, and a no-holds-barred commitment to employment success.

———

Given the lack of city buses, Isaac's shift at the warehouse—Monday through Saturday, 9:00 p.m. to 2:00 a.m.—required him to ride his bike twenty-five round-trip miles (about two hours) from his home on the north side of the city to the distribution center in the south, across what he described as the most dangerous parts of downtown San Bernardino. "You have to do what you have to do," he told me. "I thought about getting a car, but figured I should get a roof over my head first. Plus, riding my bike and the bus keeps me humble. I have to stay patient and know I'm blessed, and stay humble." Positive attitude notwithstanding, Isaac had realized that in order to get a roof over his head or get a car, he would need to round out his income with a second job, and this was easier said than done. He had been a star student in the welding course the Hub had arranged in collaboration with a local community college, but unfortunately, this entry-level training was not proving sufficient to actually land a job as a welder. He had later tried a mechanical engineering class, which career counselors claimed could lead directly to moderate-wage employment, but the class ended at 4:00 p.m. on Saturdays and the warehouse had just changed his start time to 5:00 p.m.—too tight to reliably make it to work. He would not risk losing the job.

Earlston was another person who exemplified these remarkable qualities. When I met him, he was in his early fifties, and had been working for nearly one year as a packager of incoming and outgoing goods, at a different location of the same specialty grocer that had hired Roshuan. He came into the Hub periodically to collect the monetary incentives offered by the organization to participants who have gotten hired and managed to remain employed, and often stopped by my desk to talk philosophy through topics such as car troubles, the challenges of marriage, and worksite politics. For example, he reflected that

> you must not let negative people rob you of your joy. Isaiah 55:9 says, as the heavens are higher than the earth, so are my ways higher than your ways. . . . What I get from that scripture is that my ways aren't going to work, and so let me not go on *my* understanding but rather on yours [forearm motioning skyward]. You must figure out how to remain calm and cool, and not let others affect you so much that you're thrown off-kilter.

Earlston was describing a group of young hotheads who worked alongside him at the warehouse and had been threatening to throw him off-kilter. They tended to take things personally, he said, and were eager to backstab and gossip. In particular, the guys who unloaded and reloaded the trucks were frequently stressed by their quotas, moving too quickly and ignoring safety protocols. But Earlston was determined to "take the high road." Despite a five-year parole term, with perfect behavior, he explained, he could discharge after three. Laser focused on freedom, Earlston's twenty-six years spent navigating difficult personalities at Folsom prison had equipped him to follow the course of action that would most quickly lead to his full release from captivity.

At the same time that criminalization produces systemic joblessness, it makes room for partial and contingent inclusions, often in places in the economy providing little long-term security, remuneration, or benefits. And so while it would be easy to read these men's mental fortitude and quick incorporation into the labor market as evidence that prisons "work" as rehabilitative institutions, that antiblackness is not as absolute as is claimed, or that success-ful reentry awaits all of those who apply themselves, it should instead elucidate the cruel reality that employers profit from the resilience of those who survive imprisonment and the work they've done to cultivate these qualities. Mean-while, the terms of employment often keep them from fully actualizing their potential or sharing those hard-earned qualities with their communities.[48]

Anything but That

More than any other category of criminalized job seeker, people with sex-related convictions struggle to obtain employment, and overall, represent the category of convicted persons most radically marginalized. Nearly seven thou-sand laws across the United States restrict the movements and activities of people convicted of sex-related crimes, dictating where and with whom they can live, work, travel, or simply "be," and making it extraordinarily difficult to find housing and employment, or access social services.[49] Most are also re-quired to register their whereabouts on public databases, despite overwhelm-ing evidence that while such registries do much to generate fear and stigma, they do little to protect vulnerable people from harm.[50]

Where the law leaves any wiggle room, public attitudes toward people with sex-related convictions do the rest. At the Hub, job seekers whose convictions were not related to sex frequently spoke disparagingly against those with sex-related convictions, using them as a baseline from which to distinguish and exonerate themselves. Reentry and workforce professionals across the region also regularly made disparaging remarks and expressed discomfort with hav-ing to assist people with sex-related convictions. Employers I interviewed said things like, "We're not equipped to handle that here," "I have a right not to deal with that," and "Anything but that." Memorably, one employer stated, "I don't *believe* in pedophiles." Despite the clearly personal nature of these attitudes, employers often framed the motivation to exclude in terms of a responsibility to protect other employees or "minimize exposure"—the structural reinforc-ing the personal, and the personal reinforcing the structural.

———

One morning I found Gabriel in the computer lab, eager to work on the ap-plication for Friendly Dollar. Having assisted so many others with this applica-tion in past weeks, I already knew that the process could take up to two hours, depending on the state of his résumé and whether or not he had a retail-focused cover letter ready to adapt. This degree of focus would be challenging for Gabriel, who had a sunny personality, and was constantly fidgeting, cracking jokes, and chatting.

The first step was to create an online account. I was somewhat surprised when he selected "American Indian" in the optional race and gender questions. In this computer lab, most nonwhite applicants selected "prefer not to answer" in hopes of warding off racial discrimination. Next, he struggled to choose a required account security question to verify his identity in the event of a forgotten password. The options were embedded with assumptions of personal and economic stability as well as privilege. He didn't remember the name of his elementary school. He did not know his birth mother, much less her maiden name. He had never had a pet, nor owned a car, and having never been on a vacation, had no "favorite vacation spot." Finally, he found a question he could answer: "city of your first school."

Gabriel's path to employment had been arduous. After several months of applications and interviews, he was finally hired at Sophia's laundry, but when his parole officer learned of the job, he was forced to quit because of the plant's proximity to a school—a violation of the restrictions associated with his conviction.[51] A few weeks later, he had been thrilled to be hired by a small auto mechanic shop, his ideal line of work. Yet when he showed up for his first day of work, he was informed that the employee whose resignation had created the vacancy had returned to reclaim the job.

Eventually, Gabriel had been hired to stock parts at Levit Plumbing Supply's warehouse through a local staffing agency and been working there consistently for nine months. Though grateful for the job, Gabriel wasn't getting the number of hours he needed to cover his living expenses and child support. For this reason, he was trying to find a second job, though he wasn't sure how he would manage if he were actually to get one because his manager expected him to be available at all times, even though he rarely surpassed twenty hours in a week. "They fire you for every little thing," he explained. "They don't need the temps, they can replace you in one minute." The constantly changing schedule also prevented Gabriel from taking classes at a community college to pursue his desired career in auto body work. Still, he was hopeful that if he "stuck it out," the company would eventually convert him to a full-time or at least permanent part-time employee.

Gabriel's hope ultimately materialized, and Levit Plumbing Supply decided to bring him on as a permanent employee. He and all the staff at the Hub were elated, but no one was aware that in order to convert his status, the company would run a background check. Though not required for temps, drug testing and background screening, it turned out, were standard protocol for all "regular" employees. When Gabriel learned of the pending checks, he crossed his fingers and worked harder than ever.

A week or so after Gabriel had received the good news about his promotion, Levit's HR team reached a verdict: not only would he not be converted to permanent employee status, he was fired. It was hard to believe, even in this setting where denials and disappointments were commonplace.

The firing seemed legally unjustifiable in that it completely ignored the EEOC's requirement for a clear nexus between type of conviction and job duties, not to mention an already monthslong demonstration of fitness for the job. As I will discuss further in the following chapter, however, it is precisely in the ambiguity about what constitutes a reasonable basis for discrimination, coupled with the reliance on employer discretion, that the law falls short. Regardless, legal action was out of the question. The Hub's relationships with employers—which range from simple knowledge that a particular employer does not conduct background checks to deeper engagements with employers willing to overlook some or all types of criminal convictions—depend on their reputation as a good partner. Organizations like theirs cannot effectively build and maintain positive relationships in the business community while simultaneously holding employers accountable to the law. There were also other high-stakes jobs on the line, including that of a young man with tattoos covering his entire face for whom getting hired by any employer had been a significant struggle as well as that of an immigrant from Southeast Asia who hoped to use his new janitorial position with Levit to petition for his wife and children to join him in the United States.

And so rather than challenge the decision, an absolute bewilderment at the company's conduct overcame us all. It was difficult to imagine a legitimate risk associated with stocking parts alongside other adults in a supervised group setting. If this occupational setting was too risky, what setting would be considered safe?

What happened to Gabriel is a reflection of the state's disbelief in the potential for the ethical reconstitution or reintegration of certain subjects, and choice to instead opt for incapacitation, surveillance, and control.[52] Decisions like these to exclude people with sex-related convictions are supported by the widespread belief that unlike other kinds of wrongdoing or harm, the capacity for sexual harm is rare, intrinsic, and irresolvable—a belief contrasted by the overwhelming evidence that sexual harm is in fact pervasive within families and communities, learned rather than innate, and significantly less likely to recur than other criminalized behaviors.[53]

Gabriel's maltreatment was also the result of the absence of a critical theoretical framework out of which to build more effective policy. As feminist scholars and survivors have long argued, vengeance and punishment— including the aggressive social and economic banishment of people convicted of sex-related acts—does not protect but rather compromises community safety, exacerbating as opposed to solving problems of sexual and gender violence.[54] To end or even significantly reduce sexual harm would instead require decriminalizing child and teen sexuality, investing in radical sex and gender education, and building accountability and healing practices as well as engaging in the deep social and cultural work of undoing the patriarchal and heteronormative ideologies that encourage and condone interpersonal harm and violence.[55]

Great Lengths

As the scenes presented here have made plain, looking for work with a recent felony conviction is an often exhausting, discouraging, and exasperating experience, requiring the highest level of inner resolve. Job seekers with criminal records go to great lengths to find work, demonstrating a hunger for and commitment to work that notably surpasses that of many workers without criminal records. When they are lucky enough to get hired, criminalized people frequently endure labor arrangements lacking adequate compensation, protection, basic accommodation, or respect. For at the same time that criminalization produces systemic unemployability, it produces workers who are willing to accept and embrace the disempowering conditions of their employment.

Criminalization demotes a person's status in the job market. People who previously worked in skilled occupations get relegated to general pools, those who worked in administrative or customer service positions get relegated to manual labor, and those who were never incorporated into the formal job market become even more marginally positioned. The use of criminal records as a sorting mechanism diminishes economic mobility, the possibility of advancement, and along the way, people's hopes about the possibilities for the future.

As this chapter has emphasized, not everyone is having the same experience. When people with recent felony convictions prepare for and go out into the job market, they face overlapping constraints, compounding devastations, and unique positionalities that defy easy categorization or resolution by any singular policy or social service program. There is no unitary subject "person with a criminal record," and by extension, no universal experience of "looking for work with a criminal record." Rather, criminalization's interaction with long-standing social hierarchies produces numerous variations in how it is lived and felt. Combined with one's prior relationship to the job market, the sector in which one is seeking work, and the type of conviction one has, the effects of criminalization may be more or less severe, more or less permanent, and wreak more or less havoc on a person's employment prospects and life.

Importantly, those lumped into the somewhat forced universal categories "formerly incarcerated" or "justice impacted" do not necessarily see their identities or fates as linked. Prior workers do not see themselves as similarly positioned to people who have never had a job. Black job seekers correctly perceive their "level of alienation as qualitatively greater" and their relationship to the job market as distinct.[56] And people whose convictions are not sex related often do all they can to disassociate themselves from those whose convictions are so classified.

This complexity and difference does not diminish the importance of generalizations reached by quantitative study, or eliminate the need for unitary identity categories frequently necessary for strategic political action.[57] But it does mean that efforts to challenge criminal record employment discrimination or otherwise improve employment outcomes for criminalized people must somehow grapple with the ways criminal records land as well as stick differently for people who are differently positioned along axes of power and difference. As I will discuss in the conclusion, this becomes especially significant when it comes to policy, which so easily leaves and/or sells some people out.

———

When I met Jaime, the concrete journeyman, three years later in the same parking lot, he was driving a beautiful new truck and holding a paycheck that justified it. He had found a way to shake the shame of his stigmatized condition enough to pursue better opportunities, despite his continued fear of exposure. This determination, combined with his adeptness, had facilitated a near-full professional rebound. But a deeper loss remained. Jaime had given up hope of reuniting with his family and cut ties. While he had found a way to move forward with his life, he remained haunted by the past.

Don, the heavy equipment operator, became overwhelmed with the strain of debt along with his inability to get back into the union or any other high-paid job, and checked himself into a drug and alcohol rehabilitation program.

Ronaldo, the fencer, wasn't long for the Hub. One afternoon on his way home from a parole-mandated public speaking class, he spontaneously decided to stop in at a factory near his house that makes plastics. Actually, he told me, he didn't really know what it manufactured when he stopped, but felt like taking advantage of his professional attire to take a chance and ask if the factory was hiring. Ronaldo had started talking to a random worker on the yard when by chance, the owner of the company came riding by on a forklift. Motioning him to approach, the owner, a white man in his late sixties, initiated a job interview on the spot. The owner cut right to the chase, asking the details of Ronaldo's work experience, how much he was looking to make per hour, and whether he'd been in prison. Ronaldo answered all of these questions forthrightly, grateful for the frank exchange and encouraged by what he described as the owner's lack of pretentiousness. The owner asked him to return the following Wednesday at 3:00 p.m. Though Ronaldo and I lost touch after this exchange, I have no doubt that whether at the plastics factory or elsewhere, he succeed in reintegrating himself into the workforce.

After a short period of reincarceration, Brian, the youngster who had been arrested in the computer lab, came back to the Hub and got hired as a groundskeeper by a government-sponsored nonprofit organization.

Arturo's birth mother had been a "no-call, no-show." The next time I saw him, he was plodding along slowly, his body slumped forward.

Isaiah, the one who had fallen asleep in the van, ultimately lost the custody battle for his nephew and was eventually discharged from the Hub program when it was discovered that he hadn't been making it to his parole-mandated classes.

When a fire caused by substandard housing conditions led to the tragic and sudden death of two young children in his extended family, Clifford, the man who had been forced to quit welding training because of his eye, sank into a state of emotional crisis so acute that looking for work became an impossible focus.

Courtney, the would-be nurse, never did get a callback from Sophia's laundry, but was soon hired by a major retailer through a staffing agency that had recently lowered its bar from seven years since the date of conviction to five. She eventually quit this job because the shifts interfered with one of her parole-mandated classes, and like many others at the Hub, instead took the nine-dollar-per-hour job doing janitorial work at the big warehouse.

Isaac's willingness to go to such lengths for the warehouse paid off. Within nine months, he was converted from the staffing agency to a direct employee of the company, and at the one year mark to "ambassador," tasked with traveling to satellite warehouses to train other employees. Though he worried the conversion to permanent status would ultimately result in less money than he had made through the temp agency (given the combination of part-time hours and required pay siphoning to cover his benefits), Isaac continued to accept every arrangement the employer offered with gratitude.

Not long after Caleb's time at the Hub expired, a housemate told him about an opening at a nearby pallet production facility. Staffed predominantly by undocumented Mexican immigrants, the employer was unconcerned about credentials of any kind and put Caleb to work building runners, the two-by-four structures inside pallets into which the forks of the forklift are inserted. For ten dollars an hour, Caleb built one hundred or so runners each day for almost a year until one morning, when he arrived for work, the general manager was standing at the entrance with final checks in hand. They were closing the shop. Caleb collected unemployment all summer. Then one Monday evening in November at his mandatory parole meeting, he learned that a temp agency was hiring for a popular specialty grocery store. Caleb was up-front about his parole status, but it didn't matter; a drug test by mouth swab was the only stipulation for the job. Stationed in the refrigerator with a lab coat and rubber gloves for eight hours per day, his job was to set blocks of cheese under a wire cutter, slice them into various shapes, and arrange them on trays. The trays were then stacked on a cart and rolled to the next station for shrink-wrapping and labeling. Caleb didn't like the cold, but the main issue was that it was becoming increasingly difficult to stand so many hours on his swollen feet. As he would soon learn, he was suffering from type 2 diabetes as well as congestive heart failure. But before his health would end his job as a cheese cutter, an incident in the parking lot did. Parking was scarce, so employees had to arrive well in advance and line up to wait for spaces to open up as the shift rotated. On this particular morning, another driver cut in front of him, and when Caleb pulled up aggressively behind her to make the point, she called the cops, saying he had hit her car. Luckily, the police dismissed her claim, but the company's security was alerted, and Caleb was suspended indefinitely. Caleb registered for both temporary state and long-term federal disability benefits. The former paid a percentage of his weekly earnings at the time of disability; the latter paid an average based on his lifetime earnings. Neither amounted to much, and Caleb would have much preferred to work. He remained mildly hopeful that once his parole was terminated, health notwithstanding, he would be able to return to a desk job of the sort he used to enjoy.

Roshaun eventually gave up on the restaurant industry and got hired by a staffing agency to load loaves of bread at the warehouse of a grocery chain with locations across the southwest. Though he was faring better than most earning thirteen dollars per hour, the wage was dependent on his ability to accurately fill a minimum number of orders per hour, especially exhausting given the shift that ran from 2:00 a.m. to 10:00 a.m. This shift time also meant he had to catch the 14 bus at 9:34 p.m. in order to reach the Fontana Metrolink that departs at 10:00 p.m. and then catch bus 61, a twenty-minute ride that would take him within walking distance of the warehouse. This series of transfers got him to work at 11:00 p.m., three hours early (there was a later bus 14, but the last 61 bus left at 10:17 p.m.)—a ninety-minute commute that would have taken twenty minutes by car. In any case, his employment at the grocery warehouse was short-lived. He struggled to tolerate the racial taunts of a young, white, fellow employee, who said things to him like, "Wrap the pallet, boy." Roshaun stopped speaking to the youngster, making an effort to let it go by reasoning that perhaps the youngster didn't know better and didn't fully understand the weight of his words. But the kid wouldn't quit poking, and the conflict eventually escalated into an argument in the break room. Overhearing, a supervisor fired them both.

Gabriele went AWOL. He never returned to the Hub, and none of us heard from him again. The sting of the ease with which Levit Plumbing had disposed of him after nearly a year of loyal service was just too much.

As for Jamal, Gary, Miranda, Ricky, Ezra, and many others, I never knew their outcomes.

2

The Making of Common Sense

Doing a background check is a sound business decision. You want to know a little bit more about a person that you're going to bring into your company. Criminal records can show a history of good or bad decision-making.

Sometimes companies end up doing background checks on existing employees because it's required by a new contract or something like that, and sometimes they find scary stuff. But you really can't fire someone at that point and get away with it; that ship has sailed. . . . Obviously, you'll watch them more closely, and you won't promote them.

We really do need to find employment for them, within reason.

—BACKGROUND SCREENING PROFESSIONALS

ON THE THIRD FLOOR OF a glass-faced high-rise, fifty HR professionals gathered for a training sponsored by a Southern California branch of one of the biggest and most well-established HR organizations in the United States. It was 7:30 a.m., allowing participants to arrive ahead of the traffic and still get to their offices at a reasonable time afterward. Attending these kinds of events allowed me to meet HR professionals from a range of industries, learn firsthand their practical and theoretical concerns, and hear the advice given. I was especially keen to hear this day's featured guest speaker, Tonya Jenkins, vice president of a midsize commercial background screening firm, Gold Star, Inc.

Turning to the front of the room, Jenkins clicked to display the first slide in her PowerPoint presentation, "Background Check Basics."

"Hopefully everyone is doing background checks and using a third-party screener," she began. "First, let's talk briefly about why companies should do background checks."

1. Avoid a bad hire. Hiring the wrong candidate can cost thirty percent of the employee's first-year earnings.
2. Prevent theft. Nearly 30 percent of all business failures are caused by employee theft.
3. Reduce violence. Workplace violence costs US businesses $56 billion annually.
4. Avoid a negligent hire lawsuit. The average settlement for a negligence case is approximately $1.5 million.
5. Foster a drug-free workplace. Substance abuse costs employers billions in losses due to absenteeism and reduced productivity.
6. Identify honest candidates. Seventy-five percent of job applicants falsify education records or credentials.

Jenkins read the slide with a nonchalant matter-of-factness, her tone flat—like a high school teacher reviewing material for an upcoming test. This was not an introduction to new ideas or even really a sales pitch. Each justification for background screening was treated quickly and lightly, as if requiring little explanation. The HR professionals listened politely, raising their eyebrows at appropriate moments in appreciation of some of the more sensational statistics. I could barely contain myself, shifting uncomfortably in my chair, my mind countering each rationale based on my firsthand observations of job seekers and existing research. Even momentarily setting aside the problems with the standard categories of "crime" and "violence" described in the introduction, on their own terms, the arguments didn't hold up.

Avoid a bad hire? Research suggests that people with criminal records generally make hardworking, dedicated employees. For instance, as early as 1973, a federal government study found that people on work release make equally good, if not better, employees than nonimprisoned employees, noting that what little difference there was favored employees with records.[1] More recently, a research team from Stanford University that studied 5,000 City of San Francisco employees found that the 800 or so employees with criminal convictions had performed equally well over a three-year period as those without.[2] Likewise, an analysis of 1.3 million people employed by the military analyzed the attrition and work termination rates due to poor performance, and found military employees with felony convictions performed similarly to those without, and were slightly *more* likely to be promoted at a faster rate and to higher positions.[3] Furthermore, a recent survey of more than 1,200 managers, non-managers, and HR professionals found that "within companies that have hired workers with criminal records, employers rate the quality of their work as comparable to those without a record."[4]

Prevent theft? No evidence supports the claim that people who have criminal records are more likely to steal on the job. Nor does common sense. In fact, one could reasonably make the opposite assumption: that people with convictions would be *less* likely to steal on the job for fear of another conviction, the scarcity of jobs available to them, and the awareness that they are being hypersurveilled. Furthermore, studies that have attempted to pinpoint the general likelihood of committing new criminal acts among those who have been convicted have found that any increased likelihood peaks within one to two years and declines thereafter. After about seven years, there is virtually no difference in the likelihood of committing a crime between those with prior convictions and those without.[5] To boot, these kinds of estimates are inherently conservative in that they don't account for the effect of a job itself. Not only is employment well-known to be one of the biggest reducers of criminal activity, as demonstrated by job seekers in chapter 1, the great lengths to which people with convictions go to get hired is proof in itself of a commitment to desist from crime.[6]

Reduce violence? No evidence links past convictions to workplace violence or otherwise counterproductive work behavior.[7] In fact, statistical data from the Federal Bureau of Investigation (FBI), Occupational Safety and Health Administration (OSHA), National Center for Injury Prevention and Control, and other federal agencies that track violent crime show that workers face higher risks of assault from strangers, customers, intimate partners, and family members than from coworkers.[8] In other words, the vast majority of workplace violence is perpetrated by nonemployees. Furthermore, comparative historical studies convincingly demonstrate that varying levels of workplace violence have less do with the psyches of troubled individuals, and more to do with contextual factors including working conditions, disparities in how the work is organized, and workers' power to determine the conditions of their work.[9]

Avoid negligent hire lawsuits? As I will elaborate on shortly, while a steady broadening in the scope of employer liability since the 1950s is indisputable, the law has never required criminal background checks; it requires that employers take reasonable care in hiring. Moreover, the actual risks of being held liable have been overstated by risk industries with a direct investment in background screening.

Foster a drug-free workplace? The idea that workplaces should be "drug free" took root following US president Ronald Reagan's passage in 1988 of the Drug Free Workplace Regulation, which required that all entities contracting with or receiving grants from a federal agency certify their commitment to provide a "drug-free workplace." But what does this mean? While most people would agree that being drunk or high at work is problematic, little evidence supports the claim that using drugs in one's personal time necessarily impacts work performance. In addition, a drug-free workplace does not indicate or require that companies conduct drug *testing*, yet this regulation served as a catalyst for the now widely accepted idea that drug testing is an important way to improve productivity, reduce accidents, and limit workers' compensation claims. What's more, while both legal and illicit drug use cuts evenly across lines of race and class, drug testing is more often conducted in blue-collar occupational settings and almost entirely absent in many white-collar professions.[10]

Identify honest candidates? The idea that "honest" workers are an identifiable type that can be distinguished and recruited is questionable. Not only is there little basis to support the idea of a fixed or innate character, criminal record-based limitations often conflate having been convicted of a crime with poor character.[11] Additionally, as I will elaborate in chapter 3, the demand for absolute "candor" about criminal records on employment applications is both unreasonable and unfair. Furthermore, the notion that lying about a criminal conviction on an application is as important as the conviction itself presumes an unfounded link between the willingness and ability to speak openly about a stigmatized aspect of one's identity, and the willingness to be open and honest in the performance of job duties.

Notwithstanding the evidence, the HR professionals nodded in lackadaisical agreement. Conjecture could be presented as fact, it seemed, because the basic premise of the presentation—that criminal background screening offers an effective solution to many workplace problems—had already been internalized by the audience as common sense.

———

This chapter asks how and why this common sense got built. Drawing from a range of primary and secondary sources, it traces key motivations, priorities, and political dynamics that have driven the collection, organization, dissemination, and discriminatory use of criminal records in employment. Throughout the twentieth century, police, judges, and attorneys; medical, corrections, and treatment professionals; legislators, government agencies, and professional licensing boards; insurance companies, media organizations, gun proponents, and victims' rights organizations; security, workplace risk, and HR management organizations; commercial background screening firms; and many others pursued criminal background checks as a way to "solve" problems and satisfy desires. By the mid-2000s, their combined interests had solidified into the idea that employment background checks should be conducted as a matter of routine, while their investments of time, money, and expertise had built the infrastructure, systems, and know-how to do so.

The historicization offered here writes against the most common explanations for the rise of criminal background screening. One is the tendency in mainstream thought to naturalize the demand for background screening as an organic as well as reasoned response to growing concerns about workplace safety and security; what one government report summarizes as "America's growing dependence on criminal record background checks to strengthen public safety by reducing opportunities for certain criminal offenders to repeat their past histories."[12] Relatedly, this account challenges the prevalent claim in risk and security literatures as well as screening industry propaganda, that widespread background screening was made necessary by changing tort law.[13] In these portrayals, the private sector innocently arose to meet demand generated by courts' changing legal interpretations:

> The rise in the screening industry, and particularly the use of criminal background checks to pre-screen job candidates, tenants, vendors and volunteers, stems in large part from the growth of claims alleging that an employer, organization or association can be negligent for hiring or retaining an individual who subsequently engages in violence. . . . Through the years, various state courts slowly expanded the tort of negligent hiring to cover a broader range of situations where the acts of an employee caused injury.[14]

While a steady legal broadening in the scope of employer liability over the past century is indisputable, the idea that the dramatic rise in background screening is largely *explained* by changes in liability doctrine is disingenuous in the sense that it is impossible to separate the effect of a changing legal landscape from the ways the law is interpreted, litigated, and publicized. The mere accounting of court decisions does not explain how those decisions are brought to life by attorneys, industries, and media outlets standing to gain from sensationalism.

The present account also avoids an overemphasis on the technological revolution: the idea that technological advances in computing power and the internet were in themselves the cause of wide dissemination of criminal records. Certainly, the computer industry's introduction of the first "third-generation" computer systems in 1965 (which enabled complex data-bases that could centralize and store enormous quantities of data as well as allow their retrieval from almost anywhere) made the wide sharing and use of criminal records technically possible.[15] An overemphasis on the role of infor-mation technology, however, can detract attention from deliberate decisions made by human beings to collect and centralize data, disclose data to others, and allow discrimination on its basis.[16]

In the less passive retelling I offer here, I interrogate rather than take for granted motivations, err on the side of outcomes regardless of intentions, and take more of an interest in responsibility than unforeseen or unintended con-sequences. As I will show, though some factors that contributed significantly to the rise of criminal background screening are happenstance, these were deliberately leveraged by actors invested in growing the practice. And while some threads of the phenomenon unfolded in relative isolation, key moments of coordination and collaboration have led me to read their combined effects as more than the result of a perfect storm.[17]

By extension, my commitment to think in terms of how various factors work together does not allow me (however tempting) to single out commercializa-tion as *the* cause. To be sure, commercial background screening vendors flooded the HR arena after the terrorist attacks of September 11, 2001, seeking to sell as many background checks as possible. The capacity they brought to the table as capitalist enterprises fundamentally changed what was possible, enabling back-ground screening at a scale never seen before. Yet I will argue the demand for the product enjoyed by the private sector was built on the legitimacy established by lawmakers who enacted discriminatory statutes and licensing restrictions, granted access to data, and constructed a legal framework holding employers responsible for employee behavior. Likewise, a major commercial background screening market would not have been practical outside the consolidation, digi-tization, and infrastructural improvements initiated for policing purposes and bolstered by firearms policy; selling background checks would not have become so lucrative outside courts' willingness to sell their electronic data to commer-cial vendors; and employers could not have effectively implemented large-scale screening programs without the guidance, know-how, and support provided by professional experts in insurance, HR management and employment law. Like a boulder rolling down a mountain through the twists and turns of the twentieth century, the combined forces of law, policy, profit, and professional expertise turned the United States into the world's most enthusiastic user as well as global promoter of criminal records as a discriminatory tool.[18]

Like most big stories, the rise of criminal background screening contains linear elements of cause and effect along with moments when distinct agendas intersect and build on one another to produce effects greater than any of their parts. My goal, then, in piecing together the ingredients of systemic discrimination is not only to understand who did what when but to the extent possible, the full recipe: how things work together and to what effect.[19] For on the one hand, why and how we came to be in a situation in which most employers conduct criminal background checks as a matter of routine is a complicated, multi-layered story of causes, motivations, and outcomes; on the other hand, it's a fairly straightforward one. In order for criminal records to be widely used as a discriminatory tool, the data must exist and be shared, their use permitted, encouraged, and facilitated, and crucially, people must be convinced of their value.

Motivate and Establish

Police are the primary creators of criminal records, and criminal records were, first and foremost, a tool of policing. In the United States, the first systems of criminal identification emerged in the late 1800s in the context of rising anxieties about increasing immigration and migration to US urban centers. Police, private security agencies, and criminologists needed new methods to manage an increasingly diverse, mobile, and anonymous population.[20] As policing scholars have demonstrated, private police agencies charged with protecting mines, factories, railways, warehouses, banks, and hotels as well as infiltrating and spying on the labor movement were the first to lead criminal identification efforts and call for better records coordination.[21] By the 1870s, the infamous Pinkerton National Detective Agency had assembled the first comprehensive database of mug shots in the United States. Soon after, public criminal history systems began to develop in Northeastern cities.

Police were not alone in their hunger for compiled data. As security scholar Charles W. Brackett has described, a wide range of professionals (both conservative and progressive) liked the idea of a single document detailing a person's contacts with the criminal legal system that could be shared across institutions.[22] Prosecutors and judges wanted to be able to identify (and harshly punish) so-called repeat offenders, while social reformers believed that criminal records could help track and target participants in organized crime. Within the prison system, wardens, social workers, psychiatrists, and other staff wanted comprehensive records to better tailor their treatments as well as plans for release.

Toward these ends, by the early 1900s multiple states had established bureaus of criminal identification, and were collecting and compiling bodily measurements and fingerprints from state prisoners. In 1918, California established the first state criminal record repository.[23] Other states soon followed suit, despite some initial slowing by opposition from labor, civil liberties organizations, and others concerned that coordinated recordkeeping would interfere with the exercise of First Amendment rights.[24] In 1924, the FBI established the first national storehouse, collecting fingerprint and arrest records from local, state, and federal agencies.[25]

A next big moment of inflection was the Cold War period following World War II. Brackett's research also highlights how the Cold War security mindset gave fodder to the idea that a trustworthy, reputable organization or profession should be free of people with criminal records. This notion was most memorably demonstrated by President Harry S. Truman's "loyalty" program, which initiated widespread criminal background investigations of government workers in an effort to rid the administration of Communists and other "subversives."[26] Large businesses and professional organizations followed suit, turning to criminal background checks as a way to demonstrate their legitimacy by proving they were not harboring organized crime, at the same time that government agencies, private organizations, and entire industries moved to pass regulations excluding people with criminal records from their ranks.[27] Relatedly, the numbers of occupations and professions requiring a special license or credential surged after World War II, and with them, the share of jobs for which people with criminal convictions could not qualify.[28]

These same anxieties about loyalty and legitimacy were capitalized on by the insurance industry, whose fundamental profitability depends on accurately predicting and grouping risks as well as minimizing the persons and events that are underwritten.[29] Sensing commercial opportunity in the postwar tension, insurers began to promote "blanket-bonding" policies: relatively low-cost fidelity and surety bonds to protect employers from fraud, theft, embezzlement, and other dishonest actions of employees in positions of trust. These bonds stipulated that employment be denied to anyone with a criminal record unless specifically exempted by the insurance company. Any violation of this provision would invalidate the employer's protection.[30]

This new trend, warned criminologist Marcel Frym at the 1956 Third International Congress on Criminology, was "spreading like wildfire" and in his view, had become "one of the darkest chapters in the history of man's inhumanity toward man in the United States." Frym's alarmed exposition explained to Congress how the stipulation worked in practice. A "box" had been placed on employment applications, and it functioned as a tool for determining who was insurable, and by extension, employable. Little did Frym know, five decades later, that this very same box would become the symbolic center of grassroots antidiscrimination campaigns. He observed,

> Questionnaires to be filled out by applicants for employment contain the question "Have you ever been convicted of an offense?" Or even "Have you ever been arrested?" and, if the answer is in the affirmative, rejection by the bonding company, even in cases of relatively minor offenses, is the rule and exceptions are rare.[31]

Debates about liability were also underway in other arenas. In particular, notions of responsibility were beginning to shift in US courts, expanding the scope of employers' liability for the actions of their employees. Whereas the early 1900s' understanding of employer responsibility had been quite narrow— employers were responsible only if something went wrong in the course of the job and another employee was injured—a new doctrine, "negligent hiring," extended liability beyond other employees to customers and beyond the course of the job.[32]

A foundational case, *Fleming v. Bronfin*, had unfolded in 1951 when a woman was attacked in her apartment by a delivery man. The court reasoned that although the act took place outside the direct scope of the employee's duties, the employer had known the employee would be dealing with the public and entering customers' homes, and therefore should "be held to the duty of hiring only safe and competent employees."[33] This verdict was the first to apply the law to a third party (i.e., not another coworker, but a customer) and extend liability beyond the "course of the job," setting the stage for the general argument that employers could be legally responsible for the behavior of their employees in and beyond the workplace.

Build and Share

Experts like Frym were not alone in voicing their concern about the mounting ethos of exclusion. A law reform movement that had first emerged in the mid-1950s started to challenge the hundreds of government-authorized penalties disqualifying people convicted of crimes from privileges and benefits, such as the right to vote, hold public office, own a firearm, serve on a jury, and qualify for public housing and student loans, and imposing sanctions like forced registration, loss of parental rights, and deportation.[34] This movement, as legal experts Margaret Colgate Love, Jenny Roberts, and Wayne Logan describe, called for "the abolition of laws depriving convicted individuals of civil and political rights," portraying them as "an archaic holdover from early times" and urging courts to adopt laws that would erase peoples' criminal records at the end of their sentences.[35] Legal reformers continued their fight against government-authorized penalties in the 1960s and 1970s, contending that the "collateral consequences of conviction," which had been part of the US legal system since colonial times, contributed to the social exclusion and political disenfranchisement of Black Americans especially, and were generally incompatible with the modern legal system's belief in rehabilitation and second chances.[36] In response, some states started to enact protections against automatic disqualifications from employment and occupational licensing, while federal and state courts began to strike down exclusionary statutes on constitutional grounds.[37]

At the same time, however, the urban uprisings and increasingly militant organizing of the late 1960s and early 1970s in cities across the United States had motivated a major buildup of policing and state surveillance capacities. Leveraging the "war on crime" as a tool of political repression, President Richard Nixon and his supporters targeted struggles for freedom and equality.[38] In particular, Black freedom struggles, which have always been a focus of domestic counterinsurgency, were among the crime war's primary targets.[39] In his classic *Lockdown America: Police and Prisons in the Age of Crisis*, Christian Parenti describes how by linking street crime to civil rights protest—"crime" to "urban" to "Black"—President Nixon and his supporters used Lyndon Baines Johnson's war on crime as a "bulwark built against the increasingly political and vocal racial Other by the predominately white state."[40] Under the guise of narcotics trafficking, local crime control could be reframed as a federal problem, enabling the use of a wider range of strategies and tools, including "no-knock" policies, wiretapping, preventative detention and grand juries, helicopters, and transfers of military equipment to police departments.[41] Additionally, as law and society historian Greg Marquis has emphasized, "Far more important than audio and visual monitoring devices to the evolution of the surveillance society" was a proliferation of computers, electronic maps, and criminal intelligence, investigation, and other databases to record information about people suspected of past crimes, or considered at risk of committing future ones.[42]

Indeed, policing and counterinsurgency campaigns depended on more than force and coercion. To restore not just order but also state legitimacy, governments at all levels began to invest heavily in police modernization and professionalization. These efforts were largely supported by the Omnibus Crime Control and Safe Streets Act of 1968, which established a federal program, the Law Enforcement Assistance Administration (LEAA), to direct funding to states and localities for the improvement of law enforcement. Embraced by liberals and conservatives alike, professionalization provided a conceptual framework for a range of policing goals, from increasing officers' effectiveness at suppressing Black resistance to reducing police violence against Black people. Modern approaches such as "community policing" worked to foster the broad idea that private citizens, organizations, and other nongovernment actors should play a role in crime control.[43]

This professionalization campaign also drove the impetus to integrate police, prosecution, court, and corrections records nationally toward the goal of a "single, coherent, smooth running informational and surveillance network."[44] A 1967 Johnson-appointed commission emphasized "the importance of having complete and timely information about crimes and offenders available at the right place and the right time," calling for "an integrated national information system . . . to serve the combined needs at the National, State, regional and metropolitan or county levels of the police, courts, and correction agencies, and of the public and the research community."[45] In response, Congress authorized the FBI to create the National Crime Information Center. This LEAA-supported electronic clearinghouse of criminal justice information sought to enable information sharing among law enforcement working at the local, state, and federal levels.[46] In doing so, the National Crime Information Center's technology made it possible to link a record to a particular person through a search using a name and numeric personal identifiers, such as date of birth or Social Security number. The ability to make this connection marked a huge advance in the practical usability of criminal records.

In 1969, LEAA also funded the creation of a new nonprofit organization comprised of governor appointees from each of the fifty states, the District of Columbia, and the territories. This National Consortium for Justice Information and Statistics, known as SEARCH, immediately undertook a massive effort to modernize and integrate criminal records, resulting in the establishment of a centralized information system linking federal and state criminal records systems. A few years later, LEAA's Comprehensive Data Systems Program funded states to create computerized repositories of criminal history information into which local courts, police, prosecutors, and probation and corrections departments could feed information.[47] This integration, centralization, and digitization raised questions about privacy and access.

Up until this point in the early 1970s, there existed a relative consensus among state legislatures, Congress, and federal agencies that criminal history was private and protected, and should be used primarily, if not only, for criminal justice and law enforcement purposes.[48] Criminal records held by the FBI were entirely restricted from public view. Though court records have always been *technically* available to the public—under the idea rooted in US common law and constitutional principles that court business should be publicly transparent—they were *practically* obscure in the sense that accessing them required considerable time and expense.[49] Retrieving court records required physical travel to local courthouses to request information about a particular person, and knowledge of a person's name, date of birth, and county or counties in which they had lived and/or been in contact with the criminal legal system.

Even into the early 1970s, legislatures were moving toward further restricting disclosure. Congress attempted to regulate that all criminal record data held by states and localities be as inaccessible as FBI data, and federal agencies like SEARCH were calling for "prohibiting public access to criminal history records except where access was required to comply with federal or state statute."[50]

At the same time, however, pressure was rising for open access to the data. This pressure was generated in part by the general atmosphere of government mistrust in the late 1960s, and amplified by the Watergate scandal along with the consequent mobilization of the Freedom of Information Act to push for openness and transparency.[51] Bowing to pressure for access to FBI data, legal scholar James B. Jacobs describes how Congress began "chipping away at the FBI's policy of refusing to share criminal record information with non-law enforcement agencies."[52] Slowly nondisclosure exceptions were made for local governments and other public entities for employment purposes, enabled by a 1972 law that allowed states to facilitate access to FBI background checks for the purposes of licensing and private employment.[53] Additionally, throughout the 1970s, Congress authorized particular entities to obtain FBI checks for job applicants and employees. For example, authorizations were granted to federally chartered or insured banks as well as state and local licensing agencies in 1972, and securities industry organizations in 1975. State legislatures followed a similar pattern, undermining the nondisclosure rule step-by-step through exceptions.

When in 1976, a Supreme Court decision, *Paul v. Davis*, established that an individual criminal record is not covered by constitutional privacy protections, the push-pull between privacy and access came to a temporary head. This ruling established the basis on which to set aside concerns about privacy and loosen restrictions on public access to criminal records.[54]

Disqualify and Make Responsible

By 1981, legal reformers' efforts to scale back government-imposed disqualifications had been so successful that the American Bar Association declared that "civil disabilities were on their way to extinction," to be replaced by more "sensible rules for evaluating how criminal behavior should affect employment and other opportunities." Relatedly, a 1984 proposal by the House Committee on the Judiciary suggested significantly scaling back felony conviction restrictions on eligibility for government benefits, programs, and employment.[55] But instead things swung abruptly in the other direction.

Legislatures and regulatory agencies turned away from the goals of rehabilitation and reintegration to embrace "a new and urgent emphasis upon the need for security, the containment of danger, and the identification and management of any kind of risk."[56] As is well-known, the "tough on crime" agendas first advanced by politicians like Barry Goldwater and Nixon crescendoed in President Reagan's 1984 Sentencing Reform Act, instituting severe mandatory minimum sentences and ushering in a punitive climate that would define the decades to come. Despite the act's written safeguards against excessive restrictions on access to government benefits and employment, new laws categorically disqualified people with convictions from civil and constitutional rights and benefits, and placed new limitations on the right to work for public agencies, under government contract, or in particular industries.[57] In some cases, new disqualifications were based not only on felony convictions but also misdemeanors, guilty pleas, and nonconviction dispositions.[58]

At the same time, governments bolstered the infrastructure to support criminal record checks. In 1983, SEARCH launched the Interstate Identification Index, or "Triple I," systematizing states' responsibility for collecting and maintaining criminal records from local courts and police departments while enabling police officers to almost instantly determine whether someone they detained was wanted or had ever been arrested anywhere in the United States.[59] Together with increasing state-mandated disqualifications, these infrastructural consolidations encouraged and facilitated wider use of background checks.

The late 1970s and early 1980s were also a time when debates about employers' responsibility for the actions of their employees continued to mount. Negligent hiring cases since *Fleming v Bronfin* were producing a general consensus that employers needed to exercise greater care and scrutiny in selecting employees for jobs that could involve risk to others. Several cases further established the idea that the greater the risk of harm, the higher the degree of care necessary.[60] For example, one important case in 1983, *Ponticas v. KMS Investments,* involved a hastily hired apartment manager who violently assaulted a tenant, and had previous convictions for armed robbery and burglary. Drawing from the by now well-established presumption that past conviction equates with future risk, the court ruled that it was reasonable to presume that a person with a history of violence could well commit another act of violence and therefore the risk of injury was foreseeable.[61] The verdict made it clear that employers could be sued for the criminal or violent acts of their employees.

Importantly, however, the courts did not conclude that employers were bound to investigate an employee's background in depth or necessarily to conduct criminal background checks. Rather, they were expected to investigate the applicant's background in a reasonable manner given the business context.[62] Even in *Ponticas v. KMS Investments* involving a violent assault by a person with prior serious convictions, the Minnesota Supreme Court held that employers were *not* bound by a duty to investigate whether or not a prospective employee had a criminal record, and strongly discouraged employers from rejecting candidates on the simple basis of criminal history:

> At the outset, we reject the contention that, as a matter of law, there exists a duty upon an employer to make an inquiry as to a prospective employee's criminal record even where it is known that the employee is to regularly deal with members of the public. *Evans v. Morsell,* 284 Md. 160, 167, 395 A.2d 480, 484 (1978). If the employer has made adequate inquiry or otherwise has a reasonably sufficient basis to conclude the employee is reliable and fit for the job, no affirmative duty rests on him to investigate the possibility that the applicant has a criminal record. There are many persons in Minnesota who have prior criminal records but who are now good citizens and competent and reliable employees. Were we to hold that an employer can never hire a person with a criminal record at the risk of later being held liable for the employee's assault, it would offend our civilized concept that society must make a reasonable effort to rehabilitate those who have erred so they can be assimilated into the community. Moreover, a rule mandating an independent criminal history investigation would counter the many worthwhile efforts of individuals, organizations and employers to aid former offenders to re-establish good citizenship, the sine qua non of which is gainful and productive employment. Liability of an employer is not to be predicated solely on failure to investigate criminal history of an applicant,

The Rise of Criminal Background Screening

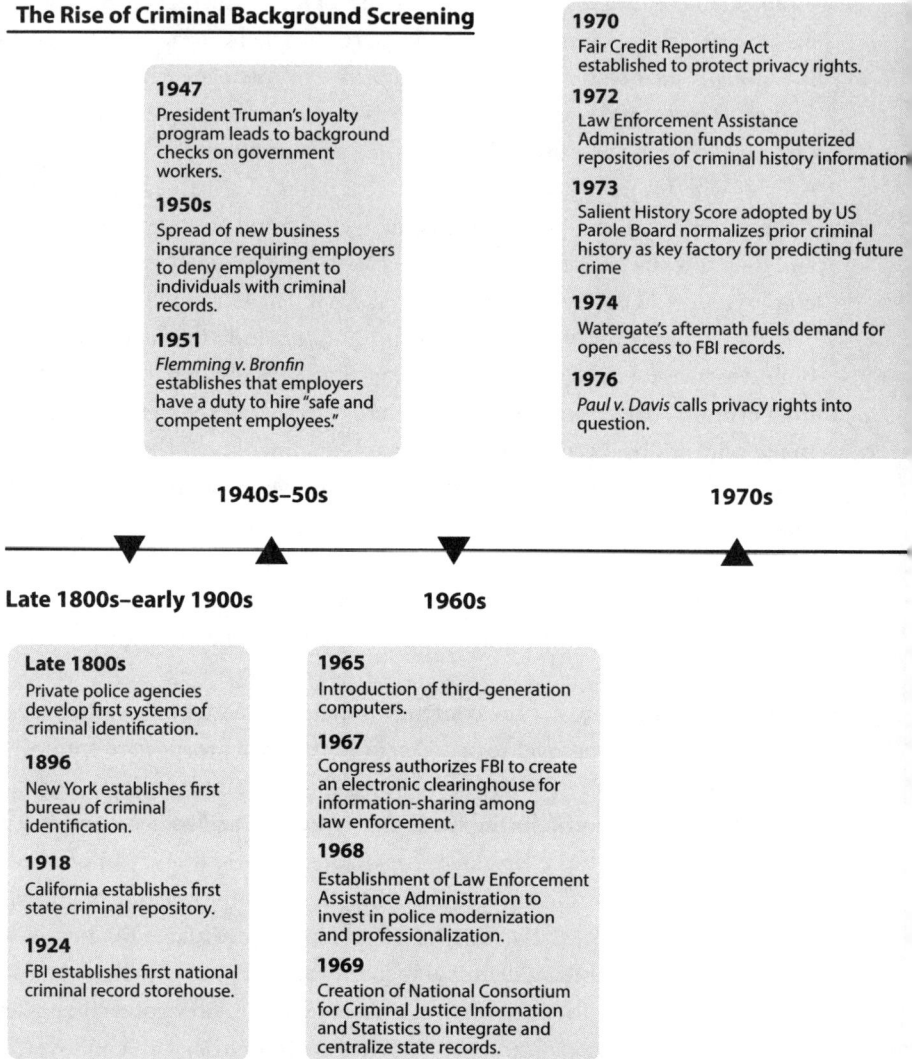

1947
President Truman's loyalty program leads to background checks on government workers.

1950s
Spread of new business insurance requiring employers to deny employment to individuals with criminal records.

1951
Flemming v. Bronfin establishes that employers have a duty to hire "safe and competent employees."

1970
Fair Credit Reporting Act established to protect privacy rights.

1972
Law Enforcement Assistance Administration funds computerized repositories of criminal history information

1973
Salient History Score adopted by US Parole Board normalizes prior criminal history as key factory for predicting future crime

1974
Watergate's aftermath fuels demand for open access to FBI records.

1976
Paul v. Davis calls privacy rights into question.

1940s–50s

1970s

Late 1800s–early 1900s

1960s

Late 1800s
Private police agencies develop first systems of criminal identification.

1896
New York establishes first bureau of criminal identification.

1918
California establishes first state criminal repository.

1924
FBI establishes first national criminal record storehouse.

1965
Introduction of third-generation computers.

1967
Congress authorizes FBI to create an electronic clearinghouse for information-sharing among law enforcement.

1968
Establishment of Law Enforcement Assistance Administration to invest in police modernization and professionalization.

1969
Creation of National Consortium for Criminal Justice Information and Statistics to integrate and centralize state records.

FIGURE 2.1 The Rise of Criminal Background Screening. Illustration courtesy of Ana Holschuh.

1993

Brady Act mandates infrastructure upgrades for quick firearm background checks.

1993

National Child Protection Act authorizes fingerprint-based background checks for adults working with children.

Mid 1990s

Slew of child protection laws require registries of people convicted of sex-related offenses.

1997

E-Sign Act allows electronic signatures for background checks.

1998

National Instant Criminal Background Check System launched.

Late 1990s

Multimillion-dollar negligent hiring settlements widely publicized.

2012

Equal Employment Opportunity Commission issues updated guidance on use of criminal records.

2012

American Bar Association launches National Inventory of the Collateral Consequences of Conviction, identifying more than 40,000 sanctions and restrictions on people with records.

2016

National Consortium for Justice Information and Statistics estimates state repositories hold records for 110 million people.

2016

Major survey finds 72% of employers conduct background checks on all new hires.

1990s

2010s

1980s

2000s

1981

American Bar Association declares collateral consequences of conviction are on their way to extinction.

1983

National Consortium for Justice Information and Statistics launches FBI database (III) linking federal and state criminal records systems.

1984

Sentencing Reform Act ushers in punitive climate.

1989

Department of Justice v. Reporters Committee for Freedom of the Press holds that an individual has a cognizable privacy interest in their criminal history record.

2001

Patriot Act mandates millions of new background checks for security and transportation positions.

2002

E-Government Act requires online access to federal court records; states follow.

2003

PROTECT Act expands scope of authorized fingerprint-based background checks.

2003

Formation of National Association of Professional Background Screeners to represent interests of commercial screening firms.

2006

First Ban the Box resolution passed in San Francisco, California.

but rather, in the totality of the circumstances surrounding the hiring, whether the employer exercised reasonable care.[63]

This kind of balanced consideration of multiple priorities, though, would soon become more difficult to uphold. As criminal records became more widely available, and background checks cheaper and easier to conduct, it became increasingly difficult in the event of a lawsuit to argue that due diligence in hiring had been accomplished without them.

Escalate

By the start of the 1990s, the foundation of criminal record exclusion had set. Databases had been created and shared among criminal legal agencies, and access had been granted to a range of users outside the legal system. Countless laws permitted background checks as well as required the exclusion of people with convictions from a wide range of jobs and professions.[64] State agencies, professional organizations, and businesses bolstered their reputations on the appearance of having excluded the right people through background checks. Insurers used criminal history as a factor to determine eligibility and premiums.[65] Often enough to cause worry, the courts found employers liable for things gone wrong. Although an important 1989 Supreme Court decision, *Department of Justice v. Reporters Committee for Freedom of the Press*, had expanded privacy protections, pressure to share the data was advancing from many directions.[66] On these pillars of law, policy, and liability, the background screening landscape began to intensify.

Moral panics related to child protection played a major role motivating the additional expansion of access to FBI data. The 1993 National Child Protection Act (also known as the "Oprah Bill" in honor of the key role played by cultural icon Oprah Winfrey) established a national database of all indictments and convictions for child abuse, arson, felony drug, and sex-related charges, and authorized all businesses and organizations employing childcare providers to access this database. Similar access was later extended to organizations working with the elderly and disabled, leading to tens of millions of new background checks.[67] Ensuing laws named after children who had been victims of sexual violence also established policies and systems for sharing sex-related conviction data. For example, the 1994 Jacob Wetterling Act allowed law enforcement to release information about people convicted of sex offenses and required states to create public registries. Megan's Laws (passed in many states in the mid-1990s) required law enforcement to release information to the public. The Pam Lyncher Act of 1996 established a national database and state-sponsored website to track people convicted of sex offenses, and made registration mandatory for ten years or life.[68]

It so happened that at the same time access was being granted to ever-more users, the biggest effort to fortify criminal records infrastructure since the policing-motivated upgrades of prior decades was underway, this time driven by a desire to quickly check the criminal records of potential gun purchasers. As Jacobs explains, the 1968 Gun Control Act used the presence or absence of a felony conviction to distinguish between the "law abiding" (who should have easy access to firearms) and the "criminal" (who should not). But before the passage of the Brady Handgun Violence Prevention Act in 1993, retailers had no way to verify.[69] Gun purchasers simply filled out a document swearing they'd never been convicted of a felony. Now with the infrastructure in place, legislators wanted to require background checks for gun purchasers. This didn't sit well, however, with the National Rifle Association and others that objected to the idea that purchasers would have to wait for background check results. To appease the National Rifle Association, a provision was added to the Brady Law requiring that by 1998, the US Department of Justice develop a National Instant Criminal Background Check System that could produce results for firearms dealers within three days. State-level criminal record systems were not sophisticated enough to enable the promise of "instant" checks, thus triggering the federal investment of nearly half a billion dollars to yet again upgrade as well as improve police and court records.[70] Naturally, upgrades for gun buying smoothed checking for other purposes.

Alongside expanded access and improved infrastructure, the number of disqualifying statutes and institutional policies continued to proliferate. Now, in many cases, these policies not only permitted but also required exclusion.[71] For example, legislation such as the 1996 Housing Opportunity Program Extension Act required police to check the records of public housing tenants and applicants on request. In what became known as the "one-strike" rule, these checks were used broadly by federally funded housing authorities to evict tenants and deny applicants on the basis of even a single arrest, including the arrest of guests and household members not on the lease.

The 1990s were also a time of intensification with regard to employer liability for employee behavior. Courts continued to expand the scope of employers' responsibility, but equally important, *awareness* of negligent hiring claims as a cause of action in cases of workplace violence grew.[72] Like the moral panics around child protection, media promotion of exceptional legal settlements holding employers responsible for the actions of employees played a major role.

One oft-repeated horror story that captured the popular imagination involved an Oakland-based pediatrician, Kerry Spooner-Dean, who was murdered in her home by a carpet cleaner. The company hadn't checked references for Jerrol Glenn Woods before hiring him, and his record of felony robbery convictions thus went undetected. The case settled in 2000 for $11 million, putting the company out of business. Another dramatic case, *Ward et al. v. Trusted Health Resources, Inc., et al.*, involved a man who had been hired by a home health agency to care for a thirty-two-year-old with quadriplegic cerebral palsy and the client's seventy-seven-year-old grandmother. Jesse Rogers had missed several shifts and been removed from the job by the agency when he returned to the home, apparently with the intent to steal, and for reasons unclear, murdered the patient and grandmother. After Rogers had been sentenced to life in prison, a Boston-based attorney took on a negligent hiring case, successfully contending that had the home health agency conducted a background check, they would have discovered Rogers's history of theft-related felony convictions. The defense attorney for Trusted Health Resources argued that conducting criminal background checks was not an industry standard, and that because Rogers's prior convictions were theft related, the murders could not have been foreseen. However, the plaintiffs successfully maintained that because background screening was standard in other businesses involving people going into the homes of others, it "should have been common sense."[73] The company was sued for $26.5 million—the second-largest jury verdict in a negligent hiring and wrongful death case in Massachusetts history—and was forced to close as a result.

Yet it wasn't so much the verdicts themselves as their repeated rehashing in the popular media and trade literatures that shifted practice.[74] Though these kinds of horrific cases and outsized settlements represented but a small slice, their impact reverberated throughout business, legal, and public policy communities, and negligence lawsuits became well-known. Criminal history became a standard part of the evidence for plaintiff-side attorneys seeking to drive up settlement costs. Defense attorneys encouraged their clients to conduct preemployment background checks, advising them that while a background check may not be required under the law, it would be easier and cheaper to conduct them than to try to defend not having done so after the fact. Public support also increased for state-required employment background screening. For instance, the national attention gained by *Ward v. Trusted Health* prompted many states to enact statutes requiring criminal background checks in all home care agencies.[75] In all, tragedies like Rogers and Spooner-Dean became cautionary tales, leveraged by employment law firms, background screening, security, and HR professionals to generate hyperawareness of liability as well as build a lasting narrative around the idea that tragedy, expense, and embarrassment could be prevented through background screening.[76]

By the end of the 1990s, the desire to use criminal records as a discriminatory tool, it seemed, had become a higher public priority than protecting individual privacy. The overwhelming tendency was to permit access to FBI conviction records for a range of noncriminal justice purposes and increasingly make rap sheets accessible online.[77] Courts too, overwhelmed by requests, were in many states compiling and selling batches of bulk criminal record data to technology vendors.[78] At the same time, despite declining crime rates, in the seven-year period from 1991 to 1998, the number of state and federal prisoners rose by 59 percent—a higher rate of imprisonment than ever before seen in world history.[79] It was in this context of fear, litigiousness, and unprecedented criminalization that background screening truly came into the mainstream. President Bill Clinton's 1997 E-Sign Act ended the time-consuming and cumbersome days of faxing consent forms back and forth, streamlining the process, and thus making preemployment background checks more feasible and economical.[80] As an expert in the security industry explained,

> The E-Sign Act changed everything. Before that, background checks were allowed, but really hard. You used to have to fax consent forms back and forth, etc. E-Sign transformed all industries, but definitely also background checks. With E-Sign, people started seeing they could make money from background screening. . . . Then 9–11 happened.[81]

The terrorist attacks of September 11, 2001, and the government's response to them, set ablaze the already widespread idea that there were clearly identifiable bad guys who could be kept out of one's organization by simply running a criminal background check.

Commercialize

There are risks to highlighting the role of money in systems of surveillance, prisons, policing, or confinement. Once announced, the mere presence of a profit motive tends to shrink analysis, downplaying the role and motives of state and other actors while implying the problem can be solved by merely eliminating profits. This shrinking is due in part to the persistent fantasy of a clean divide between public and private interests, the idea that commercialization is a new and external force, and the notion that profit can somehow be isolated from the other motivations.[82] The overarching problem to be avoided is thinking that profit *explains* the problem.[83] Besides, from an anthropological perspective, more important than the fact of commercialization, or how big and profitable an industry gets, is *how* an industry changes the landscape—the quality of the intervention and the difference that a profit motive actually makes.[84]

———

No evidence suggested that background checks could have prevented the tragedies in New York City and Washington, DC, and yet the events prompted the single-biggest surge in state-mandated criminal background checks to date. Within a few weeks of the attacks, Federal Aviation Administration administrator Jane Garvey ordered criminal background checks for up to a million workers with access to secure areas in US airports. By October 2001, the Patriot Act mandated employers involved in hazardous material transportation to conduct background checks for an estimated 3.5 million employees, and new congressional mandates for airport workers, airline personnel, port workers, and truck drivers resulted in millions of new background checks and related restrictions.[85] Other new laws required checks for people in other transportation positions as well as people with access to controlled areas of maritime facilities or access to biological agents, and those working in airports, or as airline personnel, air marshals, and private security officers.[86]

Employers and others in positions of responsibility were encouraged to embrace criminal background checks and exclusions as a primary means to mitigate workplace risk. Whether located in industries requiring new background checks by law or compelled by the bandwagon effect, after September 11, 2001, many employers who had not previously done so endeavored to run background checks on new employees, existing employees, and outside vendors coming onto their properties.

Spotting commercial opportunity in the fearful wake of 9–11, as had insurers in the anxieties of the Cold War, background screening vendors rose to capitalize on new demand. An industry professional described the shift. "Before the late 1990s, there was no mature industry . . . maybe some sea level folks, but it [background screening] was really a thing of law enforcement. . . . [A]fter 9–11, the industry EXPLODED." They added,

> There were already some big players. Sterling, which had started out as [an] insurance company in 1975, then fully pivoted to background checks. A ton of people started jumping into the market. Suddenly everyone wants background checks and everyone is selling background checks. It was the Wild-Wild West. There were laws, but no one was following them or enforcing them.[87]

Indeed, one major firm reported an increase in criminal background check requests from approximately three thousand in November 2001 to nearly twenty-five thousand by February 2002.[88] The money to be made, people realized, was in developing the systems and know-how to facilitate access to the criminal record data. Governments had motivated the use of background checks and made it legally permissible to access the data, but they lacked what urban planning scholar David Thacher helpfully describes as the "collective capacity that actuarial social control requires."[89] Digitization had produced a big pile of "messy" data that could be scraped from government websites, purchased cheaply in bulk, or obtained by the Freedom of Information Act, but for lay potential users, comprehensive background checking was still challenging, costly, and time-consuming.[90] To effectively implement or expand screening programs, employers needed quick access not to raw data but instead to neat "consumer reports": documents summarizing and compiling the salient as well as legally permissible aspects of an individual's past contact with police, courts, and institutions of confinement.

Producing a tidy, comprehensive report in a timely manner—and at a price point employers would be willing to pay—was not easy at first, however. In fact, when I spoke to Tonya Jenkins after her presentation, she mentioned being upset because her firm, Gold Star, had just lost a potential contract to a company of approximately twenty-five hundred employees. The owner had decided to forgo background checks altogether because of the expense. Many employers wanted to view the criminal records of potential hires, Jenkins explained, but "didn't want to pay much for the privilege."

For a sense of the economics, at the time Gold Star was processing between six hundred and one thousand criminal background reports per day, at a cost (to the employer, landlord, or other user) of fifty to seventy-five dollars per report. This price was justified by the quality of the product. In contrast to the growing trend toward batches of aggregated information often marketed as "national background checks," Gold Star screeners took the time to check Social Security numbers in order to determine the counties in which a person had lived and worked, and then search for criminal records in each of those counties, hiring additional local researchers in about 20 percent of the cases. Additionally (and unfortunately for formerly imprisoned job seekers), the company also reviewed Department of Corrections records to determine release date from prison, using this date as the benchmark from which to begin counting seven years rather than the easier-to-calculate (and thus more commonly used) date of conviction. Jenkins was resentful of industry giants garnering much of the business by bidding cheap and cutting corners, while smaller firms like hers aiming to transcend the industry's reputation for sloppy reporting, struggled to build market share.[91] Like any businessperson, she was convinced of the value of her company's product and disappointed the buyer couldn't see it. "Employers need to feel the pain," she said with an edge in her voice, by which she meant that employers opting to forego background screening because of the expense would ultimately learn its value through a workplace incident or negligence lawsuit.

Another factor impeding market growth (and a constant source of irritation for screeners) was the mixed-message regulatory landscape—support for screening, on the one hand, and second chances, on the other. "Luckily, the EEOC is losing most of their cases," Jenkins quipped. "They would like to see no background checks at all! Same with the Ban the Box stuff; it's a matter of integrity. Employers should be using that question just to see if the person is honest about it or not."

A trade association formed in 2003, the National Association of Professional Background Screeners, to more coherently espouse the value of background checks, build a consensus around the need for background checking, and reduce technical and legal barriers driving up the cost of producing accurate reports.[92] With profit as a backdrop, the association and its members vigorously promoted the idea that any legitimate business should be conducting routine background checks on all hires. This agenda, which depended on quick, easy, and cost-effective access to the data, could not help but involve arguing against the privacy and due process rights of people with criminal records:[93]

> It is critical for employers, legislators, the courts and public officials to understand that background screening companies are not in the same category as data miners and other entities that are "data profiteers." Employers

depend on bona fide, relevant pre-employment information to make safe hiring decisions and avoid litigation. The bottom line is that unreasonable restrictions on the ability of screening firms to access public records on behalf of employers . . . only benefit[s] criminals, terrorists and cheaters.[94]

Commercial screening vendors came late to the stage, and therefore to borrow Gilmore's language, could arguably be understood as "parasites" on the process.[95] But they have also been drivers. By going straight to court data (bypassing federal restrictions on access to FBI data), the industry effectively upended the "practical obscurity" of court records.[96] By leveraging their commercial capacities, vendors built the systems to make the data cheaper, faster, and easier to access, and thus more practical to use. By deploying fear-based risk narratives to challenge antidiscrimination efforts, they stymied thoughtful public consideration of what role, if any, criminal background checks should play in employment.[97]

Professionalize

Still, more help was needed to enable widespread, routine screening. Though employers were increasingly convinced that background screening was necessary, they needed practical help to integrate screening into their hiring processes without slowing things down, legal support to interpret and use the data without getting sued, and frameworks to help them integrate screening in ways congruent with existing systems. To meet these needs—for information, systematization, guidance, and expertise—background screening was thrust into the HR management milieu, where professional standards and best practices are developed and formalized.

Security and HR experts W. Barry Nixon and Kim M. Kerr describe the moment in their 2008 hiring risk management manual:

> Suddenly human resource and security professionals were expected to be experts on background checks, including the rapid changes in technology, law, and societal values associated with establishing and protecting identity in the workplace. A massive educational effort has been taking place to meet this expectation.[98]

A perusal of the plethora of reports, textbooks, manuals, and articles in popular HR magazines, specialty trade journals, and legal journals reveals that the so-called educational effort was really more of a campaign, overwhelmingly recommending that employers conduct background checks as a matter of routine.[99] Indeed, one comprehensive review of legal, scientific, and popular HR literatures found that nearly all HR textbooks published after the mid-1990s discussed and recommended criminal background screening.[100]

Relatedly, trend surveys, often conducted in collaboration with the screening industry, seemed intent on making background screening appear ubiquitous, publishing claims such as, "Employers universally using background checks to protect employees, customers and the public" and "Nearly all HR professionals conduct background checks of some kind."[101] Likewise, background screening became a regular topic at webinars and seminars, marketed to hiring managers and other HR professionals with fear:[102]

> Mitigate your risk, learn how to avoid a bad hire!
> There's nothing worse than having a "bad hire" slip into your company. You want to reduce criminal activity at work, you have an obligation under OSHA to provide a safe worksite and you can also be liable under negligent hiring law. Make sure your company is mitigating these risks by performing thorough background checks on all employees.[103]

Preventing a negligent hiring lawsuit served as the primary rationale.[104] Although courts had repeatedly held that employers were *not* necessarily bound by a duty to conduct criminal background checks—some even going so far as to discourage employers from excluding candidates on the basis of criminal history—as legal scholar David McElhattan's comprehensive review of the HR literature shows, "the HR trade discourse invert[ed] this position, framing criminal record checks as the default practice for screening prospective hires irrespective of occupation-specific criminal risks."[105] This disconnect between what the law requires and what HR professionals have promoted, argues McElhattan, is made possible by the "structured uncertainty" of legal standards. Because the law does not spell out precisely how one should exercise "reasonable care," and instead examines each complaint after the fact and on a case-by-case basis, overcompliance can appear the most surefire way to insulate oneself from liability. In the face of this uncertainty as well as the relatively low cost of background checks, the HR field latched onto criminal background screening as a clear, actionable solution around which to rally.[106]

The decision to respond to structured uncertainty in this way must be understood, as anthropologist E. Summerson Carr has contended, as action. Correcting our common tendency to view expertise as a property that elite

individuals have or hold, Carr urges us to instead think of expertise as something people *do*. Expertise is enacted in real-time interactions and struggles,
and in relation not only between experts and their objects of expertise but also
between experts and laypeople. In other words, people do not possess and
dole out expertise; it gets coconstructed "in real-time interaction, as actors
and institutions struggle to author and authorize powerful texts that will be
read as such by others."[107] Furthermore, these "enactments of expertise" con-
fer value, not only on the objects in question (whether real estate, wine, dis-
ease, or gold, as Carr suggests, or background checks, as we discuss here), but
on the experts themselves. Indeed in the distance between expert people and
potentially valuable objects, a space is created for moneymaking.

Like insurance industry actors, lawyers, and commercial screening firms,
the professional field of HR management did not merely support but also
helped to construct the screening landscape and grow the reliance on background checks.[108] By providing oral and written guidance, facilitating access
to legal advice, conducting research, and training their members and associates
on how to incorporate criminal background screening into hiring processes,
HR professionals packaged it, made it manageable, and institutionalized it as
a best practice, all the while positioning their services and expertise as essential to the task.

———

Back in the presentation room, Jenkins offered her final warnings to the HR
professionals in light of recent litigation outcomes. Home Depot had been
sued for failing to provide disclosures, Whole Foods for failing to obtain written consent, and Verisk Analytics for reporting inaccurate information. She
advised the audience to avoid advertisements promising "national" background checks they can't deliver as well as the use of social media as a screening mechanism, which can easily violate the Fair Credit Reporting Act or
result in discrimination against protected classes, and to be be aware of Ban the
Box laws, which "like it or not, [were] sweeping the nation and [would] soon
become law for private employers in California." Though I had been fixated on
Jenkins's unsubstantiated rationales, I realized in hindsight that the bulk of
her presentation—at least fifteen of the twenty or so slides—had been dedicated not to *whether* or *why* employers should conduct background checks but
simply *how* to conduct them in ways compliant enough with the law to ward
off lawsuits.

An Unfounded Link

This chapter has revealed the power of policy and law to establish the ground rules on which oppressive systems are built, and the power of private sectors to grow them. By the mid-2000s, an unfounded link between criminal records and workplace risk had been firmly established in the popular imagination— so firmly in fact that whenever something bad happened, the response was more background checks, whether or not people with criminal convictions had been associated with the harm, and regardless of whether background checks could have prevented the harm.[109]

For example, a 2008 *Los Angeles Times* and *ProPublica* investigation reported that "dozens of registered nurses convicted of crimes, including sex offenses and attempted murder, [had] remained fully licensed to practice in California for years before the state nursing board acted against them."[110] The investigation revealed holes in the nursing board's background screening process, such as a failure to flag new arrests. Yet rather than focus on actual harm done to patients, much of the attention was directed toward the mere fact of past arrests and convictions.[111] From the investigation's perspective, the problem was "escaping scrutiny," conflating having been convicted with medical incompetency.[112] The Board of Registered Nursing's primary response was to require the fingerprinting of all of its licensees, shutting many competent nurses out of the profession.

This kind of state-sponsored exclusion was widespread. Whereas a national survey conducted in the early 1970s had documented 1,948 statutory and licensing provisions barring or restricting applicants with arrest or conviction records from employment in professions such as childcare, education, security, nursing, and home health care, by 2012, the American Bar Association had identified approximately 40,000 collateral consequences of conviction, more than half of these affecting access to employment or occupational licensing.[113]

Pressure to conduct criminal background checks and exclude on their basis was further reinforced by insurers' escalating use of criminal record data in underwriting.[114] With criminal history data readily available, insurers could easily incorporate it as a factor to estimate risk levels, determine the insurability of potential employees, and set premiums.[115] Additionally, as criminal background *screening* became more commonplace, insurers could also consider a company's screening habits to determine premiums.[116] By codifying this largely unfounded link between past conviction and future risk in coverages and premiums, insurance companies further cemented the idea that employers alone would bear the burden and expense of potential liability.

FBI-Based Background Checks for
Non-criminal Justice Purposes

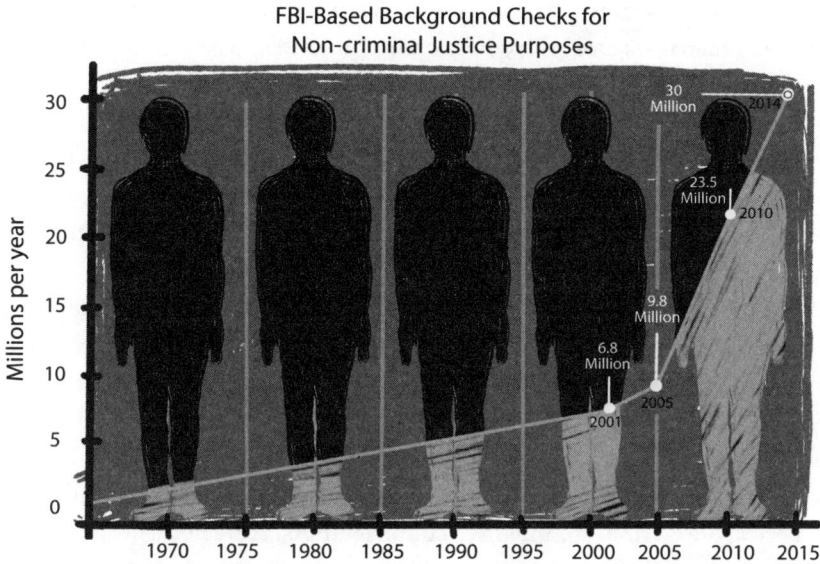

FIGURE 2.2 FBI Background Checks for Noncriminal Justice Purposes.
Illustration courtesy of Carolina Jones Ortiz. Estimates for 2001 and 2005
are derived from *The Attorney General's Report on Criminal History Background
Checks* (Washington, DC: US Department of Justice, 2006). The 2014
estimate is taken from an internal memo from Jeremy M. Wiltz, FBI deputy
assistant director, Information Services Branch, Criminal Justice Information
Services Division, to the chair of the Senate Judiciary Committee, Charles E.
Grassley, September 21, 2015, https://www.wsj.com/public/resources
/documents/9-21-15WiltzreIdHS.pdf. An estimated 17 million FBI-based
checks for employment and licensing purposes were done in 2012. See
Madeline Neighly and Maurice Emsellem, "Wanted: Accurate FBI Checks
for Employment," National Employment Law Project, July 30, 2013, https://
www.nelp.org/insights-research/wanted-accurate-fbi-background-checks-for
-employment/.

Though by the mid-2000s, notable efforts were underway to temper the
most egregious forms of discrimination, employers on the front lines of everyday decisions were operating in a context in which it was taken as common
sense that a responsible employer would use background checks to protect
their business and the public. With few pressures or incentives to behave
otherwise, the vast majority of US employers had taken false comfort in the
incorporation of criminal background checks into their hiring processes, using
them as a quick, easy, and cheap sorting mechanism.[117]

Indeed, by the 2010s, a consensus had all but consolidated. Major surveys of hiring managers and HR professionals found that nearly three out of four conducted criminal background checks for all applicants.[118] In 2014, more than half of all FBI-based background checks (thirty million) were conducted for purposes other than criminal justice——with more than seventeen million of these for purposes of employment and licensing—demonstrating a culture of criminalization in which millions of people were relying on conviction history as a data point in their operations.

This trend was not limited to the United States. Between 1999 and 2011, employers more than doubled their use of background checks in Sweden, more than tripled them in the United Kingdom, quadrupled them in the Netherlands, and sextupled them in Australia.[119] Though few data exist on the use of criminal background checks beyond Western and English-speaking countries, one analysis of fifty-two countries in Europe, Oceania, North and South America, the Caribbean, and three countries in Asia revealed a near universal rise in criminal background screening between 2002 and 2019 for noncriminal legal purposes.[120]

3

Criminal Stigma
and the Politics of Helping

No employer *wants* to hire someone with a felony. If you just sit in your office and ask them if they hire felons, the answer will definitely be no. I have to tell them, "Stop the noise, I'm not going to send you Charles Manson!"

You can't change an employer's perspective. They either share your perspective or they don't. I'm just selling the job seeker: I have a qualified, prescreened person for the job.

I tell them [job seekers] your record is the F on your report card . . . but that was yesterday, it's the past. I teach them not be ashamed of it, to check "yes" [in answer to the conviction question on the application], "Eager to discuss."

We need to stop sounding like we're asking employers for a favor to consider people with criminal records, when in fact they are required legally to do so . . . to stop reinforcing the idea that this is optional.

—INLAND EMPIRE JOB DEVELOPERS

SASHA PARKED on the street in front of a cluster of tin mailboxes leaning to the side on their old wooden posts. She had graciously invited me to join her on an impromptu visit to Archibald Stonework, a fifty-year-old business with a long-standing reputation for hiring laborers with criminal convictions. The driveway was sandy with gravel so loose and broken down that a decade must have passed since it was first spread. It was almost midday, and the sun was shining brightly, illuminating dust pockets produced by the occasional pickup truck, forklift, or front-end loader rolling by. A few paved areas provided stable ground for piles of stone, pallets, steel shelving structures, and sheds. Sasha headed toward the closest building, a trailer with a sign taped in the window that read, "Applications accepted between the hours of 8:00 a.m. and 1:00 p.m." She had come in person, rather than continue to try to fax the applications, in hopes of reestablishing a relationship with the company, because unfortunately, the HR point person had changed. Sasha had no professional experience with job development before joining the Hub, but had been hired with confidence that her local knowledge from having grown up in the area and warm-but-no-nonsense persona would be well suited to the task of connecting job seekers to local employers. She had bonded easily with the previous HR person, who like her, was young, female, and new in her job, and had offered to keep a special folder for Sasha's potential job candidates. Now Sasha would have to begin the courtship again from scratch.

Standing at the window, Sasha waited for several minutes before a woman opened it and said hello. "Hello Marissa," Sasha replied cheerily, but it turned out she didn't quite have the name right. It was Maritza, not Marissa. This seemed to mildly annoy Maritza, especially coupled with the fact that she had apparently not been expecting a visit. The awkwardness was further compounded by some confusion about whether Maritza was in fact the HR representative who had been communicating with the Hub about current openings as well as some confusion about who Sasha was because Maritza had been speaking with Kristen by phone. Although the account technically belonged to Sasha, she had been out of the office on the day when Maritza called about the job openings. Instead of making an employer wait for a callback, Kristen had taken the call—a smart decision (you don't want to keep employers waiting)— but too many cooks in the job development kitchen can lead to the kind of muddle and territorial murk now unfolding here. Given that each job developer was accountable for placing a certain number of job seekers in positions of permanent employment each month, it mattered who got credit for what.

Sasha started talking fast in effort to iron out these bumps, clarify matters, and establish a professional connection. This was not easy because Maritza wasn't terribly friendly or direct, making it difficult to discern the source of the disconnect. It almost seemed as if she hadn't heard of the organization, despite three days of back-and-forth telephone conversation. Nevertheless, Sasha was an impressive talker. Quickly and efficiently, she explained who she was, what the Hub was and could offer, and the detailed profiles of the two applicants she had come to promote. "Both have administrative and customer service experience and aren't afraid to labor," Sasha emphasized. "Didn't you mention you'd had trouble with supervisors who were unwilling or unable to do the physical part?"

Sasha's awareness of this personnel challenge caused Maritza to warm a bit.

"Do you have their résumés?" she finally asked. "Shit," Sasha self-scolded under her breath, then out loud, "I'm so sorry."

Unfortunately, she had only thought to bring the carefully completed applications that for some reason were not transmitting via email or fax. Now seated at her desk a few feet away from the tiny window, Maritza pulled up one of the emails on her computer monitor to demonstrate to Sasha that there were indeed no attachments, while also gesturing to the empty tray where a fax would have come in.

"What do you guys do?" Maritza invited Sasha to repeat.

Sasha was clearly bewildered by the question, given the long-standing relationship between Archibald and the Hub, but grateful for the bite.

"Our goal is to place them in permanent jobs. First, they work for us, as a kind of job-readiness training, three days a week on a landscaping crew. We get to see how they work, and coach them on interviewing and work habits. . . . Everyone we work with has background issues." To this last bit, Maritza nodded both up and down and side to side, as if to say: that doesn't matter to us. Sasha continued with a rundown of what she and/or the Hub could offer, and how the relationship could work:

> If you guys need any positions filled, we have at least sixteen guys at any given time, all with different kinds of skills, the majority general labor, but others have different experience, like these applicants. . . . Also, if you need somebody quickly, we can likely help you out. We can bring them out here for an interview. We can get you their application, and if the attachments aren't working, we can bring them out to you. . . . We're in the area a lot meeting with other businesses.

I could sense Sasha's discouragement that Maritza only wanted to talk through the dusty little window, especially given that she could see the male HR director with whom she had previously met face-to-face inside the trailer. She was also conscious of the fact that she was doing most of the talking, a no-no according to Larry Robbin, the esteemed California-based workforce development consultant whose all-day seminar on how to persuade businesses to work with you she had attended some weeks ago. But at least, according to Robbin, she was saying the right things. Robbin had recommended that in their communication with employers, job developers focus on how partnering with their program could add to a company's profit margin, save them money, and reduce stress by streamlining their hiring process and helping them find good matches. In this regard, Sasha may have actually overstated what she could deliver in hopes of drawing Maritza into a close working relationship. Truthfully, it was inefficient to drive all the way out here to hand deliver two applications, particularly when in terms of a "match," the candidates' qualifications for the positions were a bit of a stretch. But Sasha needed to stretch as it was nearing the end of the month and she hadn't yet met her target quota of three placements per month—a minimum contribution required to meet the organization's then goal of seventy-five per year. In any case, Sasha hoped the time today had been well spent. Even if it didn't result in jobs won for these specific job seekers, now Maritza knew her by face and name. Perhaps over time, Maritza would treat the Hub as a trusted acquaintance, call the Hub about job openings before posting them publicly, and consider its candidates with a generous eye.

———

People who have been convicted of a crime, who bear the label of criminal, have long been stigmatized as dishonest, untrustworthy, and otherwise disreputable.[1] Indeed the connection between having been convicted and being of questionable character is taken as self-evident. Unlike stigmas that are the result of accident or birth, criminal stigma is viewed as a condition controllable by the individual, and thereby less deserving of social empathy or legal protection.[2] This chapter explores how job seekers, with the help of workforce development professionals, navigate criminal stigma in the job market.[3] It draws inspiration from canonical theorizations of stigma generated by sociologist Erving Goffman, who saw the moments of conversational encounter between "normal" and "stigmatized" individuals along with the basic problems that infuse these encounters as key moments for social analysis.[4]

Recent stigma scholarship has expanded earlier conceptualizations of stigma as merely a labeling condition affecting individual victims, toward an understanding of stigma as a social relation embedded in broader cultural norms, and shaped by the social, political, and economic contexts in which it unfolds.[5] Stigma, we have come to understand, does not just exist; it is a process in motion that gets determined interactively between perpetrators and targets.[6]

Though I center the Hub ethnographically, my analysis draws from repeated engagement with job developers employed by nonprofit and government-funded workforce organizations across the region. With some variation in how the work is approached and divided, "job development" as I use it here involves, on the one hand, identifying and cultivating relationships with employers whose vacancies roughly match the qualifications of job-seeking clients, and on the other, preparing job seekers to interface effectively with these employers—by helping to craft résumés, cover letters, and job applications, and providing guidance in terms of how best to dress, present one-self, and respond appropriately to interview questions. Approached as sales, the strategy is to get an employer to try *one* candidate, and through a positive experience, become persuaded to try others.

This middleperson role is neither easy nor straightforward. As demonstrated by the strained interaction that unfolded between Sasha and Maritza, simply making a connection with an employer and piquing their interest is a major feat. Harder still is building trust and navigating the moods, communication styles, preferences, and ever-evolving labor needs of business owners, managers, and HR staff who are frequently demanding, unevenly committed to the partnership, and not always forthright. Then add to these dynamics the frustrations of working with an ever-changing pool of job-seeking clients who are, in many cases, inexperienced, unskilled, ill-equipped, and for lots of reasons mostly beyond their control, unreliable. It's matchmaking, between two fickle entities.

These complexities, I will argue, are not only practical and interpersonal. In the daily work of brokering between job seekers and employers, job developers find themselves at the crossroads of state-sanctioned discrimination, gendered and racialized ideas about criminality, and the inequities of a capitalist job market. They are also often the first to confront employers' individual perspectives, attitudes, and biases. At these junctures, they make strategic choices—about which job seeker to send to which employer, how to respond to employers' preferences, and what advice to give to job seekers about how to discuss convictions. In this role as "stigma managers," they not only respond to the sociolegal landscape; they participate in its formation. While the hard work of helping people get hired may thus appear to be a merely practical undertaking, job development is inherently political.

Because job seeking is by definition a normative enterprise—an endeavor in which social standards, conventions, and etiquette are deeply ingrained, and their performance expected—it is exceedingly difficult for job seekers or their helpers to do anything other than reproduce and reinforce dominant ideas—about crime and punishment, who should do what kind of work, and about why some succeed and others fail. As the ensuing episodes will show, mainstream approaches to job development do not work equally well for all job seekers or developers, and tend to accommodate rather than challenge employers' problematic ideas and practices.

How to Sell a Barrier

On one of her many visits to Archibald Stonework, Sasha had decided, on a whim, to stop at a neighboring business. Balpex Systems Design was a local manufacturer of precast concrete, and unlike many of the surrounding businesses, had a nice parking lot with a clearly designated reception entrance. Welcoming appearances notwithstanding, Sasha had left with no more than a business card from the icy secretary, who had responded to her standard pitch about the Hub with about as much interest as if she had been peddling neon shoelaces.

But Sasha didn't give up. She diligently cold-called the number on the business card for several months until she eventually got the general manager, Bart Casas, on the line. To her delight, he agreed to a meeting. Some of his best people had criminal convictions, Bart told her, and not so long ago, someone had taken a chance on him. Sasha began to send Bart handfuls of applicants, and ultimately Bart placed a call at 11:00 a.m. one Wednesday to the cell phone of Lucas, a young father who'd been on the Hub's landscape crew for about a month. Luckily for Lucas, the call came in at a moment when the noise of the weed whackers and chainsaws did not overwhelm his ringer. "Can you come in for an interview at 1:00 p.m.?" asked Bart. "Yes sir," he stammered, heart pounding as he ended the call and immediately placed another—to Hub headquarters to ask if someone might be available to rush over to where the crew was working to shuttle him back to the Hub so that he could retrieve his car and drive himself to Fontana.

Bart *loved* Lucas, quickly detecting leadership potential. Though Lucas had little work experience of any kind—and knew nothing about how to mold rebar and concrete columns as needed for Balpex's current contract with a new Apple facility—he'd been honest about his inexperience and was a quick study. Energetic, hardworking, and ambitious, Lucas hadn't been on the job four months before he had set his sights on becoming a concrete inspector—a position that would quadruple his income and lift him out of the exhausting six day per week, twelve-hour shifts.

Lucas's success was exciting for Sasha, but also stressful. Now that she had won Bart's confidence, the relationship needed to be nurtured through the periodic supply of star candidates like Lucas. Delivering on this expectation was fairly difficult at the time, given the Hub's relatively small and constantly shifting pool of job-seeking clients; there was often a sizable gap between the qualities of the Hub's labor pool and employers' needs.

This was precisely the dilemma in which Sasha found herself when a few months into the relationship, Balpex landed a major new project requiring expansion in its use of heavy equipment. Bart told her he was looking to bring on eight to ten new hires. Prior construction or manufacturing experience wasn't required, but was preferred. Candidates did have to pass a basic math and measurements quiz, and given the need to make shifts beginning as early as 6:00 a.m., reliable, *personal* transportation (meaning their own car) was an absolute must.

Sasha scrambled. The job seekers on her caseload wouldn't pass muster, primarily because the handful of those who had personal transportation were already committed to start work for another construction employer that also required a private vehicle. Determined not to let Bart down, Sasha felt she had no choice but to cast her net outside the Hub for job seekers who might satisfy the Balpex demand. She contacted a partner nonprofit agency, whose clients had felony convictions too. The agency pulled together a group of eight men, to whom she presented the job duties, qualifications, employer preferences, and interview process. Of these, five expressed interest in the job, and Sasha conducted mini interviews on the spot to assess their applicable skills as well as help them to fill out applications in enough detail and with good enough grammar to make it through the eyes of Bart's HR department. In the end, while Sasha gave everyone the address and HR person's name, she did not want to fully recommend two of the applicants, who had no job experience whatsoever. To differentiate her level of endorsement, she attached her business card to only three of the applications, from men in their thirties and forties with considerable experience, and who seemed eager to work. She later confessed that she felt somewhat conflicted about this decision, especially given that the two applications to which she did not attach her card belonged to young African American men. Because it was a new account and she was trying to build the relationship, she explained, she wanted to send her best folks or at least applicants who had some experience. For the sake of future job seekers, she needed to show Bart that she could be counted on to deliver more job seekers like Lucas—hardworking, dependable, and competent.

Sasha's concern with protecting her own reputation and prioritizing the relationship with the employer was strongly supported by workforce development experts like Robbin, whose signature workshop, Are You Talking like

Businesses Think?, taught an approach to job development that put employers' needs and concerns above all else.[7] Rather than trying to get employers to see the world from the criminalized person's perspective, the seminar emphasized, the goal should be to persuade the employer that hiring your client will increase their profit margin. Sasha and Kristen had attended the workshop, which had been commissioned and paid for by one of the Hub's funders for its workforce grantees. I tagged along.

The biggest mistake most job developers make, Robbin implored, is getting so caught up in a view of themselves as advocates that they forget how to relate to businesses. "The employer doesn't want to hear how great your program is or how hard so-and-so has had it." For the vast majority of businesses, "what you need to prove to them is how this person will make them money." Robbin estimated that 95 percent of businesses are driven only by a profit motive versus 5 percent that are driven by a combination of profit and social motivation. Unless there were clear signs that a job developer was talking to an employer from the 5 percent (e.g., they have a wall in their reception area dedicated to certificates of charitable donation), he argued, they must pitch their product as if talking to the 95 percent. So strongly did Robbin believe in prioritizing the business relationship that he recommended job developers refuse, as Sasha had done, to endorse job seekers who had not demonstrated reliability or were not a good skills match.

The role of a job developer, from his perspective, was to lend their social capital to job seekers. Because the vast majority of hiring is conducted through trusted friends and acquaintances, rather than publicly advertised, knowing someone who knows someone is essential. Robbin explained, as lightly paraphrased:

> When we think about hiring, we usually focus on preparing people for interviews and work: *human capital.* But this is not the dominant factor. Conventional wisdom in hiring says the best résumé wins, but actually the 70 percent résumé may win over the 90 percent résumé if the 70 percent résumé comes from someone the employer knows and trusts: *social capital.*

In order to transfer their social capital to job seekers, Robbin continued, a job developer must first win the confidence of employers, as again lightly paraphrased:

> The important thing is to make the employer feel comfortable with your presence; to pay attention to what they like to talk about or not talk about,

to watch their communication style and match it. Furthermore, they should do 70 percent of the talking. There are only a few things the job developer should say: the age of your organization, which will interest them in terms of stability; what your organization does, phrased in terms that matter to them, such as, "We run a business that trains people to become employees at other businesses"; and finally, who your other customers are and how many others you have. These should ideally include other business that are well-known or are similar kinds of businesses nearby. Sell your references, not your services. Ask them to tell you about their hiring process, and then show them everywhere along the way that you can save them time or money—convince them that their traditional approach is not great and it would be better to go through you. Find out what their problems are in the hiring process and then fix them. Tell employers, "We are expert in matching candidates for employers; we will not waste your time sending you the wrong match." Assure them that when they hire someone from you, they can fire, transfer, or do anything, and you're not going to be involved as an advocate.

Like any negative credential, Robbin's advice on how to best navigate criminal records was unequivocal. "Stop thinking about barriers to employment. You can't sell the barrier; it's the barrier stupid! Frame the candidate as a job hunter, not someone with barriers and challenges."

This advice resonated with Kristen, who had for many years practiced an approach compatible with Robbin's that she called the "slow simmer." As a white, middle-aged, middle-class woman, Kristen saw herself as part of the business-owning community, had friends who were small business owners, and felt natural building relationships in this setting. Having worked as a job developer for many years, she was used to circulating and networking in the business community. Her strategy was to build trust incrementally with hiring managers as well as business owners by asking lots of questions about the business, demonstrating interest in their personnel challenges, and developing a warm professional affinity. Slowly, she offered bits and pieces of information about her pool of job seekers, avoiding mention of any shortcomings for as long as possible, and if needed, revealing them only indirectly.

Robbin's philosophy sat less well with Sasha, for whom it felt more strategic, comfortable, and authentic to seek out employers who could connect in some way to the idea of assisting people who had been criminalized. Young, Black, and Latina, Sasha felt uncomfortable in many business settings, and often perceived a certain mistrust on the part of white businesspeople—something that could not necessarily be overcome. Kristen's methodology presupposed the job developer had social capital to share, but Sasha sometimes felt she was going door-to-door trying to lend capital she did not herself possess. Instead, Sasha preferred to reveal the Hub's mission up front in order to avoid potential awkwardness later. She would rather build rapport eyes wide open, with employers who understood and supported (or at least didn't object to) the idea of hiring people with felony convictions. Effectively, if not consciously, Sasha's strategy was to hunt for the 5 percent of employers—people like Bart with whom she could form a straightforward connection. Not only was transparency more comfortable for Sasha, in her experience, these were the relationships that worked best over time. Such employers were more willing to take a chance on candidates with imperfect qualifications, tended to be more understanding of their various challenges, and were also generally more invested in the employees. For instance, one of her employers who had been forced to make a batch of layoffs had tried hard to avoid laying off his Hub employee because of the relational obligation he felt to make good on the opportunity.

Skills and Behaviors

"I'm not digging your research question," said Kristen casually, pausing beside my podium desk on her way back to the classroom, where she was midway through a PowerPoint presentation, "Introduction to Job Development," with an incoming cohort of job seekers. I didn't mind the directness. Since my field-work had begun, Kristen had been trying to put her finger on the intervention she wanted to make with regard to my research. I found the tension productive.

"The question shouldn't be, What differentiates employers who are willing to hire people with criminal records from those who aren't?" she said. "The question should be, What differentiates the *job seekers* who get hired from those who don't?"

I nodded slowly, taking in the meaning of her reframing. In seeking to redirect my attention to job seekers' attributes, I realized, Kristen was rejecting a structural or discrimination-focused analysis of the problem, in favor of a framework forefronting individual job seeker's skills and behaviors. This outlook was encapsulated in one of her presentation slides, titled "Reasons You Might Not Get the Job."

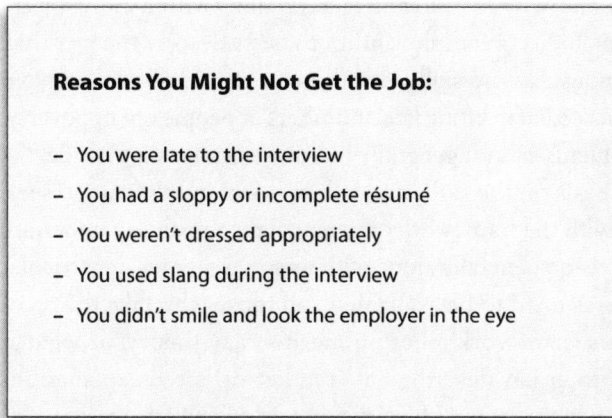

FIGURE 3.1 PowerPoint slide. Illustration courtesy of Karson Schenk.

Absent from the slide were many other reasons people "might not get the job" that I had already witnessed:

- The law prohibits the employer from hiring people with felony convictions for the position
- The employer prefers not to hire people with felony convictions, and no one is enforcing the laws that prohibit discrimination
- The businesses' insurance policy does not cover people with felony convictions
- The employer prefers to hire people of a different race or gender than the applicant
- The employer will only hire people with their own cars because public transportation isn't viable

Kristen's outlook was consistent with mainstream approaches to workforce development, which focus less on "employment" and more on "employability"—a framework in which a lack of education, training, hard skills, and "soft skills," such as punctuality, integrity, reliability, and self-presentation, are understood as primary barriers to employment.[8] Offering little acknowledgment of structural issues such as the basic absence of good jobs that pay a decent wage or allow for advancement, "employability is misleadingly considered 'an intrinsic property of individuals' rather than a reflection of the existing structure of the labor market."[9] Indeed, even when structural impediments to employment are explicitly acknowledged, recommendations often center on factors falling within individual job seekers' control. This focus on employability persists despite the fact that, as major studies demonstrate, no skill, education, or attitude-based employment program has succeeded in lifting large numbers of people out of poverty, and labor market problems cannot generally be solved on the supply side.[10]

An emphasis on the skills and behaviors of individual job seekers is also consistent with the framework of personal responsibility undergirding social service provision generally along with prisoner reentry in particular, in which success is presumed to be available to all those who take the recommended steps.[11] This framework relies on meritocracy theory, or what sociologist Deirdre Royster has described as "market-oriented explanations of social inequality," which assume a level playing field in which everyone has an equal chance to succeed so long as they study and work hard. Disparities in employment and other arenas are explained in terms of differential abilities, market demands for those abilities, and individual attitude.[12] As cultural theorist Paul Willis observed in his classic *Learning to Labor: How Working-Class Kids Get Working-Class Jobs*, "The contradiction is never admitted that not all can succeed, and that there is no point for the unsuccessful in following prescriptions for success—hard work, diligence, conformism, accepting knowledge as an equivalent of real value."[13]

This places tremendous pressure on not only job seekers but also job developers who day in and day out struggle to place clients who, for a range of reasons, may not actually be ready or able to take a job. Unequipped and unfunded to challenge discrimination, shift the terms of the labor market, or meet their clients deep needs, they instead attend to job seekers' psychosocial dispositions. To be clear, this narrow emphasis is not simply the result of a failure on the part of social service organizations to think critically or broadly. The people who work in these organizations often know what is needed, but time and money are limited by structures of funding myopically focused on immediate and tangible outcomes—evidence of return on their investment in the form of large numbers of job placements.[14]

The Conviction Question

Kristen began her weekly thirty-minute job development session with Linda, whose long work history, well put together résumé, and confident self-presentation had put her on the "job-ready" list almost immediately. Kristen was thrilled to have Linda included in her caseload, in part because of her preparedness, but also because Kristen was still struggling to make sense of

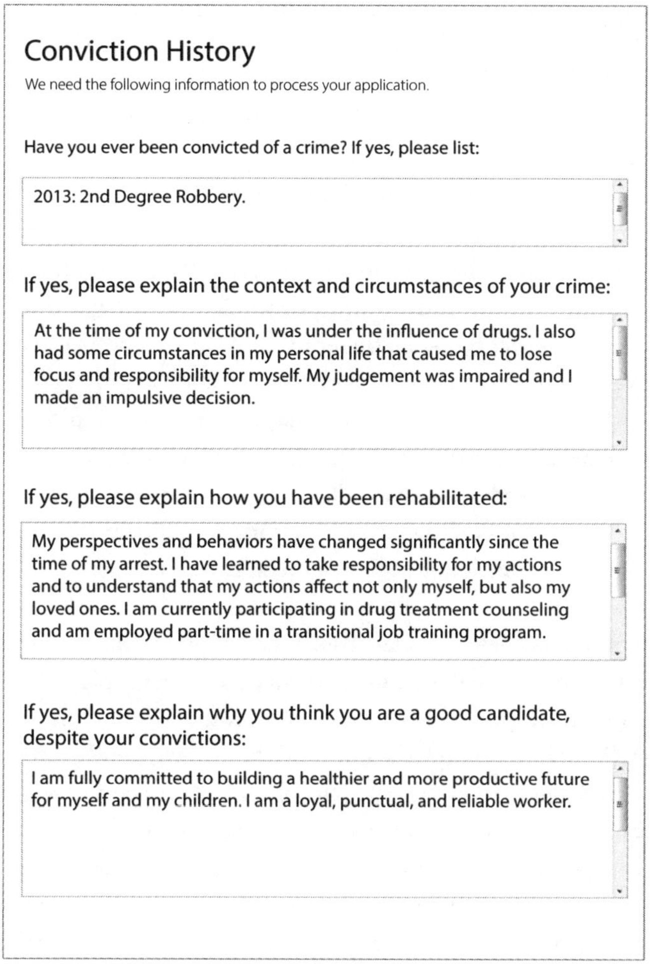

Conviction History

We need the following information to process your application.

Have you ever been convicted of a crime? If yes, please list:

> 2013: 2nd Degree Robbery.

If yes, please explain the context and circumstances of your crime:

> At the time of my conviction, I was under the influence of drugs. I also had some circumstances in my personal life that caused me to lose focus and responsibility for myself. My judgement was impaired and I made an impulsive decision.

If yes, please explain how you have been rehabilitated:

> My perspectives and behaviors have changed significantly since the time of my arrest. I have learned to take responsibility for my actions and to understand that my actions affect not only myself, but also my loved ones. I am currently participating in drug treatment counseling and am employed part-time in a transitional job training program.

If yes, please explain why you think you are a good candidate, despite your convictions:

> I am fully committed to building a healthier and more productive future for myself and my children. I am a loyal, punctual, and reliable worker.

FIGURE 3.2 The "conviction question." Illustration courtesy of Karson Schenk.

what it meant to have taken this job. While she had enjoyed and excelled at her career in job development for more than a decade, never before the Hub had she worked in a setting in which the clients were predominantly male, and in which many had been convicted of acts designated as violent that included violence against women and children. Linda provided a refreshing alternative: a case it was easy to feel good about.

Linda had already applied for multiple jobs. Hopeful that an interview was imminent on the horizon, Kristen's goal for the session was to ensure that Linda was prepared to excel. This included making sure she could easily recite a clear and polished response in the event that an employer should ask about her criminal record. Initiating the rehearsal, Kristen offered the standard prompt: "I see here on your application you indicated you have a criminal conviction?"

Linda replied directly. "Yes, back in 2009 I was charged with assault on a person with a firearm."

Kristen was taken aback by Linda's bluntness.

According to conventional wisdom, not only had Linda committed the faux pas of naming the conviction too directly, she had failed to strike the appropriate balance between too much and too little information. Although job seekers must not dwell on the conviction—and thereby amplify its significance in the mind of the employer—they also must offer *enough* information to satisfy the employer's curiosity and assuage any concerns. A simple "yes, that happened" would run the risk of producing a stream of specific questions that could cause her to lose control of the dialogue, while "yes, that unfortunately happened six years ago" would more likely avoid what Goffman called "performance disruptions."[15] The tricky part was to read the interaction in the moment, and make quick decisions about how much and what kinds of information to offer.

To determine this delicate balance for Linda, Kristen asked her to say a little more about the events that led to her conviction. Linda explained how, in the heat of a domestic dispute, she had fired several rounds toward the ceiling of her apartment. Although no one was hurt and the ex-boyfriend preferred not to press charges, the judge had convicted her of "assault on a person with a firearm" and sentenced her to five years in prison, expressing a need to use the case to set an example, particularly given its occurrence in an apartment complex where others might have been hurt. Linda felt the sentence was unduly harsh, especially because she had no prior criminal record. She also rejected the judge's classification of her behavior as "assault," correctly pointing out that not long ago, prior to the punitive sentencing turn that began in the mid-1980s, her behavior would have been characterized less inflammatorily as "brandishing a firearm."

Intrigued, Kristen asked, "Was the gun registered in your name?"

"Yes, it was," said Linda, adding that her ex-boyfriend was a linebacker, more than 6 feet tall and 280 pounds, and had physically attacked her one week prior to the incident that led to her conviction.

At this point, Kristen leaned out of the tiny office to summon Sasha's assistance. Sasha joined Linda and I on the opposite side of Kristen's desk. Kristen asked Linda to repeat the basic details of her story, then directing herself toward Sasha and I, proposed, "You know, the more she talks, the more sympathetic I am to her story. In this case, saying more might *help* her job prospects."

Sasha hesitated, unsure what to say and uncomfortable with being suddenly privy to the painful details of Linda's experience within the intimacy of the small room. Still, it became apparent that Kristen was not so much soliciting diverse opinions as looking for affirmation. Her gut feeling told her the uniqueness of the case warranted deviation from the usual rules of narration.

Kristen asked Linda to try the script again, this time in a way that reframed the events so as to portray her more sympathetically. Sharp and analytic, Linda easily grasped the needed adjustments. "Back in 2009, my boyfriend at the time had attacked me. I was afraid, I brandished a firearm, which was registered to me, and was sentenced to four and a half years in prison."

This reframing, all agreed, was ideal. Linda had diminished the significance of her conviction by reframing the criminalized behavior as an act of gendered self-defense. Though not white, Linda's small frame and light skin could be leveraged to draw from socially constructed notions of white women as submissive, domestic, and nonthreatening. She had substituted the inflammatory word "assault" with "brandishing a firearm," a label that she found more accurate and fair, and most important, that registered as less alarming. Additionally, Linda had directly countered her interpellation as criminal by including in her script the gun's registration. By emphasizing legal gun ownership, Linda portrayed herself as law-abiding, and subtly invoked the widely held belief in the right to bear arms and defend oneself. All in all, Linda had been coached to downplay and deflect her own criminal stigmatization, without challenging the legitimacy of criminal stigma itself.

———

There was perhaps no aspect of reentry workforce development more prone to reinscribe problematic ideas about race, crime, and punishment than the issue of how to respond to employers' questions about convictions. The overarching question on the table was how job seekers could concede the immorality of their actions, without dwelling on, saying too much about, or drawing attention to an incident that however awful, was generally unrelated to their ability or suitability to perform a given job.

The job developers and coaches I spent time with had mixed views about the extent to which employers "deserved" explanations of criminal records, but most agreed that in interview contexts where the employer already had *some* information, curiosity must be anticipated and managed in the most efficient and strategic way possible. To prepare, job seekers were coached to craft and then rehearse "conviction scripts"—preformed mininarratives that succinctly packaged the conviction(s) in as neutral and digestible a format as possible.[20] Together with job developers, they engaged in a process of "anticipatory interpellation" that aimed to predict what the employer expected to hear and help job seekers craft presentations to actively confront negative stereotypes.[21] The stakes were high—many an interview had gone sour on this presentation—and the margin of error was thin.

In the job development community, it was generally agreed on that job seekers should look the employer in the eye, and get in and get out—that is, answer only what was being asked and then redirect to one's greatness, just as you would with any other sticky question in a job interview. But it had to be handled just right. While job seekers typically sought to refrain from offering too much information, employers often pressed for more detail. Thus job seekers needed to be prepared to describe in brief, general, and nonalarming terms what had happened. Doing so was of course easier said than done given that the situations being narrated were frequently linked to unresolved emotional trauma and sometimes to ongoing interpersonal dynamics. Furthermore, a compelling performance depended on one's ability to speak with confidence and in nuanced ways during the stress of a job interview—not necessarily a well-developed skill for many of the Hub participants.

Notwithstanding differences in style and emphasis between individual coaches and across organizations, good conviction scripts were presumed to contain the following core components:

1. Acknowledgment
2. Responsibility
3. Remorse or regret
4. Transformation

Communicating transformation could be taught fairly easily. The goal was to convey assurance that whatever had happened in the past would not happen again in the future. This could be achieved by simply naming accomplishments and commitments that signal widely accepted categories of cultural value, such as work and self-sufficiency. As one job developer explained in a coaching session,

Remember there are two parts in the "one-minute-me": owning it and then describing what you're doing now. I suggest you try something like, "In the past year, I have held two steady jobs with an excellent track record, enrolled in school, and completed rehabilitation classes. I also have stable housing and transportation."

To satisfy the "acknowledgment" component, most coaches recommended simplifying and generalizing the conviction so as to make it sound less alarming. "Theft" or "robbery" would translate to, "I took something that wasn't mine," just as "assault" may be better phrased as, "I got into a fight with someone," or "I was involved in a situation in which someone got hurt." It was also advised to drop qualifiers like "intent to cause great bodily harm" or "intent to sell" that make the conviction sound graver. "Drug charges" would do. One middle-aged man who had been at the Hub for several months had gotten this entirely wrong when after hours of processing with a temporary staffing agency, the administrator at the last moment had asked, "What did you say your conviction was again?" He had answered simply, "Street terrorism." The administrator's eyes dilated, and the offer was immediately rescinded.

Part of the acknowledgment conundrum had to do with the fact that many people bear conviction titles that misrepresent and/or sound more dramatic than what actually happened.[22] For example, "street terrorism," a term that was adopted with the 1988 passage of the Street Terrorism Enforcement and Prevention Act by the State of California, makes it a crime to participate in a street gang, and further, makes it mandatory to sentence anyone who commits a felony for the benefit of a gang to additional prison time—whether or not the individual is a gang member, and whether or not they are the individual who was most directly responsible for the felony act. In other words, the same behavior would be named and treated more severely if a person were allegedly associated with a gang.

Though seemingly straightforward, the personal responsibility component could also be tricky to coach.[23] According to convention, responsibility (alternatively referred to as "ownership") was best communicated through the use of the words "mistake" or "bad choice." But there were many cases where the complexity, longevity, or gravity of the criminalized behavior left the language of "mistake" or "bad choice" sounding a bit hollow as well as disingenuous. Behaviors such as assault, stalking, rape, or child abuse are not generally "mistakes" (i.e., an oversight, blunder, or miscalculation), and while these behaviors are certainly "bad choices" (i.e., a selection or option), their underlying causes and motivations exceed these terms. Job seekers with these kinds of convictions struggled to formulate truthful and satisfying explanations of what happened, and why, in the brief, nonalarming ways expected.

In all cases, but particularly when a conviction defied easy explanation, it was essential to clearly convey remorse and regret. This sentiment needed to be communicated through careful word choice along with the proper management of facial expression and tone—the crucial test, as Goffman argued, of one's ability as a performer.[24]

> JOB DEVELOPER: OK, since we got started late, let's cut right to the chase. I remember you were OK with your conviction history question, but maybe still a little rusty?
>
> JOB SEEKER: Yes, still rusty.
>
> JOB DEVELOPER: OK, let's practice. So Mr. Davis, I see here you answered "yes" to having a felony conviction. Can you tell me about that?
>
> JOB SEEKER: My felony, yes, that was a mistake. I made some bad choices. Now I'm trying to better myself by working with the Reentry Community Partnership and the Hub.
>
> JOB DEVELOPER: Well, Mr. Davis, I normally like to hear more words, but I have to say that even though you didn't use many words, you *sounded* remorseful, I really felt it. And that's what employers will be looking for.

All in all, when delivered well, a conviction script closely following this rubric would sound logical and satisfying. In fact, a good script almost felt ceremonial in that, as Goffman observed, "when a performance highlights the common official values of the society in which it occurs, [it] may be seen . . . as an expressive rejuvenation and reaffirmation of the moral values of the community."[25] And yet this very capacity to uplift and celebrate dominant social norms was frequently called into question when "the moral values of the community" were at odds with the values of those it had criminalized. Many people rejected the application of criminal stigma to their identities, contested the very idea that the past should continue to haunt them, and questioned decontextualized notions of personal responsibility as well as easy distinctions between right and wrong.

Take, for example, Brian, who the reader will recall was arrested in the computer lab on his third day at the Hub. Brian explained that he did not regret the act that had resulted in his conviction of attempted murder. There had been an altercation between his family and another family in the neighborhood with which there was a long-standing beef. Under threat, Brian had used violence to defend his family and felt this decision was justified. This decision did not seamlessly lend itself to sympathetic appeal, thereby making it all the more important that he effectively communicate remorse. As Brian attempted to script the conviction, however, he and his job developer could not help but confront the fact that a decision can sometimes be both "bad" and "right."

SASHA: Let's try it again, but this time, try to express a little more remorse.

BRIAN: But I'm not remorseful and I don't regret it. I regret them coming down my street and threatening my family, but I don't regret doing what I needed to do to protect my family and I'm not sorry about that. . . . We were having a family thing. We weren't bothering them.

SASHA: How about handling it a different way, though, so that no one got hurt?

BRIAN [thinking on it]: I mean, in this situation, there was really no other way, at the time. . . . If I were faced with the same situation, I would do it again and that's just the way it is.

Brian stood by his decision to break the law and face negative consequences in pursuit of self- and familial defense, rejecting the assumption embedded within the script structure that criminal acts are simple decisions between right and wrong.[26] While for many job seekers, it was a welcome relief to master a simple narrative, for others, the stakes of narrative felt higher, not only for managing the perceptions of others, but as a matter of self-making. The stories we tell matter for how we see ourselves, what we think we deserve, and how we imagine the possibilities for our futures.

The Candor Trap

Ché Oliveras's big personality coupled with four years of restaurant cooking experience had landed him a prized position as a cook with a major food service chain that contracts with universities across the Southwest. In spite of his unkempt appearance—uneven mustache, scraggly goatee, and missing front tooth—he was magnetic and gregarious, the kind of person who walked into a room and instantly made everyone feel more relaxed.

Yet Ché's first day on the new job had been a bust. On arrival, the manager, Mr. Jansen, had informed him that he was unhired, effective immediately, because he had failed to fully disclose his conviction history. Ché had explained in his application the circumstances leading to the felony charge for which he had just completed a prison term, but had failed to reveal a handful of petty drug and theft convictions from about six years prior. Jansen mentioned an appeals process, but stressed that in a case like this, such an appeal would go nowhere. Making matters worse, on landing the job, Ché had turned down another offer as head cook at a Denny's restaurant on the outskirts of town.

This situation was also a job developer's nightmare. Kristen had worked hard to increase Jansen's openness to Ché's application, talking up his competence and positive attitude, and eventually, cajoling him to overlook the recent felony conviction. And now this.

Because criminal stigma straddles the distinction Goffman made between stigmatized conditions that are visible versus those that can be concealed, it produces complicated "disclosure dilemmas." Ché had fallen victim to a disclosure dilemma that reentry attorneys have called the "candor trap."

The concept was developed through attorney's work representing clients with criminal records who were seeking expungement, certificates of rehabilitation, and professional licensing approvals from review boards. In pursuing these remedies, they had noticed a common practice: applicants being asked about their past convictions, and then having their answers (even more so than the convictions themselves) used as a gauge of rehabilitation, trustworthiness, and character. Failure to properly disclose conviction history was frequently taken as prima facie evidence of dishonesty, and in many occupational licensing contexts, constituted grounds for denial of the license. In a working paper on the topic, attorney CT Turney explained:

> The commonly understood narrative of rehabilitation holds that if someone is rehabilitated, and therefore trustworthy, they will be upfront and honest about past convictions. If the information provided by the applicant does not align with what shows up in the background check report, this is evidence that the applicant is not trustworthy.[16]

Turney outlines the many shortcomings of this logic. First, the candor requirement ignores the relatively strong possibility of errors on the background check, including the appearance of arrests, convictions older than seven years, and dismissed convictions, which should not legally appear on third-party background checks in California. Second, many applications require not only admission of the conviction but elaboration of the underlying facts and circumstances too. Given the prevalence of plea bargaining and other kinds of negotiations that arise in the process of criminal prosecution, many people's charges and convictions do not accurately name or match what actually happened. In other words, the "facts" represented on paper may not have been proven in a court of law, let alone be true. Additionally, a person's explanation of facts and the surrounding circumstances may be compared to police and probation reports as a means of verifying their veracity, without regard for the subjective nature of such accounts. Third, the candor requirement ignores the numerous legitimate reasons for job seekers to not fully disclose conviction history. Many, for example, do not remember conviction history in accurate detail, particularly those struggling with addiction or mental illness at the time of conviction, or whose encounters with the legal system span a long period of time. Additionally, while job seekers are intuitively aware that informal disclosure requirements often outweigh those proscribed by law, the complexity of the laws governing background reporting leave applicants unsure of whether or not they should disclose various aspects of their criminal records.[17] Finally, applicants know from experience that openness and honesty will frequently prevent them from being hired, and thus sometimes deliberately choose not to disclose in hopes that the employer won't find out, or by the time the conviction(s) are discovered, they will have had a chance to demonstrate their abilities and develop a relationship.[18]

Be that as it may, in situations like the one facing Ché, none of these inconsistencies, complexities, or injustices could be brought to the employer's attention. If there was a sliver of hope to overturn the revoked offer, it lay not in challenging the policy or explaining its flaws but rather in taking full responsibility, expressing unequivocal remorse, and begging for forgiveness.

Kristen called Jansen immediately to apologize and discuss the situation. To her relief, Jansen was more frustrated than angry. He needed a cook right away and believed Ché would excel in his kitchen. Hence contradicting the hopelessness he had conveyed to Ché some hours earlier, he urged Kristen to send an appeal letter by email—and ASAP. From Kristen's many years' experience working with employers, she knew there was rarely a means to recover a job offer gone bad. But it was unusual for a manager to tell you about an appeals process, she said; this was the kind of information a job seeker (or attorney) would normally have to dig for. As such, while not especially hopeful, she pursued Jansen's request for a written appeal with total seriousness.

Somewhat hesitantly, Kristen invited my assistance. She was still not entirely comfortable with my involvement in job development activities. Given our radically different outlooks, there was a way in which my observation sometimes felt critical or evaluative to her, despite my constant effort to demonstrate my desire to participate rather than assess. She also worried that my participation would in some way undermine her approach, which, I had to admit, on several occasions it had, though without intention. Nevertheless, seeking solidarity in her predicament, the three of us took a seat in her office, where she immediately went out of her way to assure Ché that he could "say no" at any time to my participation. "We'll have a sign in case I start talking about something you don't want her to hear," she promised. Ché shook his head while raising his brows to indicate he wasn't the least bit concerned about my presence. I verbalized, again, that I was there only to help. "That's a better way to think about it," she agreed, and together we began to think about how to help Ché write an appeal. It needed to be perfect, but the kind of perfect that sounded genuine and like it came from him.

Ché wrote in blue ink on a lined piece of paper, scratching things out and starting new sentences as we brainstormed. He was open to feedback and editing, and after a while, the three of us began to enjoy the collective process of searching for the best words, content, and structure. How to "own it," yet deflect the characterization of the mistake as an indication of dishonesty. Whether or not to speak to drugs directly as a workplace issue given some of his charges had been drug related. And above all, how to reassure the employer that the convictions would have no bearing on the present. Rough draft in hand, I followed Ché to the computer lab in case he needed help typing it up. Though I could tell he wanted me to do it for him, I encouraged him to take the first stab. He banged it out in about twenty-five minutes, I made some minor adjustments, and we emailed the draft to Kristen. Then we went back to Kristen's office, where she swiveled her monitor so that we could all see the document. With a few more tweaks, we decided we liked it.

Kristen emailed the final letter back to Ché, attaching a letter from Janine on behalf of the Hub, attesting to his exceptional characteristics and recent "Job Seeker of the Month" award. Back in the lab, I walked him through the steps of downloading the letter and reattaching it to a new email, explaining that it's best not to "forward" in important situations like this because of the danger that even if you think you're cleaning up the email, there is a chance it could look like a forward. It absolutely needed to look like it came directly from Ché. Since he seemed to appreciate this kind of detailed information, I also shared my tip to fill in the "to" field last, thereby eliminating the danger of accidentally sending an email before it is ready—a common problem in this lab.

The moment the letter was sent, the three of us piled into Kristen's SUV. There were no guarantees that the letter would work, so we were headed ten miles north up Interstate 215 toward the mountains to drop Ché at the Denny's so that he could reinquire about the job opening there. Ché did not want to do this. He was embarrassed to reinquire about a job he'd just turned down, and worried that if things by some miracle worked out with Jansen, he'd have

appeal letter

CO me <Ché Oliveras>   1:16 PM   ⋮
to <jansenm@foodservicecompany.com>

Dear Mr. Jansen,

I am writing to appeal your recent decision to suspend my
employment. I sincerely apologize for failing to fully
disclose my conviction history. I mistakenly assumed that
you would only be interested in my most recent and
serious conviction. It was not my intention to withhold any
information about myself. I am interested in this job
because my skills are a perfect match for the position. I
also understand that the job is on a college campus and
that drugs in particular are a sensitive matter. Please
know that I am fully committed to a drug free lifestyle.

Thank-you for your consideration. I look forward to your
response.

Sincerely,
Ché Oliveras

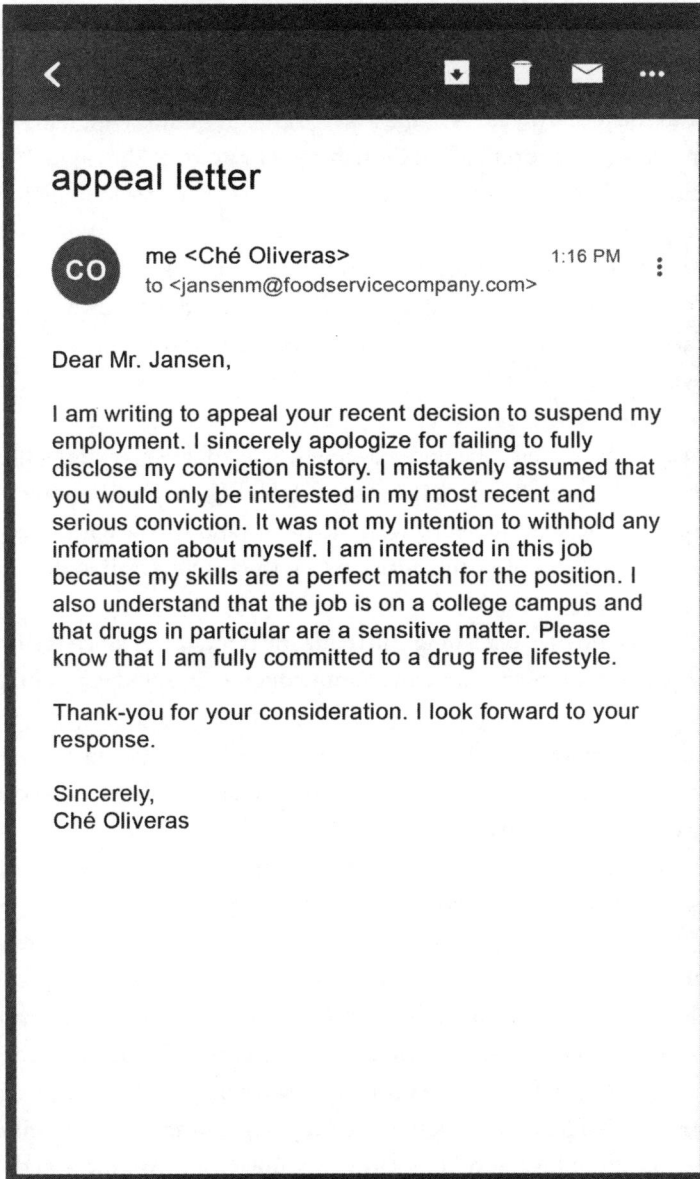

FIGURE 3.3 Letter of appeal. Illustration courtesy of Karson Schenk.

to further jerk the Denny's manager around. As we drove, Kristen tried to talk
Ché out of his reluctance, assuring him it was entirely ethical to pursue two
jobs at once, glancing in her rearview mirror to gauge his reactions. Ché eventually conceded, but the point, we soon learned, was moot: Denny's head cook
position had already been filled.

White Man's Burden

Kristen's eyes scanned the list of names on her whiteboard, head cocked in thought to the left. "Any ideas?" she asked. A former Hub client had stopped by this morning to report that San Bernardino Framework, the cabinetry company where he has been employed for almost one year, was looking to hire a few new "gluers."

"Most of these people are not on my happy list," Kristen commented. "They're all about to be suspended or sent back for more coaching. And it's a new relationship, so I really want to send someone solid, someone the employer will be happy with."

"What about Jeff?" I proposed.

"I *should* consider Jeff," she nodded slowly. "He's doing everything he's supposed to do, but my gut tells me he's not solid; I think he may still be homeless.... I also don't want to send someone with too many tattoos," she continued, with reference to Frank, whose name was next on the list, "even though I want to believe in him."

While this kind of gatekeeping still made me twitch, ever since the Robbin workshop, I better understood and to some degree accepted it as a matter of strategy. Whether to produce the ideal "reformed" candidate, narrate the events of criminalization in particular ways, or cater to unnamed racial preferences, the pressure job developers felt to accommodate employers' expectations in order to get people jobs was real.

Looking at the names on her whiteboard, I could empathize with the hesitation to send Gary or even Devon, neither of whom would be likely to impress the employer. Gary was a bit slow of thought and speech, and potentially unreliable. Devon would be great if he decided to be, but it was not yet clear if he actually wanted a full-time job. There were signs he was mostly using the Hub as a place to earn a few interim dollars rather than being invested in the program's goal to place him in a permanent position.

Kristen invited Sasha to weigh in. Luckily, she had someone in mind that she thought might be a good fit. "Do you know Gordon?" she asked. "He's twenty-one years old, Caucasian.... I don't really know why, but I just feel like he's the type the company would take well to."

Kristen agreed this was a good option, so Sasha mentioned the opportunity to Gordon. When Gordon expressed interest, Sasha quickly put a call in to Derek, the company owner's right-hand man. Sasha relayed the conversation. Derek had explained that gluer turnover had been high. He'd been letting people go because they "show up late, don't have the right attitude, aren't driven," and so on. "What would you do, Sasha, if your employee wasn't showing up on time?" she impersonated mockingly, rolling her eyes, and noting, "He was asking me to empathize with the problem of poor job performance from a supervisor's perspective, but I happen to know that his attitude toward employees is also problematic."

Sasha had of course not said as much to Derek, but instead politely cut this part of the conversation short by revealing that she might have a good candidate. Derek responded eagerly.

"Send him on Monday at 9:00 a.m., dressed in work clothes with no logos, wearing work boots, and [bringing] that little report card thing you guys give them that speaks to their work habits."

Sasha was caught off guard. It was Friday afternoon, and she would need to circle back to Gordon to see if Monday at 9:00 a.m. would work for him. But sensing that any hesitation on her part would be ill received, she agreed to the terms on the spot. "On second thought," Derek revised, "tell him not to ring my doorbell one minute before 9:15."

"Perfect," Sasha mustered as she hung up the phone and started to panic, remembering from past experience that part of the interview would be a measuring test. She knew Gordon had been studying for the GED and struggling in particular with the math. He had complained he had no one to help him learn the concepts. How am I going to teach him the basics of measurement over the weekend? she asked herself, knowing it was not her forte either. Improvising, Sasha began searching for instructional videos on YouTube and constructing a long email to guide Gordon toward interview success:

Sasha and I had the kind of working relationship and comfortability with one another that allowed me to later ask, "I'm curious, did Gordon's whiteness have anything to do with why you thought he would be a good fit for this employer?"

"Yes!" she replied, surprised. "How did you know he was white? . . . Did I mention that?"

MELISSA: "You did."
SASHA: "Yeah, the other guy from the Hub who works there is white too."
MELISSA: "Have you toured the plant? Do they mostly employ white guys?"
SASHA: "I don't know, they won't let me back there. . . . It's a hard hat area."

Sasha leaned back in her chair. "How can I explain why I felt this way, without sounding like a racist?" she reflected. "I just felt they would think of him

INSTRUCTIONS FOR MONDAY

CO   SJones@theHub.org   6:33 PM   ⋮
to me <gbshafer@yahoo.com>

Hey Gordon,

So, super important that you follow ALL of these
instructions for Monday!
Show up at 9:15 a.m. SHARP. I would start ringing the bell at the door
at like 9:10 a.m. if I were you.
PLEAAAASE DONT BE LATE :) Feel free to call me if there's a problem.
Set your alarm for this day too!!!
Make sure you dress in a white clean T-shirt WITH sleeves, and regular
work pants (I guess jeans) and work boots.

You are going in and asking to speak to Derek. Tell them that Sasha
sent you from the Hub. This is definitely where you fill out an
application and you may or may not interview with Derek on the
spot. No matter who you come in contact with there, be super polite
and really personable—light joking, don't be afraid to start
conversation, I know you know this stuff but it reaaaaallly matters
with them, especially Derek. This whole encounter is going to be
65 percent personality.

On the application, make sure you show up with your résumé and
report card in hand—if they don't ask, make sure you offer it up, but
only if they interview you. The application is going to include a
section about your conviction. Make sure you are honest here, write
down what it is, and write "would like a chance to discuss this in
person." I already told him what it was and that it was non-violent.
Make sure you also write that it was non-violent as well.

When discussing this, it is important that you acknowledge your
conviction as a big mistake that you learned from. You can talk
about how your dad helped turn you in (like you told me) and how
you are completely done with that lifestyle and regret it. Then move
on to talking about all of the positive things that you are doing now,
(classes you are taking which can be moved to Saturdays if needed,
your participation at the Hub, working with your grandpa, etc.)

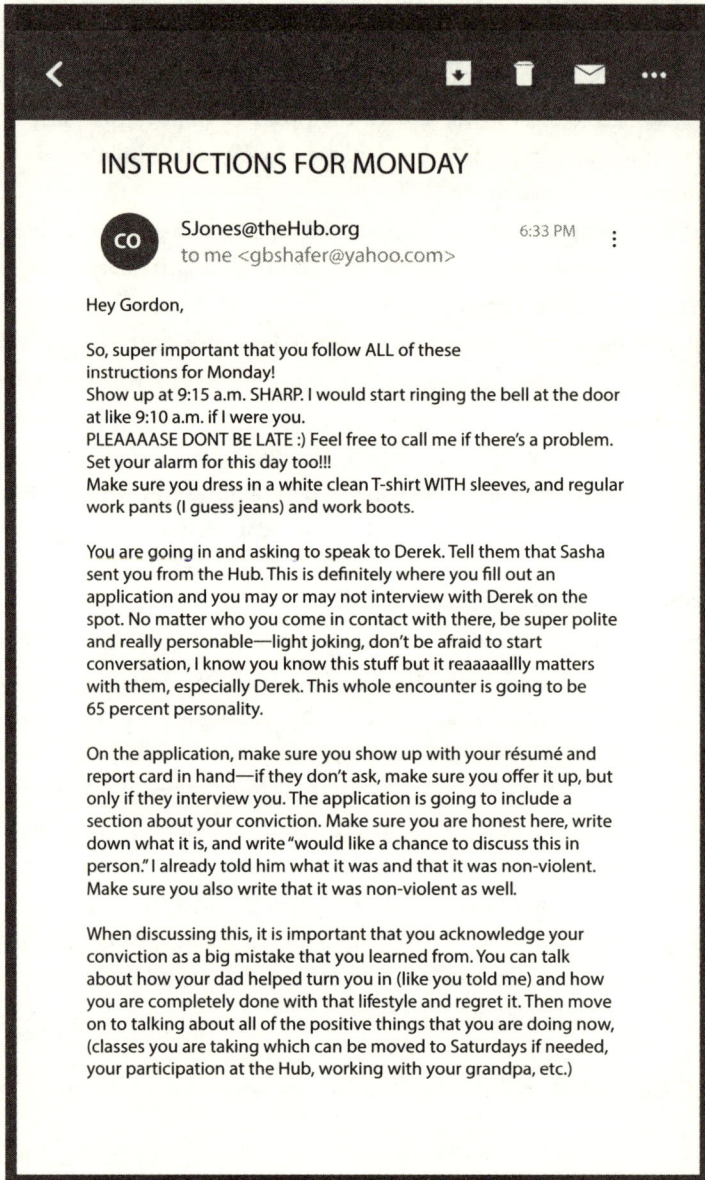

FIGURE 3.4 Instructions from a job developer. Illustration courtesy
of Karson Schenk.

The application will also include a section on measurements, make sure that you review the links below, and I mean SERIOUSLY review this because I'm not sure how hard the questions will be and they're not gonna offer you the job if you can't do the measurement portion well enough!!

http://themathworksheetsite.com/read_tape.html (this one is cool because you can create an answer sheet to make sure you're doing it right)
Make sure you practice ALL the measurements 1inch, 1/2 inch, all the way to 1/32 inch). Google "tape measurement practice" on YouTube for extra help. PLEASE DO THIS even if you think you already know it..!
Watch https://www.youtube.com/watch?v=pPJBGN7PqeM and also https://www.youtube.com/watch?v=4mMCpc0SfN0

Please practice this stuff every day of the weekend: Friday, Saturday, and Sunday ...
Derek told me if he has time he will interview you, or "talk" to you on the spot and if not, he will schedule you for an interview later in the week. If you do interview with him, make sure you talk to him about your interest in the job first. RESEARCH THE COMPANY (here is the link http://www.sanbernardinoframeworks.com) You can tell him that you heard there is a gluer position open, but make sure you stress that you are open to anything because you are a hands-on worker, love the type of work and hear that they are a really good company and want to be a part of that. Stress that you are always on time to work, and that you are serious about proving that you are a hard and dedicated worker. You can bust out your Report Card here. Talk about your Firecamp experience in detail and make connections to the hard work you did, and your SAFETY skills in Firecamp. PLEASE PLAN TO GIVE ME A CALL ON SUNDAY SO WE CAN DO A QUICK RUN THROUGH OF THE CONVICTION QUESTION TOGETHER. TEXT ME IF I DON'T ANSWER.

This is so much info, but very important for this employer, this could be a great job for you! Please let me know immediately if you have questions or concerns.

FIGURE 3.4 *(continued)*

as 'American,' a perfect second-chancer who made some mistakes when he was young. This feeling I get from them is hard to describe, but in the meetings I've had with them, something about the way they handle the idea of a second chance. . . . It's like that thing, what's it called again? . . . The white man's burden, isn't that a thing?"

To refresh our memories, Sasha googled "The White Man's Burden," a poem, originally written by Rudyard Kipling in 1899 about the colonization of the Philippines. Used as a justification for European colonialism, the concept white man's burden calls on white people to accept their moral responsibility to "civilize" nonwhites and thereby impart a supposedly superior culture.

"But in this white man's burden equation," she theorized, "the Blackness for them is only the prison."

Sasha elaborated on how this employer seemed to feel a sense of duty to extend employment opportunities to people with criminal records, but then "cherry-picked" to the extreme. The company was willing to hire someone with a conviction, but only if that person was otherwise unblemished, with their conviction the only flaw in an otherwise flawless profile. For example, a few months ago, another person from the Hub had applied and made a good impression. Something came up on his drug test due to a medicine he was taking for a back injury, which he had the prescription to legitimize. Derek had asked for a note from his doctor indicating his readiness to return to work—a note that required him to take time off from his current job in order to devote most of a day to traveling to the doctor's office on the bus and from there over to company headquarters. On arrival at San Bernardino Framework, another manager decided they would also like the note to say he was no longer taking the prescribed medication. The candidate missed another day of wages to go back to the doctor's office once again, but when he returned with the perfect note, they said, "I'm sorry, but we've already moved forward with another candidate."

Derek had specified that any candidate sent by the Hub should be "one who really wants to change." In doing so, the company framed its job opportunities as prizes reserved for the sufficiently repentant, self-motivated, and otherwise socially admirable—and bestowed itself with the power to determine the winners.

A few days later, Derek called Sasha to report that the interview went well, affirming Sasha's gut feeling with uncanny precision: "I really liked Gordon. He's a good kid; seems like a hard worker. . . . I feel like he represents the American dream."

Just as Sasha had suspected and hoped he would, Derek had perceived Gordon as a person who had made some mistakes, yet was now ready to redeem himself and climb the ladder toward prosperity. Her reading of the situation rested on a critical understanding of how ideas about criminality intersect with ideas about race. Without overthinking it, Sasha understood this employer's "openness" to criminal records was filtered through broader social ideologies, including color-blind meritocracy, the idea that success is determined by hard work alone, and cultural pathology, the notion that people's culture and habits perpetuate their subordinate position.[19] It did not behoove Sasha to question or challenge this employer's perspectives. Her complicit participation was needed in service of the immediate goal to get as many people hired as possible.

Double Crossings

For the first time in the Hub's two years of operation, a major employer—a staffing agency from a town twenty miles west—was coming to interview potential candidates for "packer" positions in a local warehouse. Springer Staffing urgently needed as many as twenty people, so it made sense for the company to come to the Hub to interview multiple candidates at once rather than schedule individual job seekers to come to it. An inside tip had informed the Hub staff that no background checks would be required for the packer positions. Sasha and Kristen were excited. Hosting a major employer at its offices would help the Hub to build its profile and credibility in the business community. Job seekers too were enthusiastic, especially those who had not yet had a job interview since their release from prison, or ever.

A man named Arnold arrived more than an hour early, smartly dressed in black slacks, an Easter-blue button-down shirt, and a striped tie acquired from the Men's Warehouse donations closet in the back room. A black leather folder containing copies of his résumé was tucked under his right arm. His left hand alternated between his pocket and side body as he paced nervously around the large, empty suite. Sasha suggested that he pass the time practicing some interview questions. I reviewed the basics with him: Tell me about yourself. Why did you leave your last job? I see here you marked "yes" that you have a criminal conviction? Arnold managed to rattle off the appropriate responses to reinscribe his value: I'm a reliable employee. . . . I like to stay busy. . . . I left that job because of a personal situation. . . . And yes, I did something I deeply regret, but that's in the past, and I'm working hard to improve myself and put that behind me. As we practiced, more job seekers trickled in, similarly well-dressed, anxious, and optimistic.

Hub staff would also be taking advantage of the assembly of so many job seekers to hold the "Participant of the Month" award ceremony, in which two job seekers would be praised for their efforts or accomplishments in job searching and/or their performance on the Hub's work crew. The first would go to Isaac, the job seeker from chapter 1 who had been successful in getting hired at BGM, and the second to Linda. Though she had not yet been successful in getting hired, she had submitted a formidable number of job applications in the past month with little coaching or nudging from job developers. Moreover, it had been challenging for her to adjust to working alongside so many men at the Hub, but now she was excelling on the landscaping crew, enjoying the work and camaraderie.

On arrival, Linda marched straight to my desk. She was upset about a recent denial by the same warehouse where Isaac was employed. Having heard about his success, she had decided to try her luck, plus her prior experience as a dispatcher in a major warehouse made her a perfect fit for the position. Linda explained how she had disclosed having a felony conviction on the job application, yet progressed quickly through the process, making an excellent impression at the interview, where she had frankly discussed her conviction. "A criminal record is not a bar to employment at our company," she had been assured with a wide smile. The hiring manager made a formal offer of employment and set a tentative start date, but on the conditions that she pass the drug test and background check. One week later, she had received a standard email. She pulled it up on her phone.[27]

Linda questioned, "Why did they waste my time . . . and theirs? Why pay for my background check? . . . I told them about it! Couldn't the person who interviewed me have surmised that I wouldn't pass?"

Overhearing this, Isaac wandered over. "It seems there's a bad omen over the organization right now," he commented, referring to a slew of negative employment outcomes that had unfolded in the past few weeks. A construction company had hired seven men from the Hub (including Ezra, the person who had been struggling to obtain a hard hat from chapter 1), some at a rate as high as sixteen dollars per hour, but then kept them dangling for weeks on end, citing construction delays beyond their control, and when a few finally did start, they didn't get paid in full or on time, and the foreman often showed

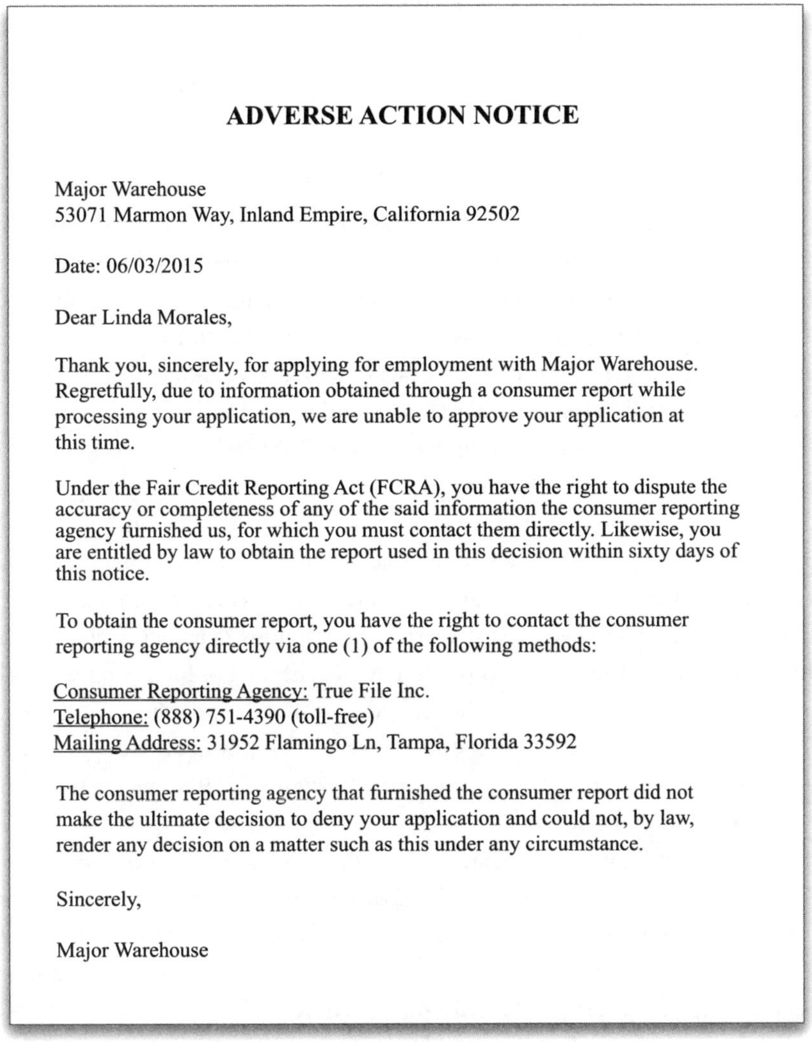

ADVERSE ACTION NOTICE

Major Warehouse
53071 Marmon Way, Inland Empire, California 92502

Date: 06/03/2015

Dear Linda Morales,

Thank you, sincerely, for applying for employment with Major Warehouse. Regretfully, due to information obtained through a consumer report while processing your application, we are unable to approve your application at this time.

Under the Fair Credit Reporting Act (FCRA), you have the right to dispute the accuracy or completeness of any of the said information the consumer reporting agency furnished us, for which you must contact them directly. Likewise, you are entitled by law to obtain the report used in this decision within sixty days of this notice.

To obtain the consumer report, you have the right to contact the consumer reporting agency directly via one (1) of the following methods:

Consumer Reporting Agency: True File Inc.
Telephone: (888) 751-4390 (toll-free)
Mailing Address: 31952 Flamingo Ln, Tampa, Florida 33592

The consumer reporting agency that furnished the consumer report did not make the ultimate decision to deny your application and could not, by law, render any decision on a matter such as this under any circumstance.

Sincerely,

Major Warehouse

FIGURE 3.5 Adverse action notice. Illustration courtesy of Karson Schenk.

up to the jobsite drunk. Additionally, the staffing agency providing janitorial services to the warehouse where Isaac worked had hired five Hub participants within the past month, but then fired three of them after retroactively running background checks. The policy change had ostensibly been prompted by a series of thefts at one of the company's locations, though only one of the people fired even had a theft-related conviction, and he had not been employed at the location in question.

———

Precisely because things had been going badly, Sasha and Kristen had not yet had the heart to tell the assembled job seekers what they had learned yesterday afternoon: that the opportunities at Springer Staffing may not be quite as inclusive as they hoped. Yesterday, Sasha had accompanied Kristen to Springer Staffing's office in person to predeliver seventeen applications and finalize details for the job fair. Rather than speak again with the administrator by phone, they were directed to the general manager and invited to further describe the work of the Hub. At some point in the conversation, Sasha had asked how she and Kristen should prepare interviewees to answer the conviction question. The manager snapped, "Do you mean to say that the people on this list will not clear the background check?" The small room filled with an uncomfortable tension. For their agency, the manager explained, to "clear" meant no convictions within the past seven years, seemingly oblivious that such a blanket exclusion is illegal under Title VII of the Civil Rights Act of 1964. Kristen swallowed a lump. "In that case, no," she replied, "most of our people will not clear." The manager demanded to know how they got the impression the agency was open to applicants with criminal records. Kristen hesitated, not wanting to reveal her personal relationship with the owner of the company for whom Springer was staffing and who had told her directly there were no background checks for packing positions. This kind of miscommunication was common in the field, where as we have learned, job developers are taught to avoid too much direct discussion of the "barrier," and various actors frequently understand or implement criminal record policies differently.

In effort to save face, Kristen turned to Sasha and said, "You have some people who will pass, don't you, Sasha?" Playing along, Sasha paused and then exaggerated a little. "Yes, maybe four or five." Truthfully, at this moment there were only a few job seekers at the Hub whose convictions dated back further than seven years, and most of them were already employed. "Well, I have one or two," Kristen continued, "so together that's six to seven. . . . We'll make sure those who can pass are there and make it a learning opportunity for the rest." Though with notably dampened enthusiasm, the manager had agreed to proceed.

But now, as 4:00 p.m. neared—the time the job fair was scheduled to begin—there was no sign of Springer Staffing representatives. Frantic, Kristen placed a call, then another, and yet another. Finally, a Springer representative returned her call to say that the agency was experiencing an internal emergency, some sort of payroll snag, and wouldn't be able to make it after all. Kristen was flabbergasted. In her twenty-plus years in job development, an employer had never canceled a job fair at the last minute; it just wasn't done. While a payroll issue seemed plausible, it was not an excuse to cancel. Surely, she and Sasha agonized, they could have sent *one* representative.

Kristen and Sasha speculated there may have been a power struggle between the manager and the lower-level employee who had initiated the partnership; it was common for background check policies to vary within a company at different levels of the chain of command. There also could have been a miscommunication between the staffing agency and the actual employer; it was not unusual, for example, to get a tip about a "felony-friendly" employer from a fellow job developer, only to later find that the employer was in fact quite particular about the type or age of conviction. Nonetheless, they likely would never know the true reason the agency had decided to bail and more pressing than speculation was the need to inform the seventeen hopeful job seekers waiting in the next room.

Instead of being the bearer of such bad news, however, Kristen made a quick and rather brilliant decision to cash in on one of her "slow simmers." A few weeks ago, she'd gone to deliver a dozen donuts to the office of Ricardo Moretti, the owner of a highly successful roofing business located only a few miles away. The lead had come from a Hub client who had been hired there a few months back. When Ricardo had mentioned an opening to Kristen, she had presented him with Ritchie Gonzales-Lopez, barely twenty-five years old, strong, fit, and highly motivated to work. Ricardo had fallen in love. Ritchie was exactly the type of kid he wanted to help. Ricardo, it turned out, had spent almost a decade cycling in and out of the prison system himself, and after starting his business, had become part of Robbin's 5 percent mission-driven employers.

To Kristen's relief, Ricardo had taken her call and agreed to come over to the Hub. If not interviews with Springer Staffing, at least the job seekers would get to interact with a real-live employer.

Ricardo stood in front of the group. At first, he didn't have many words.

We run a roofing company.
Roofing is really hard.
And dangerous.

We're busy.

If you want to work, come down and talk to us.

The audience was quiet, but attentive. Ricardo relaxed a bit:

> We've hired a few guys from here, and it has worked out. I used to be on parole, forever. One day I woke up at California State Prison and I was like, Where am I, what am I doing? I got out. I worked hard. I started my own business. That was back in 2007. It was a blessing. So life is what you make it. I don't know what else to tell you guys . . .
>
> You have to tie off. If you don't, you're fired. I had an OSHA violation a few years ago, cost me twenty grand. A competitor saw that we weren't tied off and called them. First time it's a fine. Second time they take my license.

"Ricardo," Kristen interjected from the back of the room, "if they do decide to fill out an application and you call them for an interview, one of the most common fears we hear around here is having to answer the conviction question. Do you ask about that?"

> I don't care. I'm not part of that segment of society that judges you. I don't care what you did in the past. I care about what you're doing today. I already know you're convicted. I'm convicted too. We screwed up. You can't hold onto that; you have to let it go and move on. Nobody's better than anybody else. Treat me with respect, and I'll treat you well too. If you're a knucklehead, you have to get out of my way. The problem with some of us who have been locked up is that we're knuckleheads. [Pause.] Am I right? We have trouble listening to people. But on the roof, somebody is in charge, and you have to be OK with that. A couple of times guys have come to me talking about a supervisor who disrespected them; you gotta let all of that go. It's a job. Just come to work, support yourself and your family, go home.

Shoulders dropped and breath exhaled as Ricardo's comments registered throughout the room. Though the immediate prospect of a job had been lost, it seemed his no-frills talk provided even better medicine.

Major employment agencies like Springer Staffing that can afford to pick and choose their workers hold tremendous power in the labor market. They the call shots and set the terms of employment. And while job seekers, and especially those with criminal convictions, are held to the highest standards of integrity, candor, and etiquette, none of these standards are required of employers. To simply be addressed honestly, frankly, and with respect was in itself refreshing.

Beyond Stigma Management

This chapter has explored criminal stigma as a dynamic social relation that gets developed and determined interactively, and expressed in real-life, historically specific encounters.[28] Across the United States, hundreds of organizations engage in this dynamic social relation, interacting with employers who may be reluctant to hire criminalized workers, and coaching job seekers to present themselves in the most strategic and self-advancing ways possible. As we have seen, the work of stigma management necessarily involves talking about, and coaching others on how to talk about, crime along with its causes and solutions, and in this sense, broadly shapes how criminalizing processes are perceived and understood. I have thus argued, alongside other critical stigma scholars, that the way stigma is managed is a matter of politics with broader social consequences.[29]

Unsurprisingly, workforce organizations tend to steer job seekers toward well-oiled conventional narratives that align with an assumed demand for remorse, personal responsibility, and rehabilitation. These entirely individualized framings leave no room for a critique of historical or ongoing systemic marginalization, the structural inequalities that render some people much more vulnerable to criminalization than others, or the unjust conditions of the labor market. Instead, criminalized people are encouraged to portray themselves as exceptional, and as uniquely worthy of inclusion, by differentiating themselves from others who may appear "less reformed"—to dissociate from, rather than challenge, criminal stigma. Such distinctions sometimes make direct or implicit use of racialized and gendered stereotypes.

Portraying oneself as sympathetic, or "less bad" than the next person with a criminal record, is a tactic that may work and even sometimes be necessary for individuals attempting to get hired, or gain access to other privileges and resources. Yet a politics of empathy and relative innocence that seeks to paint particular criminalized individuals as uniquely deserving of second chances (e.g., those who are young, grew up in troubled homes, or whose crimes are easily classified as economic, nonviolent, or drug related) leaves out the many criminalized people who lack access to social categories that can be interpreted as docile, normative, and deserving.[30] Not every criminal act is explainable in a way that can render a sympathetic judgment. Thus attempting to elicit an empathetic response necessarily reinforces the condemnation of those who cannot or choose not to make such claims.[31]

Tactically, job development can end up relying on a theory of social change that workforce leader Sarah Glenn-Leisitkow has likened to "exposure therapy": a belief in the possibility that through introducing diverse individuals to one another and having that be a positive experience, we might change individual perspectives, and slowly, those of society more broadly. Not only is such an approach impractical as a primary basis for societal-level change, says Glenn-Leisitkow, it leaves intact employers' capricious power to determine whether the engagement has been "moving enough," and if the denigrated person in question meets their norms of how a person worthy of access, participation, and respect should act/be.[32] Exposure therapy furthermore leaves open the possibility that rather than radically shift their perspectives or practices, employers can become convinced that certain people are acceptable and redeemable while many others remain irredeemable.

Ultimately, I came to see how getting people jobs cannot rest on changing employers' ideas about criminality. Not only is changing beliefs incredibly difficult, as long as criminalized people are presented to employers with stigma in hand, no matter how careful or nuanced the narrative, stigma perpetuation is inevitable. Truly challenging stigma must go beyond the realm of interpersonal communication between power holders, stigmatized people, and their immediate allies. It must also involve challenging the power that allows "the identification of differentness, the construction of stereotypes, the separation of labeled persons into distinct categories, and the full execution of disapproval, rejection, exclusion, and discrimination."[33] In other words, it is not just better stigma management that is needed in the long run but instead an end to the presumption that having been convicted is necessarily reflective of character or relevant to employment, as well as an end to the power to *enact* those presumptions.[34]

4

Good Sense Hiring in Small and Midsize Business

It doesn't matter whether they came from the army, college, or prison.
You must hire people you like, trust, and respect.

The oldest rule is, Don't hire a problem. . . . I would rather take a chance
on a felon than a repeat workers' comp claimer.

Hiring is about asking good questions. A good interviewer says very little,
gets them talking. If you want to find good people who are going to stick
around a while, you must do good interviews. If you want mediocre people,
just go through applications, they contain a lot of superficial information. . . .
A criminal record can be superficial. A criminal record just makes me ask more
questions.

I think the small business owner can relate to the people who work for
him. He's not up in some ivory tower.

—INLAND EMPIRE BUSINESS OWNERS

LAMONT BURKE, the mid-forties' African American manager of a local franchise for a major moving company, had only three questions in mind when considering a new hire:

1. Can they carry heavy things up and down three flights of stairs?
2. Do they actually want to work?
3. Do they have a "can-do" attitude?

Experience had led Lamont to be unconcerned about size, sex, or age, having found that women are equally capable movers, people over fifty are more careful, and "big" does not necessarily equal strong. He was specifically committed to hiring Black workers whenever possible given the racial discrimination he had experienced in the labor market in his own youth.

When I asked Lamont about criminal records, he shrugged. "It's fifty-fifty. A criminal record doesn't mean they'll be good or not good."

Lamont was struggling to adjust to a demographic shift in employees resulting from both a tightening of the labor market in the economic recession and recent changes to the company's criminal records policy. Like most moving companies, the business had historically barred only people with recent convictions related to violence or theft. But in 2010, the corporate legal arm of the company had sent a memo to regional managers and directors as well as HR personnel outlining changes that under the guise of "business necessity," would bar people with almost any kind of felony conviction from employment. Lamont observed that recent applicants came with higher-quality credentials and demanded better pay, but were unwilling and unable to perform physically in the ways traditionally expected of professional movers. For example, he complained, whereas movers used to take breaks either when the job was done or they were tired, today's employees stopped in the middle of a job, simply out of awareness that the State of California requires employers to provide breaks every 4.5 hours.

Carlos Salcedo, the thirtysomething-year-old Chicano manager of a twenty-two-person high-end cooking equipment production shop, shared Lamont's rejection of criminal records as a meaningful filter. "A criminal record just isn't an issue," he said. "It's just not a determining factor at all." Rather than conduct background checks, Carlos looked for traits in the interview process that could be problematic and the two key things that *did* matter to him: fit, energy, and controllability.

> Bringing someone into the plant is like a marriage. If they're not comfortable, it's not going to work. My shop has a flow. I'm very careful about who I put into my shop. Strong-willed is good in a way because it means you have direction, opinions, but you also have to be able to take direction. . . . Background or no background, you have to be teachable, humble. . . . I like people who can't sit still. I like enthusiasm, energy. But also a relaxed attitude, not too easily offended. . . . I need people I can control.

Brian Lorey, the white, mid-fifties owner-manager of an art supply business, described hiring as a difficult task that had to be repeated over and over, and was hard to get right. A few particularly bad recent hires had eaten up time and money—people he'd brought on quickly to fill a gap, despite his gut feeling that something was off. But Brian "wasn't a big fan" of background checks either, he told me, preferring not to add this layer of hassle and expense to his hiring process when he was unconvinced that it would solve his personnel problems. In Brian's view, a criminal record represented—at best—a partial record of past behavior, when the more pertinent question was, "Do you have problems *today* that may interfere with your ability to show up for work on Monday?" In Brian's experience, a criminal record could be a red flag, but no more so than the many other conditions he had witnessed impacting work performance: personal debt, alcoholism, drug addiction, medical issues, children, divorce, and custody battles.

———

This chapter explores the perspectives and hiring approaches of owners and managers of small to midsize businesses in the Inland Empire who did not rely on background checks as a primary tool of candidate selection.[1] Drawing from firsthand observations of hiring and dozens of semistructured interviews with Inland Empire employers, it unpacks an orientation to criminal background checks that differs sharply from that promoted by the criminal record complex.

At bottom, these employers did not believe that background checks would help them to determine who would and would not be a good worker. For example, when I asked James Allen, the owner of a large garden supply company who had been in business fifty-three years and hired more than a thousand people, whether he hired people with criminal records, he waved his hand back and forth in a dismissive manner and said, "It doesn't matter whether they came from the army, college, or prison. You must hire people you like, trust, and respect." James insisted that the key to successful hiring was to focus not on past events and circumstances but rather a person's current state of affairs. James explained, "The job must mean everything to them. It must give them a sense of worth, a chance to be part of something." In evaluating a new hire, he tried to discern, "Does this person have passion? Is the job an opportunity for them to do something they want to do?"

Not only were these employers crystal clear about the qualities they were looking for and trying to avoid, they exhibited a remarkable confidence in their own abilities to assess them. As one hiring manager posed rhetorically, "Is my judgment sometimes wrong? Oh sure, but I'm almost always right."

These employers expressed deep skepticism about what they called "textbook" evaluation mechanisms, including credit checks, résumé keyword finders, and background checks, instead holding their own intuition and insight in higher esteem.[2] They stressed the importance of "gut feelings," and many claimed to have a "radar" for certain qualities. Carlos, for instance, claimed to have a radar for short tempers—a quality he would not tolerate. James admitted that laziness—his least favorite attribute—was difficult to detect in an interview, but he did believe that a person's essential character could be detected. "The spots on a leopard never change," he told me, by which he meant that character was evident in childhood and changed little over time.

Of course, a mental rejection of actuarial mechanisms did not shield these employers from the constraints of policy and law, but it was my observation that they tended to question, challenge, and work around barriers rather than simply accept them. For example, when a federal regulation excluded people with felonies from working in warehouses certified by the Customs-Trade Partnership Against Terrorism after 9-11, Arnie Shaw, the owner-manager of a major warehouse operation, reorganized its entire production flow so that one of his warehouses could accommodate workers with convictions. Shaw also repeatedly argued and negotiated for an exemption with his insurance underwriter when the annual policy renewal inevitably included a clause requiring background checks along with the exclusion of people with certain felony convictions.

Though just as concerned about potential threats to the business as any other employer, rather than try to anticipate and prescreen for every possible problem, these employers' main vetting methodology was to start people at the bottom and slowly move them up. One employer explained that he would never hire someone directly into an administrative position or one dealing directly with customers. Instead he brought everyone in at lower-level positions and promoted them once they had demonstrated trustworthiness. In contrast to the hyperregulated, by-the-book, no-mistakes-allowed mentality of big HR departments, these employers were in touch with the actual, on-the-ground hazards of the business, and from this grounded vantage point, were not afraid to take informed chances or try new things. They knew how to pivot quickly when things didn't work out too.

As one would expect, these employers were not immune to widely held stigmas about certain kinds of convictions. Yet they seemed to understand something criminologists have long known that is often lost in conversations about criminal records and employment: that "crime" is highly place, time, and circumstance specific rather than expressive of anything essential. In contrast to the automatic exclusions to which Hub job seekers were so accustomed, they tended to weigh potential risks in nuanced ways. For example, when I asked one business owner if their company would hire someone with a sex-related conviction, they paused in a way that suggested they understood the social weight of the question and then replied, "Well, there are no little kids around here." Exceedingly pragmatic and empirically oriented, they were more concerned about drug problems (which can affect work performance) than murder (which does not), and more worried about workers' comp claims (a common problem) than negligent hire liability (a rare occurrence).

Many of the business owners and managers I encountered clearly derived satisfaction from using their businesses to help people improve their circumstances. Whether framed in terms of religious benevolence, racial uplift, class solidarity, or community service, they spoke passionately about using their businesses to uplift people and do good in the world. For example, Carlos described with considerable emotion an instance in which a young man had presented himself at the plant, desperate for work and complaining that no one would hire him because of his criminal record. Carlos didn't really have an opening, but felt compelled to help. He offered the young man a job cleaning the shop and eventually promoted him to long-distance delivery—one of the company's most trusted positions. "To see someone start walking around like they have a purpose, like they're needed," he said, "I love seeing that happen. . . . That's what a lot of these guys feel is that nobody needs them."

More frequently, however, these employers' talk—about hiring generally and criminal records especially—came across as remarkably *unemotional*. They emphasized that social concerns could not drive their approach to hiring, and their businesses could not be places for social work or rehabilitation. As Brian put it, "When it comes to business, the question has to be, What is best for the business?"

This chapter demonstrates that despite the seeming ubiquity of criminal background screening, a significant segment of the business community does not believe that having been convicted defines a person's character or negatively affects their suitability for work. Importantly, employers have reached this conclusion not out of political or social commitments but because hiring people with criminal records works for their businesses. With the possible exception of Shaw, who commented when we first met, "Atilla the Hun thinks I'm right wing, but I believe in second chances," the employers I met did not appear to have taken up the banner of criminal justice reform.[3]

In what follows, I explore these core elements of a more grounded approach to hiring and criminal records—what it looks like in practice, how its practitioners conceptualize it, and some of the factors impinging on its viability. As I have argued throughout and will further demonstrate here, rather than an urge to discriminate, at the heart of criminal record discrimination are a set of policies and laws animated by ungrounded risk logics as well as vested interests that benefit from the erroneous assumption that people with criminal records present a danger in the workplace. Focusing on employers who, through experience, have found that the characteristics they're looking for in an employee have little relationship to criminal records, throws those external risk structures and their flimsy logics into plain relief.

Alternate Routes

I had been embedding myself in the local business community as best I could, attending networking, professional association, and government workforce meetings across the region, and interviewing every employer who was willing. But I needed to figure out how to build deeper relationships with employers. I wanted to see what hiring looked like in practice, how decisions got made, and how criminal records figured in those decisions. On learning of my research agenda, the friendly members of a local workforce investment board all agreed, "She should go talk to Paul." Paul Weber was a respected local business owner whose trucking business, they said, was known to hire people with convictions. A week or so later, I worked up the gumption to call.

"Martin Luther who?" he chuckled heartily at the absurdity of my suggestion. Weber had just agreed to meet with me at his company headquarters, but it was Friday afternoon, and his secretary, Suzanne, had already left for the weekend so he advised me to call her back next week to schedule the visit. I had casually suggested that perhaps Tuesday would be the best day to try back given Monday's holiday.

"We will be here on Monday," he assured me, "and I go by Paul."

MLK Day was apparently not a holiday that stops construction trucking. I kicked myself for the mistaken assumption as I hung up the phone, anxiety rising at my lack of business acumen and questionable ability to pull off this aspect of the ethnography. I wanted to make the right impression, to be accepted as the kind of person it could make sense to have around. This self-doubt was not fully founded. I was at least tangentially familiar with the business world, my own mother having spent most of her forty-year career in industrial and hardware sales and management, including a major manufacturer of commercial ropes and twines.[4] But as she would sometimes critique, the social justice orientation I had solidified since my teens had led me to deliberately disidentify with the capitalist ventures that had paid my way through college. Now I had cultivated a strategic interest in better understanding businesspeople—what they value, their concerns, motivations, and influences, and how they weigh decisions like hiring.

The assurance that Weber Trucking hired people with convictions was not sufficient to level my unease as I set out with my Google map that early February morning. For starters, the landscape is desolate. The major avenues that exit the freeway are wide, as many as six lanes across. There are many more trucks than cars, no pedestrians, and few trees but for a sprinkle of dwarf fan palms and other desertlike scrub. A mix of industrial and commercial establishments are set on wide-open stretches of flat land to the east and west as one heads north toward the picturesque San Bernardino Mountains. Well, they haven't always been picturesque. People who grew up in this area remember the days when the mountains were barely visible and kids had to stay indoors, before California tightened its air-quality regulations, a topic about which the Webers would have plenty to say. As I traveled along in the right lane, just under the posted speed limit, I noted small liquor markets and gas stations, many places to buy tires, a tractor trailer sales yard, a truck leasing company, a transmission, clutch, and parts shop, a waste management facility, an electric plant, an industrial steel facility, a scrap metal yard, a place to buy concrete block, multiple collision centers and forklift sales establishments, a massive distribution warehouse surrounded by barbed wire, and a neon sign advertising Oriental massage.

I watched for street numbers or a company sign, and spotting the latter, pulled into the gravel drive, finding an empty space alongside the handful of cars parked next to a small building marked "HR Office." A middle-aged white woman sitting behind one of three desks directed me to another building across the yard where the owner's office was located. I thanked her and set out walking within the yellow-painted safety pathways as instructed. There were big trucks and heavy equipment everywhere, machines I could not begin to name or explain. I knocked on the metal screen door of the little bungalow, and a woman invited me inside. Suzanne was friendly, perhaps in her mid-forties, and like most of the employees, wore blue jeans, a plaid button-down shirt, and white sneakers. I could hear two men talking in the adjacent room.

That must be Weber's office, I thought to myself—Paul's office. I was nervous, for the obvious reasons related to meeting people for the first time and wondering how my research questions would be received. Additionally, I was trying to fight off a familiar Black girl feeling I had experienced growing up in mostly white environments. I worried I would not look as expected from my telephone voice. A grad student from Texas was probably supposed to be younger and whiter. A few moments passed, and I was motioned in and introduced to Paul. He was silver haired, maybe in his late sixties or early seventies, seated in a black rolling chair before a large glass-topped conference table.

"So Melissa, how can I help you?" he asked calmly, "if I can even help you."
"Oh, you most certainly can," I replied (probably too eagerly), restating some elevator version of my research topic. "Maybe you could start by telling me a bit about your history with this company."

Luckily, this was a topic Paul was more than happy to discuss. He proceeded to recount in captivating detail how he had built Weber Trucking into one of the largest and most sophisticated low-bed carriers in Southern California, moving heavy equipment, transporting bulk materials to and from the ports of Los Angeles and Long Beach, and in 2014, grossing approximately $30 million in sales per year and employing 225 people. A true capitalist, Paul spoke in numbers: revenue per mile, margins per ton, gross income, operating margins. It began with his first childhood for-profit venture selling onions from a wagon. Then there was the pivotal moment when he coaxed his mother into forging his father's signature on a loan so he could buy his first truck. His late teenage-hood and early twenties were a dizzying succession of hay-hauling and cattle-raising transactions, including harrowing and near-miss driving accidents. Along the way, Paul learned to drive ever-bigger and more complicated trucks. He also attended technical college, pursuing a degree in animal husbandry, which required him to leave home at 4:30 a.m. with his dad, drive seventy miles to drop him at work, then double back twenty miles to his school, and back again to pick up his father at the end of the day, getting home around 7:00 p.m. Paul remembers fondly those morning drives, when he and his dad would listen to the Loman and Barkley talk show and argue politics— his father a big government Roosevelt Democrat, and he "already becoming a right-wing Republican conservative." Eventually, the demands of college along with the realization that only those who had inherited large parcels of land could succeed as ranchers had compelled Paul to abandon his hay-hauling ventures and take a job with a trucking company. Before long, a friend of his called saying that a guy in a nearby township was looking to sell his trucking business.

Paul invited me to a tour of the yard. We circled around at five miles per hour in his SUV as he explained the company's diverse operations: hauling bauxite, cement clinker, fertilizers, allium, expanded shale, petroleum coke, and dry-periled sulfur plus iron ore; mining silica sand, kaolin clay for white cement, gypsum for agriculture, and clay for alumina use in cement and limestone; excavating and grading for stormwater and water-retention basins; transloading (rail to truck or van to flatbed); and more. The company's success, Paul believed, was attributable to a willingness and ability to take on new opportunities as they presented themselves.

As we rolled along, he stopped periodically to chat with employees at work. One asked for his recommendation on how to best move a pile of iron ore from point A to point B in the yard; another for a thumbs-up on a requested schedule change; and another for a clarification on the repairs needed to a particular truck. His involvement in these details as the company owner surprised me, as did the racial diversity of the employees in the yard—a mix of Black, white, and Latino men roughly matching the local demographic. I wondered if racial diversity was common for the industry, and whether it had always been this way, but didn't yet know how to ask.

Personnel Problems

Admittedly, I had left that initial meeting with Paul somewhat perplexed by the idea that a white conservative business owner would be open to hiring criminalized people and would hire so many people of color, including Black people. My mind seemed to expect that I would be able to draw straight, quick lines between employers' personal categories of belonging or political affiliations and the hiring decisions they would make. This expectation is not entirely unfounded; research suggests, for example, that Black employers are more likely to hire other Black people than their white counterparts.[5] As I was quickly schooled by circulating within the predominantly Right business class of the Inland Empire, however, there is no necessary or predetermined correlation between social categories, political or religious affiliations, and hiring practices, and leftist politics are certainly not a prerequisite for hiring people with criminal records. As Stuart Hall emphasized, ways of thinking and acting do not themselves have political or ideological connections; they get organized in particular ways at different times and under different conditions.[6]

———

Intrigued by Paul's personal history, the employee diversity, and the company's alleged openness to hiring people with convictions, I asked Paul's permission to return to Weber Trucking. He graciously agreed, and a few weeks later, with all of my big questions in mind, I posed a simple one: "So what does it take to be a trucker?" Paul took the question in the direction he imagined I wanted to go.

> Well, they can't have a felony that's violent or anything that could be used to blackmail you. They're in and out of the ports and other sensitive areas, so things like poor credit or a gambling addiction, issues that could be used to pressure someone to give up sensitive information. . . . No recent moving violations, no high blood pressure or diabetes . . . and a track record of working somewhere—someone who will give them a reference.

As Paul paused for a moment in thought, I contemplated the list of restrictions and unacceptable felonies he had just rattled off—a rather long list, it struck me, for an employer with a reputation as "open." But before I could inquire further, Paul called out loudly to the next room.

"Peter, would you say we have less problems finding drivers than mechanics?" Peter Weber—vice president of Weber Trucking and Paul's son—hemmed and hawed before settling on a response.

"No," he called back, "we just have personnel problems."

Virtually every employer I spoke to across industry, sector, and type of business complained about how hard it was to attract as well as retain competent and reliable employees—people who would show up consistently and on time, work hard, and stay until the job was done.

The topic compelled Peter to get up from his desk and step into the room where Paul and I were seated.

"Watch this," he said, making eye contact, "I'm going to get my dad all riled up." Then turning to his father and pausing for dramatic effect, he said, "I just saw on the news that Brown has a 61 percent approval rate."

"The people in this state are just stupid," Paul retorted. "How on earth do you justify spending $90 billion on a high-speed rail line from Modesto to Bakersfield?!"

In his first two terms as California governor in the 1970s, Jerry Brown had been the darling of many of the younger and more progressive Democrats, an heir of sorts to the Robert Kennedy crown—enacting protective legislation for farmworkers, refusing to live in the governor's mansion, and driving an old Plymouth. Late in his second term, he decided to deal with California's grossly overcrowded prisons by designing small "rehabilitation centers," but before ground was broken, George Deukmejian was elected and Brown's little prisons became the five-thousand-bed monsters that blight the landscape today. Now in his third and fourth terms as governor, Brown had two major legacy projects: one, a massive tunnel in the Bay-Delta to bring more water into the Central Valley and Southern California, and two, the high-speed train.[7] In the Webers' view, out-of-whack spending priorities like these took money away from efforts to generate jobs and grow businesses. Peter elaborated:

> Sacramento doesn't understand small business. Their motto is, "I defy you to make money in this state." You've got rich people coming up with ideas to save the poor, but the ideas don't affect them. The tax laws are aimed at people trying to make money [income] rather than at those who *have* money [wealth]. At the end of the day, companies like ours don't have money to invest or grow. We are not getting rich; we are the type of people who put everything we earn back into the company.

Air-quality and environmental protection regulations enacted in the mid-2000s were a particular sore spot for the Webers and others in the transportation industry. The Los Angeles Harbor Commission passed the Clean Trucks Program, nearly putting many companies out of business by requiring them to retrofit old trucks or purchase new, more ecological fleets. At one time, Paul noted, they were paying $2,200 per month per truck on 102 trucks in order to bring their fleet into compliance.[8]

Similarly, the Webers blamed California's zeal for regulation, coupled with misguided international trade policy, for the loss of local blue-collar jobs: three thousand when Toyota moved to Texas in 2014; another sixty-five hundred when Tesla Motors chose Nevada over California and other competing states for the siting of its new battery "gigafactory"; and most memorably, forty-five hundred in 1983, when after forty years of production, the Kaiser Steel mill was physically dismantled by approximately three hundred Chinese workers, and its parts loaded and shipped to China.[9] Peter reflected,

Not far from here, seven thousand people used to work at Kaiser Steel. They have now been relocated to China. There are no tariffs on stuff coming into our ports. Free trade agreements were a bad idea; now we have no manufacturing left. Now we have the working poor—some of them here—earning $14 an hour.

Like a number of employers I met, the Webers blamed liberal governance for their personnel problems. They saw the loss of US manufacturing along with subsequent downturn of the economy, increased taxes, and regulation as having produced a situation in which smaller businesses could no longer afford to provide the kinds of wages and benefits that would attract the best workers. Coupled with government aid, this had led workers to become unmotivated, wanting to earn higher wages, but seeming not to understand that wage increases are made possible by improvements to the bottom line. Peter, now ranting, continued,

> People don't want to work anymore. The more liberal the government, the more handouts, the worse the work ethic. The other problem is that kids have no discipline. They need boundaries. They don't go up to someone successful and ask them what it takes to be successful. They have no guidance. So they barely get through high school, or they drop out, take a few courses at the community college that their parents pay for ... [and] that passes their time, but then they realize they're never going to be a successful whatever, then their girlfriend gets pregnant, and they get a job. They end up making fourteen dollars hour. They're stuck working, but poor ... and they're mad at the world.

Though some might argue the underlying reasons for declining enthusiasm about work have less to do with free trade or excessive government support, and more to do with the crises and fluctuations inherent to capitalism, few would deny the challenges of running a business, or the struggle to find good workers.

Junkyard Dog

Given these challenges, and especially in tight labor markets, employers are looking for ways to expand rather than shrink the labor pool. Many cannot afford to limit their labor pools unnecessarily.[10]

> MELISSA: I noticed the workforce around here is pretty diverse, in all kinds of ways. Is that common in trucking?

PAUL: Yeah, I think it is. And there is a reason for that: everybody is short of people. . . . We have two or four female drivers, gal drivers. The perfect one is a woman who is forty-five years old, raised her two kids, they are gone or maybe the youngest one is eighteen and still living at home, or in the junior college or whatever. And she is divorced, and she needs to make some money, and she's figured out that no matter how many hours she works for a fast-food place, she gets up to $10 an hour and she just can't get it together with $10 an hour.

MELISSA: Right.

PAUL: So she needs a place where she can make $20 an hour. Then all of a sudden things start to come together. So we've got, I don't know how many right now, but we've got . . . How many female drivers do we have working for us now, Peter?

PETER: Three or four maybe.

PAUL: Over time, we have added way more Black drivers than what we used to have. We probably have, out of 120, Black drivers we might have 10 percent, which is probably about the percentage of the population out here.

PAUL: Our diversity is because we are tight on employees, so we hire anybody who is good.

PETER: Anybody who can meet minimum standards. Absolutely.

Given the type, size, and location of their business, the kind of work they needed done, and the compensation they could offer, people with criminal convictions were part of the pool that could meet Weber Trucking's minimum standards.[11]

> We've had a lot of second chance people here, maybe twenty of them who've done serious time, but almost everybody's been to jail a little bit. Two-thirds of the people here have probably been arrested for *something*.

For my benefit, father and son proceeded to conduct an impromptu review of past and present employees with criminal records. They recalled an applicant whose domestic violence record had worried the HR team because a calm, even temperament is critical to safe truck driving. When another employee vouched for him, however, they had decided to overlook it, and he turned out to be an excellent driver. They also spoke proudly of a man they currently considered to be their best driver who had been exonerated following two decades on death row.

PAUL: We've had very good luck with convicted felons. One guy named
    Beaker—a descendant of the *real* Beaker brothers [a famous local
    family that had been engaged in a violent feud with another clan
    dating back to the turn of the twentieth century]—he comes to work,
    works very hard, stays 'til the job is done.
PETER [agreeing]: Loyal as a junkyard dog.

Of course, not every experience was positive. For instance, they had once
hired a driver with a five-year-old DUI conviction who was caught drinking
on the job.[12] These experiences, good and bad, had produced some nuances
in their thinking.

PAUL: In my experience, the more serious the conviction, the better the
    worker. One big mistake is better than a bunch of small ones.
PETER: Right. Murder is not an addiction. It's a bad choice in a bad
    situation. . . . Drugs are problematic because they change a person's
    mental thought process. The chemical imbalance produced in the
    body has a big overall effect on people.

Paul's preference for "one big mistake"—singular and seemingly situation-
specific convictions—versus "a bunch of small ones"—which might indicate
troubles of lifestyle, temperament, or disposition—was common throughout
the business community. The reasoning was this: Was the guy with the domestic
violence case generally a hothead or were his problems specific to the home?
Was the guy with a DUI record an alcoholic or had he simply driven one night
when he shouldn't have? They seemed to understand that while a conviction
could indicate an ongoing problem, it was not necessarily or even likely so, and
moreover, not every problem affects the workplace. Markedly practical in their
talk, they seemed not to be asking themselves, "Do I empathize with the circumstances that led this person to conviction?" or "Do people deserve second
chances?" but rather, "Is this person likely to be a good employee?" Criminal
records were only of interest insofar as they might articulate with a person's ability to perform well on the job, and on balance, their experiences with criminalized workers had confirmed what researchers continually find: people with
criminal convictions perform equally well, if not better, than those without.

PETER: Honestly the former convicts, once they get into a routine here
    for a couple of months, we have a lot less trouble with those ones
    than the ones who are on their way to jail. . . . I guess what it comes
    down to is convicts who come out don't have an entitlement. I haven't
    experienced any of them having a real entitlement issue of, "You owe it

to me." Everybody else, though, there's a lot of entitlement issues where, you know, when they do get fired or they don't get a raise, they do a crappy job or they want to steal from you afterward, or whatever the case is. . . . Man, they're like a junkyard dog. They're just happy to be fed and have a bed to lay on.

MELISSA: Right.

PETER: And they're thankful for it.

MELISSA: Right.

PETER: That's what my experience has been with them.

The long list of disqualifying convictions Paul had shared in our initial conversation, I learned, were imposed not by Weber Trucking, but the Federal Motor Carrier Safety Administration's Compliance Safety Accountability Program, which concerned itself with trucker's health and driving records, and the Transportation Security Administration, which restricted access to airports and ports since Congress had enacted the Maritime Transportation Security Act following the events of September 11, 2001. The Transportation Security Administration's disqualifying convictions included sedition, espionage, treason, terrorism, murder, transportation security incident, and anything to do with explosives.[13] Additionally, the most highly paid driving jobs (about fifteen of ninety) required a Department of Defense secret carrier clearance because they involved transporting military equipment. People with any kind of felony conviction could not get this clearance. For their part, Paul and Peter were simply looking for people who could get the job done.

PAUL: Many of our positions come down to, Can you be honest and can you show up to work?

MELISSA: And how do you screen for that?

PAUL: You find out after they start . . . [starts laughing] and don't be afraid to fire someone!

A Road Test and Handshake

It hadn't always been difficult to find good workers. Hiring happened informally, and a person used to be able to get into trucking organically, as Paul had, without formal training or licensing. The first person Paul hired back in 1977 had been the son of the original business owner. The second had presented himself serendipitously one year later, at a moment when he needed another driver. Paul picked up the phone and dialed.

PAUL [on speakerphone]: Hi, Moses. Hey, Moses, I was thinking that you were, after Rusty, about the next driver we hired around here. I know there had to a couple other guys in between, but a gal is doing an interview, trying to find out what Weber Trucking's like. You want to tell me about your job interview process, when you came to work here?

MOSES: Yeah. Starting with the way that I . . . Do you want me to go over to your office?

PAUL: Sure.

MOSES: I'm on my way.

Moses's demeanor was mellow, warm, and unusually sincere. He wore blue jeans and a light-gray Weber Trucking T-shirt underneath a Dickies button-down that reached the elbows of his sun-drenched forearms. A chain made of little silver balls—the kind used to dangle army dog tags—suspended a heavy cross pendant midway down his chest. He'd grown up in a mixed American Indian and Mexican family, in the midst of orange and olive groves in rural San Bernardino. His father worked for Union Pacific, and used his earnings to buy seven acres of land, build a house in the middle of it, fence it, and develop it as a small ranch.

Like Paul and most of the old guard at Weber Trucking, Moses had gotten into truck driving through happenstance. He had been working for a company that made plastic packaging for the military, lifting crates up onto a dock, when one day, his boss pointed to a 1.5-ton stake-bed truck across the yard and said, "Go get it." Moses had never driven something so large before, and the experience excited him. A few years later while working as a forklift driver at a Pepsi plant, he set his mind on driving the company's 18-wheeler. He rode shotgun at night and on the weekends for over a year, an unpaid internship of sorts, learning the gears and the precise revolutions per minute intervals at which to shift. At twenty-three years of age, he landed the job, which he performed proudly for eleven years until the franchise was bought out. When the Pepsi plant had shut down, Moses considered his options. Having always thought the Weber trucks were "classy" and being an acquaintance of Paul's brother, he'd gone over to inquire about a job.

Moses recounted the story. The truck yard had been empty that day, he said, except for a pair of feet he'd noticed sticking out from under a trailer. Approaching, he'd called out, "Excuse me, is there anyone here I can talk to? I'd like to fill out an application." The feet scuttled out, followed by legs and a torso covered in overalls. "I'll go get him," said the full body, disappearing quickly into a little building. A few minutes later, a young man emerged, hand outstretched. "Paul

Weber," he greeted. Moses shook his hand, puzzled. Minus the overalls, he was almost certain this was the same person who'd been under the trailer. "Let's go for a drive," Paul invited, smiling to himself at his little prank.

At Weber Trucking, the road test had always served as the primary preemployment screening methodology. Through this test, a great deal could be learned about a person's personality and temperament. Would they set off quickly or take their time checking the many indicators on the machine? How would they respond to being cut off by an inconsiderate driver? To heavy traffic? Would they take the yellow light or decide to stop?

Moses had climbed into the driver's seat of a two-axle Peterbilt tractor pulling a set of bottom-dump trailers. Paul rode shotgun, holding a clipboard in one hand and pencil in the other, and began to scribble furiously. As you can imagine, this was unnerving for Moses, who was doing his best to demonstrate his superb driving skills as he made his way steadily around the block. "Am I doing OK?" he eventually broached with trepidation. "Oh, yeah," Paul replied distractedly. "I just noticed those screws on the dash are loose and I need to see about that door, it's rattling."

Over the years, Paul continued to hire just about every qualified person who came through the door, in a manner longtime employees described as "pretty off-the-cuff." This openness was supported by federal assistance under the Job Training Partnership Act of 1982, which aimed to prepare young people and unskilled adults for entry into the workforce as well as offered job training for economically disadvantaged people and others with barriers to employment. These monies allowed Weber Trucking to provide a training program— about three months of classroom instruction and three months of one-on-one training on the road—at no cost to the company, growing its workforce by approximately thirty-two more drivers.

People Who Hire People

In his thirty-seven years with the company, Moses had worn many hats—driver, mechanic, safety official, shop foreman, body and paint repair, dispatch, compliance manager, Department of Motor Vehicles (DMV) registrations, and driving instructor. One of his current jobs was to hire new drivers and prescreen shop mechanics—a job he approached with careful deliberation. Though many things had changed since the days of a road test and handshake, my days of job interviews, road tests, and application processing at Weber Trucking demonstrated that in important ways, Moses and the other managers at Weber

Trucking still hired much as they had been hired: by making a human connection, and using their own knowledge and experience to size a person up.

———

I arrived at the HR office for a day of interviews and road tests, a few minutes before a trucker seeking to get hired in the flatbed division was scheduled to arrive. The day was gloomy and overcast, a cool fifty-five degrees. I took a seat to wait for Moses, studying the wooden welcome sign screwed onto the propped-open door at eye level. Above the welcome sign, a poster warned in big red letters:

> If it's not safe, don't do it!
> . . . Someone expects you home for dinner.

Below it, a ten-inch long pink ribbon sticker signaled cancer support. Janet, a longtime member of the HR team, was a survivor. Today was her birthday. The office was decorated with streamers and balloons, and everyone was making a wonderfully big deal about it.

Loud heavy metal—the Scorpion's "Rock You Like a Hurricane"—filtered into the office from the truck of a bald-headed driver whose long beard pointed well below his chin; he was idling outside the office door while jotting notes on a clipboard and punching numbers on a calculator as he inspected his dash. A mechanic popped his head inside the door as he passed by and announced, "The Queen is coming today."

"Oh, OK," replied Craig, the former driver now responsible for company safety and compliance. "I'll call Moses and let him know."

"The Queen" was a title given to the esteemed director of a help center for unhoused people in downtown San Bernardino that serves eight thousand free lunches per month and runs two safe houses for women escaping domestic violence. Paul had served on the board of directors for eighteen years, offering Weber's facilities as the charity's warehouse and distribution center, storing large quantities of donated food and other supplies in trailers until they could be used. The notice of the Queen's visit prompted Craig to praise Paul's approach to personnel management:

> So many times, I've literally seen him pull money out of his pocket because somebody needed it. . . . When I got hired, I had been saving vacation time from my other job in order to take some time off at the birth of my son. I

explained this to Paul, and he told me to go ahead and take it. The HR ladies were all worked up because I hadn't accrued the time, said it couldn't be done, but Paul told them to make it work.

Moses came to the door and motioned silently for me to come along. The applicant had arrived, a tall and heavyset white man named Jimmy, about forty-five years old with many years driving experience. He lived a long ninety minutes away, but wanted the job for the reasons Paul had explained earlier in sketching the ideal company driver: approaching middle age, plenty of "over-the-road" experience, and likely a family man, eager to stay closer to home.

First was a tour of the facilities. Moses spoke with the enthusiasm of a museum guide as we walked around the gravel yard, pointing in various directions as he overviewed operations and business history. He spoke proudly of the company's best characteristics: self-sufficiency in washing, fueling, and servicing its own trucks; mastery of a wide range of logistical challenges along with a reputation for safety and precision. Also job security—employees tended to stay a long time (the average employee eight years, and many much longer). Even during the 2008 recession, Moses boasted, they survived with relatively few layoffs.[14] The applicant nodded and maintained eye contact, but said little, as if he already knew how things worked or was already sold on the company. Moses led him back to the HR office to fill out the application. The two of us walked outside to give him some space. Sensing Jimmy's lack of chattiness was a bit of a turnoff for Moses, who was such a people person, I asked in a low voice, "How are you feeling about him?"

Moses replied, "At this point, dead neutral."

Despite Jimmy's difficult-to-read cool, Moses decided to have Craig test-drive him on the spot rather than first send his application to the HR staff for verification of work history and background clearance, as was the usual order of things. Given that seasoned drivers were in high demand, even companies with great reputations like Weber Trucking felt compelled to court strong applicants in hopes of attracting and retaining the best. This driver had the needed experience, was ready to start, and held a current Transportation Worker Identification Credential card, required since 2007 by the Maritime Transportation Security Act to access the ports and other secure areas of US maritime facilities and vessels.[15]

"The flatbeds are all in use," reported Craig. "He'll have to drive something else."

"Good," replied Moses. "That'll let him know we're busy."

Busyness, Moses explained, was a critical labor issue in the trucking business. Because contracts for hauling are in constant flux and driver's wages are based on a percentage of the gross income generated by the loads they deliver, it was important to try to maintain a certain level of activity. It was also crucial not to let good candidates get away because of a prolonged process. When a person appearing to have the necessary experience presented themselves, the wheels were set in motion to clear them for employment as quickly as possible. Unlike the old days, however, when this clearance might have involved a few phone calls to trusted friends, now a job application more than ten pages long asked detailed questions about everything from work history to driving records and criminal history, and a whole staff was dedicated to screening and verification.[16] Gone were the days when applicants were simply asked, "How many speeding tickets have you had?"—to which drivers inevitably replied, "Just one." Driving history was verified through the DMV via a record called "H-6," which shows a person's ten-year personal and professional driving record. Accident history was checked through the Pre-Employment Screening Program run by the Federal Motor Carrier Safety Administration. Inspection history for the past three years was checked through an electronic database mandated by Congress in 2005 in the Safe, Accountable, Flexible, Efficient Transportation Equity Act. Criminal background checks, recommended (though not required) by the Federal Motor Carrier Safety Administration, were conducted in-house by looking at the online court records for San Bernardino and Riverside Counties. All of these records could impact a driver's ability to be insured and therefore hired.[17] Drug tests were also required for all drivers as a result of a 1990 federal rule mandating that everyone connected with the maintenance or operation of a truck be tested for drug use. All new applicants had to be tested as well as 50 percent of the workforce every year through a software for random testing. Paul recalled how at the announcement of the new rule, one mechanic up and quit, saying, "I like my marijuana habit and I'm going to keep it!" Within a few years, though, there was nowhere else to go because every company had implemented the law.

Back from the test-drive, Craig delivered a glowing report. "He did an *excellent* job," he said loudly, in a way that seemed to signal to everyone to accelerate their level of excitement about the candidate and expedite the process. Jimmy was sent immediately to undergo a drug test, take the results to the commercial DMV for a stamp, and bring it back to the admin side of HR, where the staff promised to push for a rush clearance of his application.

The next applicant to arrive was Lewis, short and slim with fashionable glasses, cleaner cut, and younger looking than other drivers. He took a seat on a vinyl chair facing Moses's desk, next to a huge pile of food and baby supplies being collected for a driver who'd been in a motorcycle accident over the weekend. Moses looked over Lewis's paperwork. Until recently, Lewis had been employed through his family's trucking business.

> LEWIS: We went under during the recession. Used to be me and my dad and my brother, but it all went under. I've been working construction, but only getting about thirty hours per week. My wife is about to have a baby, so she's pushing me to get a better job.
> MOSES: When you lived in Adelanto, you drove transfer?
> LEWIS: Yes.
> MOSES: What kind of material did you haul?
> LEWIS: Rock and sand and base.
> MOSES: I hauled coke, this big hunk of black coke sticking up in the air.
> LEWIS: I think my dad's first transfer was one of your trucks.
> MOSES: Do you have pictures of that?
> LEWIS: Yeah, my dad does.
> MOSES: Oh, I want a copy! The first truck I drove was a 1970 and it was way underpowered . . . when I would go out to 29 Palms, oh man . . . [and] then I was doing Big Bear. I was making good money then. It was by the hour. . . . In a minute here we'll find a truck, Lewis, and go cruising, OK?

Glancing out the door, Craig said to Janet, "Here comes that guy I road tested earlier. . . . My test-drive with that guy was the best I've had in more than a year." The applicant, Valentino, appeared to be in his forties, of medium height and build, with brown eyes and hair, possibly Latino, and wearing a railroad cap, plaid shirt, and jeans.

> VALENTINO: Hi, good morning.
> JANET: You were going to go to the clinic [for the drug test], right?
> VALENTINO: Yes, I just needed my ID.
> CRAIG: Yes, you need that so they know it's you and not your neighbor.
> VALENTINO: That's a nice truck [gazing outside the door].
> JANET: Which one, the Ford?
> VALENTINO: Yeah, well both of them. My dad has one like that.

DRIVER IN THE ROOM [currently performing office work due to an injury that won't allow him to drive]: OK, you're going to go down to Walnut Ave. It'll be on your left past Hill Street. It'll say Urgent Care.

VALENTINO: OK, do I need to come back after that?

JANET: No, but make sure you take it to the DMV. . . . There's a commercial one, because the other one has a line a mile long. . . . And get an extra copy.

––––––

In contrast to the distanced HR entities generally found in larger companies, in small and midsize businesses, little separates the people charged with hiring and those they hire. At Weber Trucking, those on the front lines of hiring—all former drivers or mechanics—intimately knew the work and the qualities needed to perform it well, and directly supervised and/or worked alongside those they hired. Importantly, they also had seniority within the organization, were empowered to make decisions, and were encouraged to bend and work around rules in service of attracting as well as retaining solid candidates.

"I am looking for *the best applicant*," said Moses, as if to summarize the philosophy. But whereas in a more credential-based context, "best" and "bad" might seem self-evident—experience is better than no experience, and a clean record is better than a marked record—for Moses and the other hiring managers, the calculations were more nuanced. For example, they had hired one of the company's now most senior mechanics fifteen years prior, despite his having no experience fixing trucks. Through conversation and a few quick scenario tests, Moses had gathered that he was highly mechanically inclined. It also weighed heavily that he had been with his previous employer for twenty-seven years and was leaving only because the manager wanted to replace him with a personal friend. Another mechanic had been hired fresh out of a training program with no formal experience and could barely speak English—also against company policy. But Moses had been so impressed by this young person's personality and zip code (having noticed from his application that he came from one of San Bernardino's toughest neighborhoods) that he persuaded the shop foreman to interview him with the promise of a free burrito. By the time the foreman was done with the interview, they too wanted to hire the young man, whose tacit knowledge gained over a lifetime spent around mechanics was evident.

This holistic appraisal of candidates did not equate with a lack of discernment; they also knew how to avoid obvious problems. Despite Valentino's stellar road test, for instance, they had later passed on his application when his references had raised questions about his integrity.

As in all businesses, disagreements about applicants sometimes emerged, most often, it seemed, between people with different kinds of responsibilities within the organization. Not surprisingly, owners and upper management at Weber Trucking—those with the most power—were generally most willing to take chances on people with imperfect credentials. They frequently connected with applicants during the interview process on the basis of shared lived experience, and if they liked them personally, felt motivated to create an opportunity as someone once had for them. Interestingly, upper managers never sought Paul's direct input on a candidate, they told me. They already knew Paul's tendency toward leniency and felt a duty to exercise greater caution in hiring than he might. HR workers were the most cautious, often honing in on issues of potential liability, loss, or hassle. For example, they did not approve of a decision made by Steve, Craig, and Moses to hire a young driver with only nine months driving experience and a license less than two years old—against the company policy of requiring a minimum of two years recent driving experience. These differences in viewpoint also frequently fell along gender lines, as the hiring managers and director of HR were all male, while most functional HR roles were occupied by women.[18]

As anthropologist Ilana Gershon notes, though these differences in viewpoint and the clashes that can arise as a result are sometimes mistaken for having to do with personalities, they are better understood as relating to institutional roles. Hiring managers are often under pressure to fill a vacancy quickly and concerned with finding someone who will fit easily into the organizational culture, while as the voice of law within the organization, HR staff members are charged with organizing and overseeing the hiring process to ensure that things are consistent, fair, and legal.[19]

Similarly, just as tensions arising between people occupying different institutional roles cannot be reduced to personality, so too must institutional roles be understood as reflecting broader tensions within industries, and between industries, governments, and markets. As I began to see, a number of external pressures had started to impinge on Weber Trucking's pragmatic approach to hiring and personnel—pressures about which Moses was uncannily aware. He reflected, "Yeah, I'm pretty sure when people go to apply with other companies, they're just instructed to leave their applications in the box and the conversation stops there. . . . I just hope the bosses can keep it this way."

Actuarial Creep

Craig Johnson, Weber Trucking's smart and chatty risk manager, walked me through the details of a pretrip inspection: how to look for leaks, check under the hood, check the oil, check the hoses, check that the exhaust system is connected tightly, that the trailer air connectors are sealed and in good condition, that the batteries are secure, connections are tight, and that all cell caps are present. You check all of this at the end of the day too, he explained; early morning when you are ready to go is not when you want to discover a problem. Riding around, Craig narrated how to shift the gears, how to make decisions about whether or not to stop for a yellow light, how far away to be from the curb on a right turn, and how to watch vigilantly for roads that don't allow trucks; one driver had recently been slapped with a $14,000 fine for getting this wrong.

Craig's dress expressed his dual identity as a former driver turned policy, safety, and compliance specialist: faded black jeans and white sneakers dirtied from the yard, paired with plaid button-down shirt and sport coat. Like Paul, he spoke in numbers, but whereas Paul's numbers related to prices and profits, Craig's mainly countered a negative perception of trucking. For example, he touted, 81 percent of all accidents involving trucks are caused by cars, but given that accidents *involving* trucks are always terrible, they tend to make the news and generate negative publicity—increasing the perception that trucks are the problem, and "Perception [he frequently lamented] is reality."[20]

Talking with Craig served as a regular check against any possible romanticization on my part of a hiring process flowing free from the gut and heart, unhindered by risk concerns. In fact, major liability considerations and a surveillance-enforced regulatory structure increasingly constrained trucker's discretion and flexibility. Craig complained constantly about the mismatch between actual risks and insurers' and policymakers' abstractions. The discord inspired his writing of policy letters, either on behalf of Weber Trucking or in collaboration with various trucking associations. One letter he had recently written began, "For the construction trucking industry, lunchtime requirements are like trying to put toothpaste back in the tube."

Craig worried that statistical and surveillance-based systems in the industry, such as the Federal Motor Carrier Safety Administration's data-driven

Compliance, Safety and Accountability program, were starting to override common sense. For instance, a Weber driver had recently been penalized for failing to use a specific double strap to secure a load, despite multiple additional ties in places that he knew, based on many years of experience, would make the load most secure. Drivers complained that the Compliance, Safety and Accountability records (not unlike criminal records) also sometimes depicted charges on paper that sound much worse than the actual occurrence, flattening important nuances of circumstance and context. In one incident, the driver of a car on the opposite side of the freeway had suffered a heart attack and spun to the other side, colliding with one of Weber's trucks. The car driver died, and although the accident was no fault of the trucker, the fatality had driven the Weber's safety rating into alert status. These ratings were becoming a crucial measure for companies looking to contract with transportation carriers to decide with whom to do business and affecting insurance premiums.[21]

The lunchtime requirements Craig had referenced in his recent letter were another case in point. Digital surveillance cameras would soon put an end to the flexibility to rest as needed, which as law and technology scholar Karen Levy's recent book on the industry found, may actually lead to more accidents.[22] Like other seasoned drivers, Craig was all too aware of the things that can go wrong on the road, and he believed in his own judgment about how to stay safe. "I used to take a nap at dawn," he explained. "That morning sun would hit me, and I would just feel so sleepy, I'd stop to take a fifteen-minute nap. . . . Now my logbooks never showed that, I just did it."

While algorithmically based risk systems may not directly impact hiring, law and society scholars have found that their introduction can impact the way organizations make decisions, conceptualize and address problems, and exercise discretion. They observe, "as actuarial or algorithmic styles of risk management are taken up in institutions where risk was previously managed in less formal, or more clinical, ways, the institutions change."[23] Indeed, by raising the stakes of making a mistake, and generating additional pressure to think about how the company and its employees look from the outside, actuarial systems were distracting from the kinds of actual risks that Weber Trucking had traditionally been worried about (e.g., Is someone going to get hurt or damage my truck?), and beginning to undermine its tried-and-true ways of assessing and mitigating the dangers of the profession. As I packed up to leave, I was reminded of one such internal risk mitigation measure, practiced every afternoon as drivers headed out of the gates. One by one, they tooted their horns loudly—a safety precaution put in place many years ago after someone had almost been run over by walking unseen across the hood of a truck. Stepping out into the blazing sun, Craig hollered behind me, "Watch out for the trucks!"

Razor-Sharp Margins

Sitting across from me at the big glass-topped table for what would be one of our last lengthy visits, Paul explained patiently, "Any business that is easily understood operates on razor-sharp margins." My brow crinkled to recall the meaning of this basic business maxim, and analyze its significance in the context of our monthslong conversation about business, hiring, and human well-being.

"The difference between your costs and your gross—the wiggle room," he added, reminding me that margins are especially important in the trucking industry because trucks are expensive to purchase and maintain, and also depreciate quickly.

Lately, Weber Trucking's narrow margin was on Paul's mind as he had begun to think more intensively about leaving a legacy for his grandkids. "It's so hard to start anything up and gain enough momentum these days," he reflected, glancing out the window at an unknown black Labrador running to-and-fro around the yard. The sight prompted him to digress to happy stories of how he had acquired each of his stray dogs, two of which now accompanied him every day to the office. Left at home, the fluffy, white-furred puppy irritated the more elderly dog into aggression, whereas here at the office, his juvenile energy could at least be partially redirected.

Overhearing our conversation from the adjacent room, Peter stepped into the office and asked pointedly, "Melissa, what is this really all about?" Despite months of repeated interactions, Peter was still not entirely at ease with my presence.

I took the opportunity to restate the research purpose even more explicitly than I had previously, a bit worried as I did so about the possibility that they hadn't fully understood, and would reject or dismiss it now.

> I want to help figure out how to increase job opportunities for people with criminal convictions. In order to do that, I believe we need to better understand how employers make hiring decisions and how criminal records figure in those decisions.

To my relief, no one batted an eye. Though the owners and managers at Weber Trucking did not necessarily share my commitment to this particular workforce issue, they did want to be able to take people under their wings and train them, and use the business as a means to provide opportunities as they saw fit. This, they felt, was becoming increasingly difficult to do.

The kind of casual entrance to truck driving that Paul, Moses, Craig, and other members of the old guard had enjoyed was a thing of the past. Now industry regulations absolutely prohibited the kinds of informal apprenticeships and mentoring that had taught them how to drive, and support had dwindled for formalized on-the-job training. Although on-the-job training monies through the State of California's Workforce Development program still provided some assistance, it was not as well funded as it once had been, and the training and apprenticeship programs funded by the Comprehensive Employment and Training ACT that had helped grow their large and diverse workforce had long been eliminated.[24] Additionally, drug tests, driving records, insurance requirements, and criminal record restrictions such as those required for the Transportation Worker Identification Credential and Department of Defense clearance excluded many applicants who might have been hired in times past. More broadly, new systems and policies designed to buffer risk—Compliance, Safety and Accountability program scores, mileage audits, and inspections, coupled with technological changes and regulatory shifts favoring larger firms—had increased competition, heightened the threat of litigation and reputational damage, and rendered business operations more costly, challenging, and insecure.[25] Not only had it had become considerably more difficult to find people who could meet the minimum standards, it had become much harder to take a chance on someone or train someone who wasn't all the way there, while turning a profit too.[26]

The Best Applicants

This chapter has showcased employers who have not found criminal records useful for identifying good employees. By approaching job candidates with an eye toward the kinds of qualities that matter to them—practical ability, positive attitude, relaxed demeanor, loyalty, and above all, a desire to work—these small and midsize business owners and managers have found that people who have been criminalized, and many others whose credentials may not look perfect on paper, are often loyal and hardworking. Even so, few of them would say they "hire people with criminal records." Rather, as James insisted, they "hire people they like, trust, and respect"—some of whom happen to have criminal records. The distinction is important.

Like all employers, the business owners and managers I came to know struggled to find excellent employees, and generally speaking, were looking for ways to expand as opposed to shrink the labor pool. Yet they were skeptical that scores, credentials, and records could identify the "best" applicants more effectively than their own knowledge and insights. Their hiring processes reflected this confidence in their own intuitions and judgment. They spent time getting to know job candidates personally through human-centered hiring processes and practical tests. Rather than try to anticipate and prescreen for every possible risk, they preferred to simply try people out.

Hiring in these businesses is led by people who intimately know the work as well as the skills and qualities needed to perform it well. Unlike in larger firms, where HR is frequently a separate and more specialized department, in these businesses, the same people leading interviews and other aspects of candidate selection, and who directly supervise new hires, also have the final call in hiring decisions. This proximity avoids the frustrating scenarios Hub job seekers so often experienced (recall Linda's experience in chapter 3), in which the person with whom they interviewed was keen to hire them, only to have the decision overturned by a distant and more powerful decision-maker.

In any hiring context, the freedom to decide what should be done in a given situation is exercised by people with unique standpoints and proclivities. As this book has vigorously argued, however, positive one-on-one encounters, personal attitudes, and even explicit commitments do not alone account for hiring decisions. People making hiring decisions are operating within complex organizations run by many people, and these complex organizations are in turn embedded in political, legal, economic, and social worlds. In this sense, there is no such thing as a businesses' "criminal records policy." If the context changed, so too would their policies.[27]

Indeed, the context that allowed employers like Weber Trucking to hire from their own good sense was getting squeezed. In a neoliberal economy characterized by financialization—in which it's harder to make money from production than from money—coupled with regulatory challenges, technological change, and a growing reliance on actuarial metrics of success, it was getting harder and harder to avoid the pressures to manage people according to the logics of big capital and the criminal record complex.

———

Moses's foreshadowing of a future in which open, flexible, and people-centered hiring would no longer be possible had been nearer than he knew. By 2016, the financial pinch at Weber Trucking led the company to downsize a core part of its operations, getting rid of twenty-six trucks and streamlining its workforce by forcing several long-term employees, including Janet and Moses, to retire. "The world has changed, the industry has changed, and we have to change with it or we'll just piss all of our money away," said Peter. "There are opportunities to make money in California, but not the old-fashioned way."

A change in employment law that same year eliminated Weber Trucking's incentive-based pay structure, raising labor costs by 11 percent and causing the company to switch to an hourly pay system to account for the difference.[28] While this made it easier to hire people with less experience who felt more comfortable with a set hourly wage, many of the most senior and productive drivers quit, as the hourly rate was lower than what they had previously earned on a percentage.

By 2021, the company had hired a professional background screening agency to conduct its background checks. The turning point had been an incident in which an applicant's name came up through the in-house search of county records as possibly having a conviction. The Weber team wasn't sure it was the right person, and the charge wasn't overly concerning, so they went forward with the hire. A few months later, though, the new hire got in an accident and didn't tell them about it—an act for which any employee would be fired. When the insurance looked him up in relation to the accident, it turned out he had in fact been the guy with the conviction. Although, as the new hiring manager (Moses's replacement) explained, they probably would have hired him anyway had they known about the conviction up front, the experience with dishonesty made them worry they might be in over their heads trying to screen in-house. If they had missed the conviction record, what else might they miss in the future that could lead to liability or hurt their scores? Now rather than rely on their judgment, they questioned it and took more precautions.

Conclusion

LIMITS AND POSSIBILITIES
IN THE STRUGGLE TO END CRIMINAL
RECORD DISCRIMINATION

THE WIDESPREAD use of criminal background checks evolved not because of any observed or demonstrated connection between conducting background checks and reducing harm or violence but rather because this practice became an easy, politically useful, and profitable substitute for the kinds of thoughtful programs and policies that could in fact reduce harm and violence. In this conclusion, I consider what it might take to overturn the logics, values, and material interests that uphold criminal record discrimination, and instead invest in the kinds of economies and workplaces that produce true safety.

———

Driving west on the I-10 freeway, on one of my last days in the field, I turned on National Public Radio to find the show *On Point* with host Tom Ashbrook, featuring an episode on Ban the Box. As the reader will recall from the preface and introduction, this legislation—first enacted in San Francisco in 2006 and statewide in California in 2013—required employers to remove questions about criminal history from applications for employment. Its aim was to ensure applicants with criminal records get a chance to compete on the basis of their skills and qualifications by delaying inquiries about past convictions until later in the hiring process.

While much debate has focused on the merits and drawbacks of this policy, Ashbrook's guests raised more fundamental questions and tensions that remain unresolved: Do criminal records in fact provide important information for employers and others making decisions about who to bring into their organizations? Do those decision-makers have a right to access and use the information? And for those who would answer yes to either of the first two questions, is there a fair way to consider the information? I believe our collective answers to these basic questions will ultimately determine whether the suffering and systemic disadvantage caused by criminal record discrimination continues or comes to an end.

The call-in segment began. A representative of the National Federation of Independent Businesses was the first to be put on air. Her tone was defensive.

> If we don't ask on the application, then we won't know to discuss it during the interview. It doesn't make sense to not be able to talk with the candidate about their criminal history in an interview. . . . The EEOC wants us to make an individualized assessment. How can we make an individualized assessment if we don't have the information?

The business representative was raising a familiar argument: If employers are going to have access to the information eventually, and be permitted to discriminate on its basis, why should access be delayed? My observations with small businesses had led me to understand, if not agree, with her point. Ban the Box doesn't make a lot of sense for many hiring processes. Requiring employers to delay consideration of criminal history assumes a "later" opportunity that often doesn't materialize in the rush to fill a vacancy. My direct, on-the-ground observations of hiring processes had also revealed that details like asking or not asking about conviction records, providing or not providing required disclosures, and other such technicalities had little correlation with where the decision landed. I witnessed companies that regularly excluded, while complying with the law, and companies in gross violation that hired inclusively. Regardless of their process for candidate selection, those who tended to exclude, excluded, while those who tended to include, included. Removing questions about convictions from applications or otherwise tinkering with hiring procedures to comply with emerging laws did not seem to change a company's general orientation.

On the other hand, she was missing the point. The measure wasn't merely meant to change hiring procedures; it was enacted precisely in the hope that by shifting *when* employers were viewing the records, it would shift *how* they were viewing them. This indirect approach explains the measure's positive reception among public officials in more than 37 states and 150 cities and counties. It allows governments to make a symbolic gesture that appears to balance multiple stakeholder interests. It also importantly does not infringe on employers' "right to ask/know," a widely held value recently reinforced by a Ninth Circuit Court case in Seattle upholding landlords' First Amendment rights.[1]

The next caller, a manager of a reentry program for the Texas Department of Criminal Justice, was sympathetic to the challenges facing people coming home from prison who are looking for work. The host asked her to respond to the small business representative's concern that Ban the Box is not practical for many hiring processes and thus was a bit frustrated when rather than addressing this dilemma, she reiterated common sound bites on the merits of the policy:

> The biggest barrier for people being successful in their lives is obtaining employment. The whole point of Ban the Box is to take that stumbling block away. . . . Talking to people, getting your foot in the door, is half the battle for folks who have backgrounds. I'm not saying that you shouldn't ever look at that background and decide that background is not something that you need. However, you may meet somebody who's amazing who has a background who you decide you want to give that chance to.

The reentry professional's impassioned testimony also unsatisfyingly sidestepped a point made earlier by a distressed, formerly incarcerated caller who was struggling to get hired despite the new law. Echoing so many job seekers' experiences, he clarified,

> You can get past the Ban the Box and you're still going to fail the background check. Ban the Box can get you into the front door, and you can even have the interview, but once the criminal background check comes back, you will fail the background check.

Later in the show, a small business owner from Austin similarly cut to the chase. For him, it seemed logical and fair to use criminal records as evidence of bad choices:

> Part of the equation here is that when I'm considering ten prospective applicants and I see a snapshot of their decisions over the past five to ten years, and I see nine applicants who have not made decisions that have resulted in incarceration or arrest, why can't I, as a business owner, make that decision? Are we not discriminating against the others who have not made a

bad choice? I have limited resources. I can't possibly interview everyone. So why shouldn't I look at a snapshot of the decisions they've made and use that to move forward?

A few other employers chimed in along these lines—including one from Pennsylvania who shouted, "I need the cream of the crop. I don't have time for this!"

Then Binyamin Appelbaum, a correspondent for the *New York Times*, recalibrated the conversation by calling into question the fundamental legitimacy of criminal records as a fair way to divide the world into risky and not risky, good and bad. Appelbaum said,

> People make the same choices, and some of them end up with criminal records and some of them do not. It is much easier to get arrested for possession of marijuana if you are a young Black man in an urban neighborhood than if you are a young white man in a suburban neighborhood. And so people who have criminal records for marijuana possession may not have made different choices than the people who do not. Race plays an incredibly important role in this story, to the point where the federal government has said that using background checks as a way to systematically screen out applicants is inherently a form of discrimination because it has such a disproportionate effect on Black applicants.

Five years after this radio debate, an even more robust piece of legislation, the California Fair Chance Act of 2018, required both public and private sector employers with five or more employees to delay asking about or considering conviction records until after extending a conditional offer of employment. It established a clear process for employers to follow when making an adverse decision, drove home the need to conduct individualized assessments using the EEOC's detailed criteria, outlined a formal pathway for appeals, and ensured time for applicants to provide evidence of inaccuracies in their background reports and/or evidence of rehabilitation as well as mitigating circumstances. As a result, employers became even more aware of antidiscrimination laws, and public opinion swayed definitively in favor of "second chances." Yet today, job seekers with criminal records continue to report that rejection on the basis of criminal history remains widespread. While it may be tempting to explain the problem's persistence in terms of regulatory inadequacies, loopholes, and a lack of enforcement, the clash (as radio guests revealed) is more elementary: while many feel that criminal record discrimination is unfair and unwarranted, many others operate on the assumption that criminal records provide critical information that they should be allowed to consider.

Rights, Rules, Procedures, and the Limits of Inclusion

In her brilliant treatise on the role of liberal politics in growing the US carceral state, political scientist Naomi Murakawa asserts that it is precisely a liberal understanding of racism as an irrational and misconstrued individual feeling that underlies the logic that racialized problems therefore can be corrected through state building, replacing individual discretion with codification, standardization, and formalization. By implementing carefully crafted rules, rights, and procedures, so the logic goes, the system can be protected from individuals' arbitrary biases, ensuring that prejudice does not blemish otherwise value-neutral processes.[2] This approach, as sociologist Alex Vitale has said, assumes that legal frameworks benefit everyone; that if we can just get everyone to follow the law, all will be well; and that the problem is procedural as opposed to substantive.[3] These core assumptions underlie most efforts to address criminal record discrimination thus far. In aiming to regulate when and how criminal records may be used, legal and policy reforms have placed considerable confidence in the idea that the legal structure can be fixed and properly oriented to provide protection as well as ensure equality.

Yet the law's baseline holds the idea that people with convictions pose a risk to the workplace. Not only do procedural reforms leave the power to assess, evaluate, and decide in the hands of individual employers with no training or expertise to make such assessments, they leave intact the idea that some criminal record discrimination is appropriate and necessary. For example, by tasking employers with assessing the nexus between job duties and conviction, whether a "business necessity" might preclude them from hiring someone, whether the candidate is sufficiently rehabilitated, and so on, the EEOC guidance reaffirms that there are indeed people who must be excluded—the task is only to properly identify them. By encouraging background checks, and focusing solely on delimiting the process and criteria for discriminating on the basis of those checks, even laws specifically crafted to protect against discrimination concede, accommodate, and reinforce the idea that prior convictions are sometimes a legitimate ground on which to deny employment.

Moreover, and precisely because the law does not fully protect or offer redress, as critical race scholar Lisa Marie Cacho has argued, legal recourse becomes understood as something the dominant class gives or denies.[4] At the level of policy, this "politics of value" often manifests in reforms that offer in-clusion/redemption to some in the devalued group, while forcefully denying inclusion to others. As political scientist and social activist Cathy Cohen long ago cautioned, "Strategies built upon the possibility of incorporation and assimilation" tend to "expand and make accessible the status quo for more privileged members of marginal groups, while the most vulnerable in our com-munities continue to be stigmatized and oppressed."[5] As we witnessed in chap-ter 3, when the battle over criminal record discrimination gets framed as a moral one, fought on the grounds of deservingness, it precipitates a scramble to recuperate social value at the expense of others who can be portrayed as even less deserving. In turn, claims for inclusion frequently succeed by explic-itly excluding the most stigmatized, feared, and disparaged.[6]

At the same time that such hierarchies are buttressed, most antidiscrimina-tion policy assumes a universal criminalized subject, without attention to intragroup difference. This is because, as legal scholar Joseph Fishkin explains, challenging policy's disparate impact on protected classes is only part of the basis for equal protection laws.[7] At heart is the goal of alleviating a "bottle-neck" in the opportunity structure so as to lessen the impact of a factor that is exerting an outsized impact on people's chances. The EEOC guidance again provides a case in point. Although the guidance was designed to level the play-ing field for protected racial groups, in practice it works to alleviate a barrier that affects all people with criminal records. Fishkin argues that this seeming disjuncture between race consciousness and neutrality is ultimately comple-mentary: a color-blind legal framework focused on alleviating impediments is the best way to help the greatest number of people, including those dispropor-tionately affected by the impediment.[8]

This book has shown that to truly equalize opportunities would require not only alleviating the background check bottleneck but also actively allocating resources and favoring people who have been systemically disadvantaged and targeted for criminalization. Though seductive, the idea of a universal frame-work that eases the way for all leaves a core contradiction unsullied: universal remedies tend to most benefit those already relatively advantaged. This is because value-neutral measures only help to level the immediate playing field; they do not account for compounding effects of historical or ongoing disadvantage—the fact that the field was never level in the first place. They do not, as historian Robin D. G. Kelley once put it, "magically abolish the condi-tions that produce racialized inequalities."[9] As we saw in chapters 1 and 3, people's lived experiences of criminalization vary widely along lines of race, gender, and class, and in relation to many other factors including age, sexuality, appearance, health status, level of education, access to transportation, and child-care. The layers of historical trauma as well as ongoing marginalization impacting their abilities to obtain work make plain that removing the impediment of background screening would only go so far in equalizing opportunity.

In particular, the centrality of antiblackness to projects of policing and containment means that what is good for white job seekers with criminal records may not be effective for Black ones. As research has shown, white people generally benefit more from lenient criminal justice policies than do Black people; the opportunity to meet with a hiring manager in person does not improve Black job seekers' prospects in the same way it does white job seekers' prospects; and in the absence of conclusive information about criminal history, employers may simply avoid hiring Black applicants altogether.[10] Despite the troubling convergence of antiblack labor market racism with criminal record discrimination, this ethnography has shown that the two problems are distinct and in need of separate attention. Without criminal record discrimination, Black job seekers would still bear the stigma of blackness and face pervasive antiblack bias in the labor market. Likewise, if labor market racism could somehow be eliminated, criminal record discrimination (in a racialized criminal legal system) would still produce racialized disadvantage. These layers and complexities imply that while more stringent Fair Chance policies, better enforcement of existing laws, and more refined risk assessments could certainly improve the job prospects for some, simply "putting [more] employment discrimination policies on the books" would not likely be sufficient to overcome existing patterns.[11]

A true solution to the problem of criminal record discrimination is unlikely to be technical, administrative, procedural, or even primarily regulatory. This is not simply because rules are difficult to enforce. It is because rather than resolve deeper issues, proceduralism tends to skirt them. Proceduralism is in fact "a strategy of abstinence, of not tackling, let alone settling, value conflicts in pluralist societies."[12] Besides, when proceduralism *does* engage with fundamental value conflict, the effect is often to obscure and undermine deeper claims of injustice.[13] In seeking to increase consistency and fairness, procedural changes validate the use of criminal records by reinforcing the assumption that background checks will be conducted, and limiting the terms of debate to the specific criteria and methods for enacting "just" discrimination.

Substantive change—change that actually increases social mobility—will not only acknowledge and attempt to mitigate racial *disparity* but also confront the social harms systemic racism and antiblackness have historically engendered as well as eliminate the oppressive conditions they have created and still create. Substantive changes will engage with the complexity of who is impacted and how, directing care and attention to the specific ways that lived experiences of class, gender, sexuality, type of conviction, and other factors inflect, intensify, and exacerbate experiences of criminalization. Rather than lump or gloss lived experiences, they will attend to the ways people are specifically impacted. Substantive changes will furthermore include—from the beginning—the most stigmatized and least sympathetic criminalized subjects—instead of hoping that the benefits will trickle down. As the history of criminal justice reform has shown, rarely do regulators circle back to include groups initially excluded.[14]

Substantive changes will not depend on individual employer's goodwill, open-mindedness, or ability to accurately assess an individuals' criminal risk level. They will take the mere fact of a person showing up to apply, in spite of so many barriers, as evidence in itself that the person is ready for work. Likewise, they will not depend on moral appeals for inclusion based on deservingness, second chances, or even rights. In fact, substantive changes will focus little on what individual employers think or don't think, and rather will take aim at the underlying reasons criminal records became such a salient tool, and the ideas and material forces that sustain their legitimacy.

Instead of Background Checks

Ending the reliance on criminal records is not a new idea. As early as 1956, the National Conference on Parole called for "the abolition of laws depriving convicted individuals of civil and political rights," and shortly thereafter, the 1962 Model Penal Code called for the "removal of disqualifications and disabilities," encouraging states to automatically restore voting and other civil rights on completion of a prison sentence.[15] In the early 1970s, members of a French prisoner solidarity organization took the argument even further. These activists were arrested outside a Paris prison for distributing a pamphlet calling for the abolition of the *casier judiciaire*, a system for keeping criminal records, and making them available to employers and potential employers.[16] As the group's demands reveal, it saw the abolition of criminal records as essential to the overall struggle to weaken the scope and power of carceral logic.[17]

Recent reform efforts across the United States have taken a variety of approaches—aiming to increase automatic expungements, reduce the number

1. Abolition of criminal records

2. Abolition of banishment

3. Abolition of the death penalty

4. Abolition of life imprisonment

5. Abolition of conditional release and preventative detention

6. Abolition of imprisonment for nonpayment of legal costs

7. Reorganization of prison work

8. Right to free speech and correspondence

9. Right to proper medical and dental care

10. Right to appeal and defense before the prison administration

11. Right to association within prison

FIGURE C.1 "The Eleven Primary Points of the Prisoners Action Committee." Illustration courtesy of Karson Schenk. Comité d'Action des Prisonniers, "Les Onze Premier Points Du C.A.P.," *Journal de Prisonniers C.A.P.* 1, no. 2 (January 15, 1973): 1–8. Translation courtesy of Michael Hames-García, "Are Prisons Tolerable?," in *Challenging the Punitive Society: Carceral Notebooks, Volume 12, 2016*, ed. Bernard Harcourt, Perry Zurn, and Andrew Dilts (New York: Publishing Data Management, 2017), 170.

of years a conviction may be considered relevant, recognize criminalized people as members of a protected class, protect employers from negligence lawsuits, and strengthen existing Ban the Box and Fair Chance laws.[18] Among the most significant wins, attorneys affiliated with All of Us or None sued the Inland Empire's Riverside County Superior Court for violations of criminalized people's right to privacy. They challenged the court's failure to properly destroy and redact records pertaining to minor marijuana offenses dating back to the 1970s as well as the disclosure of protected information regarding defendants in criminal cases, and most significantly, the court having permitted background screening firms and the public to search for an individuals' criminal records using the date of birth or a driver's license number. The California Court of Appeal's 2022 ruling, *All of Us or None v. Hamrick*, significantly impacted the way courts across California allow access to criminal records using personally identifying information, effectively disabling the background check industry: access to a record does not mean anything if the record cannot be found and confirmed using personal identifiers.[19] The verdict gestured toward the general attitude held by the California legislature in the 1970s, as described in chapter 2: that while court records are individually public, an individual's criminal history compiled and maintained by the government is private and protected, nondisclosure is the general rule, and when there is a compelling reason to look at criminal history, it will be specific and limited.[20]

Another radical measure was put forth in 2023 by a coalition of California-based legal service, policy, and workforce organizations. SB 809 proposed to essentially eliminate all preemployment background checks except as required by law.[21] By attempting to shift the burden of proof—from the presumption that background checks are necessary to the presumption that they are not necessary except in special circumstances, these advocates sought to erode a core idea upholding the entire practice. Though unlike the *Hamrick* ruling, this proposal did not get far through the legislative process, even the mere introduction and discussion of premise-shifting policies can produce what professor of literature Ross Chambers once described as a "disturbance" in the political landscape. Such disturbances in the system, Ross posited, can over the long run bring about changes in what people desire, which in turn can change the way things are.[22]

How we understand the problem shapes our imagination of possible solutions. This book has maintained that the pervasive and pernicious use of criminal background checks is upheld as well as driven by a convergence of law, policy, profit, and expertise, whose ideological and material investments together constitute a "criminal record complex." This conglomeration propels the use of criminal background checks for reasons untethered to objective threats. Because the criminal record complex has been so long in the making, and involves so many actors and institutions, its unraveling will require creative approaches to tackling each of its tentacles, without simplifying or reducing the problem to any one strand.

This tackling cannot only be mechanical. I have emphasized that criminal records cannot be used as a discriminatory mechanism unless they are widely available and their use permitted, but just as crucial, unless people are convinced of their value. This value has been deliberately constructed by the institutions that comprise the criminal record complex, whose ideas and theoretical frameworks have largely molded what Italian philosopher Antonio Gramsci famously called "common sense": our everyday beliefs, assumptions, and understandings.[23]

As we learned in chapter 2, the criminal record complex got built based on a hodgepodge of laws and policies with no coherent framework other than a basic presumption that a criminal record equals bad/dangerous. Substantive change initiatives will insist on a reframing of criminal records from their current misconceptualization as objective ledgers of who has *done* what to ledgers of who has been *policed and punished* for what. They will decouple having been criminalized from having poor character, and expose criminal records as a faulty mechanism for neatly dividing the world into good people and bad, risky and trustworthy, or deserving and undeserving. A criminal record, it will be widely understood, is not a reliable stand-alone indicator of future behavior, nor as many of the employers I met insisted, a meaningful measure of suitability for work.

A more sensible approach to hiring and criminal records already exists and is working across a diverse set of employers. The elements of this alternate approach along with the conditions that support it could be nurtured and spread. Chapter 4 demonstrated that the criminal record complex guts employers of their hard-earned expertise and ultimately reorients them toward approaches that may not serve their interests. Indeed, the risk practices and logics of the criminal record complex have become yet another way that smaller businesses are forced to operate in a consolidating terrain that increasingly favors bigger business. Though many employers are looking for better ways to screen and vet job candidates, they want sensible mechanisms that actually deliver useful information. To return to Brian Lorey, the owner-manager of an art supply business,

> There is a saying in business that how a person plays a round of golf will reveal what kind of businessperson they are. The idea is that golf is a game that requires a high level of personal responsibility and honesty because of its reliance on each individual to evaluate and score their own play. . . . What we need for better screening is the equivalent of a round of golf.

Building a new common sense that recasts the meaning of criminal records, pokes holes in their presumed legitimacy, and questions their relevance will require vigorous political contestation. Change efforts will be hotly contested by governmental agencies, legislators, risk industries, and others with a direct investment in screening. The post-2020 racial reckoning worked to alert background screening industry leaders to the role of background checks in perpetuating systemic racism, prompting some to attempt to reform background screening as a practice that can be made fairer through education and the elimination of human bias.[24] Yet the industry as a whole continues to actively lobby against grassroots efforts to enact substantive legal reform.[25] While I have cautioned against a reduction of the analysis to "profit," clearly the commercial background screening industry represents a significant impediment to the emergence of a new common sense.

A countermovement will thus require sophisticated messaging that goes beyond the "hearts and minds" campaigns typical in US contexts that so often rest on foundations of personal responsibility, a patronizing savior mentality, and individual exceptionalism. An effective counterdiscourse will instead assert unequivocally that no system of background screening evolving from a fundamentally unjust criminal legal system can be fair. It will chip away at the basic premises legitimizing criminal record discrimination with the most highly developed evidence-based arguments possible so as to generate a new ethos that discrimination on the basis of conviction is both wrong and ill-advised. But beyond basic moralism or convincing facts, a compelling platform will contend that regardless of how carefully administered, the practice of criminal background screening will exacerbate—rather than protect against— the problems it purports to address. Beyond a critique of the legal system, it will assert that using criminal records to decide who can and cannot be included will ultimately generate less safety, less well-being, and more harm and threat. Recall Gabriel, who disappeared from the Hub's support networks after the plumbing supply company fired him with such disregard, or Courtney, trying to support two children by cleaning warehouses for nine dollars per hour rather than continuing to build a career in nursing. Excluding people from the economy and limiting their social mobility only undermines individuals'— and by extension, communities'—stability, security, and well-being.

Ending the reliance on employment background checks is not an easy position to advocate or adopt. In 2014, an Uber driver in Los Angeles was arrested on suspicion of kidnapping and attempting to sexually assault a passenger, and a few years later, a series of incidents involving Uber drivers hit the news. On closer investigation, however, most incidents of actual harm did not involve drivers with criminal records, and some "incidents" were not incidents at all but instead (as in the *Los Angeles Times* and *ProPublica* exposé of nurses discussed in chapter 2) discoveries that some drivers had past convictions.[26] Through these classic cases of moral panic, a consensus began to build among lawmakers, the media, and general public, prompting California governor Brown to sign a law in 2016 that would require rideshare companies to have a third party conduct a national background check on all drivers and subject them to a fine of up to $5,000 for every driver found to have any of the criminal records specified by the bill.[27] In 2017, Uber began running background checks on its drivers every two years as opposed to only at the time of hiring. The panic only grew when, in 2018, a man dubbed the "rideshare rapist" was arrested and charged with sexual assault against four women in San Francisco. But again, it became clear that Orlando Vilchez Lazo was not working for Uber or Lyft when he was alleged to have committed these crimes, and rather had posed as a rideshare driver in order to pick up women.[28] To boot, Lazo did not have a criminal record. Still, Uber's response was to announce that it would start doing annual background checks on drivers, and hire a company to constantly monitor arrests and other incidents between annual background checks. California passed another law requiring local and national background checks for all app-based rideshare drivers, allowing for continual background monitoring without added consent along with exclusion of persons ever convicted of a felony considered serious or sex related.[29]

We need to develop and implement strategies, systems, and policies to build safe communities, and protect those most vulnerable from harm and violence. But criminal background checks are not the way; they simply don't deliver. Instead, background screening creates a false sense of safety by making a promise it cannot fulfill: to divide the world into those who are safe and good versus risky and bad. To the extent that there even could be a way to ensure that any person be able to ride alone with any stranger without fear of harm, background checks cannot provide that assurance. Rather, a movement to reduce the scope, scale, and power of criminal background checks along with the logics underlying them must fight for deep investment in the kinds of resources that create true safety, including basic necessities such as food, shelter, quality education, health care, and meaningful work.

This investment will include exploring, developing, and implementing effective ways of creating as well as maintaining safe workplaces. Workplace violence will be understood, as it was in earlier periods of industrial capitalism, as rooted in workplace arrangements and thus will be approached as a collective versus individual psychological phenomenon.[30] As opposed to relying on background checks as a lazy stand-in for due diligence, alternative workplace risk management will promote active supervision, open communication, mutual care, and other known ways of preventing workplace violence.

Gramsci's famous concept "hegemony" analyzed the ways dominant classes reproduce dominance and how they gain the "consent" of the subordinate classes. He theorized how social groups achieve and maintain their power through mechanisms of domination that are at once economic and political as well as intellectual and moral.[31] Hegemony was a notion, as historian Michael Denning explains, that allowed Gramsci to ask, "Where do our conceptions of the world and our norms of conduct come from, and how do they change? What are the sources of a new collective will?"[32] Gramsci believed change must begin from the preformed ideas about the world people already possess, and was "skeptical" (to borrow Denning's language) of the idea that people can be persuaded to adopt another position simply because the facts support it. This does not imply, however, that people are hopeless captives of dominant ideas imposed from above. New ideas and proposals must start from the dominant common sense, but also be rooted in peoples' "good sense"—the ideas and knowledges developed through peoples' labor and practical engagements in the world—such as the levelheaded ideas about hiring and personnel management generated through employers' practical experiences.

Cultural critic Raymond Williams's notion "structures of feeling" described the idea that at any given moment, new and different ways of thinking are vying to emerge.[33] These are not necessarily reflected in the official discourse of policy or regulation but nonetheless represent the possibility of new formations and approaches. That different common senses can be operational at the same time means that within any social formation, there is always the possibility for fresh approaches to come to the fore.

My research in the Inland Empire changed my understanding of what the problem is, where the problem originates, and what should be done about it. Yet I am acutely aware of an insight offered by Black studies scholar Edmund T. Gordon: "Intellectual production which is not instrumentalized through praxis has no liberating effect."[34] While new explanations can sometimes spark new kinds of interventions, there is no assurance that new explanations lead to mobilization or that mobilization will be effective; there is no necessary through line from new ideas to transformed practices. Deep change, history demonstrates, always requires organizing. It requires collective movements that are clear about what they want, actively experiment with the kinds of changes they envision, and come together regularly to assess, adjust, and figure out what kind of politics are needed and possible.

GRATITUDE

THIS STUDY would not have been possible without the active participation of people at the Hub who invited me to get involved in their job-seeking activities and talked freely about what they were experiencing and feeling. Working alongside you was one of the most meaningful and rewarding experiences of my life; thank you. I hope this book's documentation of your steadfast grit compels employers, policymakers, and other power holders to eliminate senseless barriers.

I am equally indebted to job developers and coaches at the Hub who allowed me, sometimes uncomfortably, to observe them in action, interfacing with job seekers and employers in their offices, over the phone, and out in the field. The research could not have succeeded without their welcome. Special thanks to "Janine," the Hub's regional director, whose support and guidance was indispensable. Beyond the Hub, workforce experts and advocates Maria Alexander, Darren Cook, Billie Hayes, Brenda Sowers, Timothy Vasquez, and Joseph Williams shared important insights.

This book would have been far less interesting were it not for the many business owners, hiring managers, HR professionals, employment attorneys, and risk industry experts who gave of their scarce time to share their outlooks and answer my endless questions. I will never forget the generosity of Paul and Peter Weber, Moses, Craig, Janet, Suzanne, and all the good folks at Weber Trucking who allowed me to hang around. Beyond their enormous contribution to the research, our conversations grew my understanding of the world in ways that continue to impact me personally and as a scholar.

I am grateful to the Wenner Gren Foundation for Anthropological Research for supporting the fieldwork. I could not have finished this book without time to devote to later-stage research and writing funded by fellowships from the Ford Foundation and the American Council of Learned Societies.

I am deeply grateful to the colleagues, friends, and family who read parts of this work along the way. My colleagues Kelly Askew and Liz Roberts, developmental editor Katie Pace, and mother, Liz Burch, read early drafts of the manuscript. Their comments helped me to find the book's structure and overarching themes. Web Keene, Stuart Kirsch, Tina Lee, Mike McGovern, Andrea Morrell, Kevin O'Neill, Damien Sojoyner, Deborah Thomas, CT Turney-Lewis, and my colleagues in the anthrohistory and sociocultural workshops at the University of Michigan read related papers and provided helpful feedback. Shana Agid, Kriszti Fehervary, Matt Hull, and Erica Meiners read late-stage chapters and provided sharp comments that improved the argumentation. Sarah Glenn-Leistikow, Priya Kandaswamy, Joshua Kim, Rehana Lerandeau, Judah Schept, and Noah Tamarkin generously reviewed the entire manuscript and provided invaluable suggestions. In many an instance, their comments showed me how to solve problems in the writing I knew I had, but couldn't figure out how to fix.

Charlotte Smith has been an indispensable research assistant. She spent countless hours looking up the details of laws and policies, conducting literature reviews, compiling statistical data, checking facts, and looking for sources to substantiate or disprove claims that I or research informants wanted to make. I thank Jordan Smith as well for the research support she provided.

I want to thank the talented artists who have made art for this book and the Afterlives of Conviction website: Shana Agid, Ana Holschuh, Carolina Jones Ortiz, and Karson Schenk. Working with you has opened new avenues for analysis and creative expression.

I am grateful to the entire editorial, production, design, and marketing team at Princeton University Press, including James Collier, Cindy Milstein, Jaden Young, and especially, Fred Appel, for taking an interest in the project.

———

Long before imagining a book project, I was grounded by communities of principled thinkers and organizers dedicated to abolishing the prison industrial complex, defending the rights and dignity of people with criminal records, and building vibrant communities.

I thank Rose Braz and Rachel Herzing for their scrupulous mentorship throughout my introduction to prison industrial complex abolitionism. Within and through Critical Resistance, I am honored to have known and worked with Shana Agid, Ashanti Alston, Paula Austin, Kai Lumumba Barrow, Ellen Barry, Dan Berger, Kim Diehl, Jay Donahue, Linda Evans, Kenyon

Farrow, Jess Heaney, Ashley Hunt, Priya Kandaswamy, Amelia Kirby, Kung Li, Rehana Lerandeau, Pilar Maschi, Erica Meiners, Sitara Nieves, Isaac Ontiveros, Brent Plater, Laura Pulido, Dylan Rodriguez, Cassandra Shaylor, Mohamed Shehk, Setsu Shigematsu, Mike Murashige, Nat Smith, David Stein, and Ari Wohlfeiler.

Special love for my New Orleans crew, where this journey began—Miriam Barrios, Rachel Breunlin, Shana Griffin, Tamika Middleton, Jamie Schweser, Khalil Shahid, Andy Sherwood, Courtney Smith, Brice White, and our elders, Althea Francois, Larry Hurst, Mwalimu Johnson, Curtis Muhammad, Jerome Big Duck Smith, and Robert King Wilkerson. And Los Angeles crew, where the journey continued—Craig Gilmore, Ruth Wilson Gilmore, Jasmine Guerrero, Kevin Michael Key, Kim McGill, Roy San Filippo, Noe Orgaz, and Micol Seigel.

Within and around A New Way of Life Reentry Project, I am grateful to have worked alongside many courageous and dedicated people, including Evelyn Ayala, Gena Gong, Gretchen Heidemann, Ruth Mayfield, Kara Minnehan, Charsleen Poe, and Flozelle Woodmore. Susan Burton taught me everything important that I know about supporting people coming home from prison. Her no-bullshit, don't let 'em git ya approach to fighting for women and running a nonprofit continues to inspire me. Marilyn Montenegro's integrity and commitment provided constant grounding. Joshua Kim's strategic vision, tireless passion, and humility made me want to do the work. It was an honor to work with Josh on the UCLA Legal Clinic as well as Saul Sarabia, CT Turney-Lewis, and Noah Zatz. I am especially grateful to have met Sarah Glenn-Leistikow, whose sharp mind, principled politics, and dedication to the work are a continued inspiration. Through the Ban the Box campaign, it was a privilege to organize with Susan Burton, Kim Carter, Maurice Emsellem, Eric Greene, and Dorsey Nunn. I thank Linda Evans for showing me how to hold the contradictions while staying true to political principles.

———

My first seminar in anthropology at Goddard College and the Institute for Social Ecology was taught by Dan Chodorkoff, whose lectures captivated me and who was the first person to suggest that I had the potential for graduate-level study. Brian Tokar was a generous and encouraging mentor. Charles Woodard fueled my love of learning—imagine that in my first semester, he encouraged me to design, build, and install a composting toilet in my dormitory!

At the University of New Orleans, Jeffrey Ehrenreich and Martha Ward's love of anthropology was infectious. Years later, Ruthie Gilmore, Dylan Rodriguez, Micol Seigel, and Setsu Shigematsu encouraged me to go to back grad school and helped me navigate the process. I blame them for exemplifying a version of activist scholarship that I aspired to emulate.

I thank Katherine Beckett, King Davis, and the Hub's then California regional director for talking to me about my research plans. Meredith DeSautels was also helpful in this regard. When I wondered whether my questions were better suited to sociology, Avery Gordon and Devah Pager, two accomplished sociologists, listened generously and steered me back to anthropology.

It was my great fortune to slide into the last slot for a PhD student in the anthropology–African diaspora track at the University of Texas at Austin at a time when the Austin school, though beginning to splinter, was still a vibrant, intense, and communal place to be. I am deeply indebted to the faculty and students who welcomed me and actively supported my process of becoming a scholar.

In particular, I thank my fellow students Mohan Ambikaipaker, Sade Anderson, Maya Berry, Claudia Chavez, William Gblerkpor, Pablo Gonzalez, Julie Grigsby, Sarah Ihmoud, Courtney Morris, Vivian Newdick, Damien Sojoyner, Elissa Underwood, Eli Velasquez, Chelsea West, and Traci-Ann Wint for the essential support and camaraderie they provided. Dissertation writing was made less grueling and at times even fun because of Shanya Cordis's companionship and solidarity. Our regular writing sessions, punctured with hot yoga and stiff margaritas, kept me going when I wanted to quit. Vivian Newdick, a cherished friend, was one of few who took a genuine interest in the details of what I was finding in the field and has continued to cheerlead the whole way through. Marcia Del Rios, Gabo Diaz Monyemayor, Sam Eddings, Shannon Eddings, Carlota Garcia, Keagan Lee, Jim O'Quinn, Madeline Pizzo, Anna Lisa Plant, Justin Pratscher, Adriana Ramos Hinojos, and Ben Wilcott were vital friends in Austin who kept my spirits lifted, and made life there feel connected and bright.

My dissertation committee can only be described as a dream team. My chair, João H. Costa Vargas, was responsive, encouraging, and had a skillful way of guiding and supporting my intellectual development without trying to steer my thinking toward his own. Above all, in big ways and small, João had my back—for instance, repeatedly offering to babysit, which I was mostly too anxious to take him up on, but appreciated nonetheless. As I formulated the project, Shannon Speed kept me grounded in ethnography as the starting point for theorization. Ruthie Gilmore's expertise was essential for pushing me to think about political economy beyond the ways my protagonists were thinking about it. Charlie Hale encouraged me to think about the kinds of research questions and ethnographic focus that might matter politically. Our conversations always left me feeling reassured that the theoretical insights generated by my research might also matter on the ground. Edmund T. Gordon was my favorite teacher. His mastery of the Socratic method is unmatched in my classroom experience, and I have yet to master it myself. Dr. Gordon also let none of the fluffery of the academy and graduate training slide. He wouldn't let you get away with phrases like "gendered racialized criminality" without making you explain what it meant.

Outside the committee, Kamran Ali and Pauline Strong's core theory course provided helpful grounding. Circe Sturm's grant writing class was instrumental in helping me to define the research questions and draft the grant that ultimately funded the project. Cherise Smith provided an essential postdoc appointment. If at any point this book is a good read, I credit Cecilia Ballí, whose inspiring course on creative nonfiction writing provided crucial tools for my burning desire to write in a way that is pleasurable for the reader. Ballí's dissertation—so gripping that I read it in one fell swoop lying on the beach—provided a model for the power of well-written ethnography.

It would be hard to overstate how lucky I was to land right out of grad school in the University of Michigan's department of anthropology. The department's blend of intellectual rigor and collegiality—not to mention exceptional nurturing of junior faculty—make it a prized location from which to launch an academic career. Andrew Shryock, the department chair for my first years at U-M, was an enthusiastic and encouraging supporter. He, along with Mike McGovern and Daphne Watkins, made a fantastic "launch committee." Kelly Askew, now chair, is the most active and dedicated supporter of underrepresented scholars I have ever known, and has been an energetic mentor and ally since day one. Liz Roberts has been an exceptional mentor since my arrival. Practical, strategic, and positive, to walk away from meeting with Liz is to feel like the seemingly impossible can somehow be accomplished, and with concrete strategies for how to do so. Many other of my senior colleagues have generously provided critical wisdom and ongoing mentorship. In particular, I would like to thank Ruth Behar, Jason De Leon, Maureen Devlin, Jatin Dua, Kriszti Fehervary, Matt Hull, Webb Keane, Stuart Kirsch, Michael Lempert, Mike McGovern, Damani Partridge, and Scott Stonington. I am especially grateful to Yasmin Moll for her camaraderie and support, and for bringing me into the Writing Wizards, which on many a morning during the writing of this book, helped me get to the desk. Thank-you wizards for the countless pomodoros!

It has been an honor to supervise the dissertation projects of Reuben Riggs Bookman and Faith Leone. I thank students in my Critical Theories of Criminalization and Urban Ethnography seminars for keeping me on my toes. Amy Rundquist and Julie Winningham have provided critical administrative support.

Faculty collaborating through the Carceral State Project supported the early development of the Afterlives of Conviction Project. I thank Jesse Hoffnung-Garskof, Matthew Lassiter, Bill Lopez, Ashley Lucas, Ruby Tapia, and Heather Ann Thompson.

Beyond U-M, I am grateful to belong to various communities of thought and practice, including the Critical Prison Studies Caucus of the American Studies Association, Critical Resistance's Abolitionist Educators, and the California Fair Chance Coalition. It is an honor to collaborate with my friend Royal Ramey.

I want to thank new friends Josh Charson, Jeff Clark, Liaa Cruz, Erica Franz, Colin Gunkel, Christine Hume, Eric Langrock, Wendy Langrock, Dan Nemser, Valentina Silva, and Cliff Williams, for keeping me sane with critical diversions in the form of ridiculous text chains, fiction and TV recommends, neighborhood walks, dance parties, hula competitions, and delicious cocktails. I thank Henry Buchtel, Carla Hines, and Katy Leep for sharing their mind-body wisdom. I thank my pickleball pals, Carol Davis, Sarah Derouin, MaryAnna Dickinson, Alan Jackson, Anne Jackson, and others at Wolverine, for the joy of whacking and dinking that little Wiffle ball around the court.

I thank Lisa Adler, Bree Edwards, Robin Ellis, Karl Jagbandhansingh, Orin Langelle, Anne Petermann, Jenni Piette, and Geneva Tien-Witzleben for their friendship over the years. I thank my dear friends Margaret Lumley and Darini Nicholas for their ongoing encouragement and support. I thank my ace girls Maya Berry and Shanya Cordis for their camaraderie throughout this journey.

I am grateful to my family for loving me without condition. I thank my sister Nichole Burch-Waldron, brother-in-law Reuben Waldron, and beautiful nieces, Dhakiya and Toccara. I am thankful for my brothers, Damon Anderson, Shannon Swan, and Ricardo Medina, and my sister Aimar Burch Morillo. My childhood was deeply enriched by my relationships with my aunts Peggy and Marion, and uncles Robert, JB, Clifford, Herman, Earlston, and David. For all they have taught and given me, I thank my uncle Alan and aunt Nell, aunt Marg and Terry, aunt Rose and uncle Paul, uncle David and aunt Linda. A big spot in my heart will always be reserved for my Granny Burch and Nana

Banana. Much love for my cousins and their partners, Deadra, Marshene, Terenay, Kim, Vanessa, Bryan, Derika, Aaron, Andrew, Dan, Bonnie, Steven, and David.

I am grateful for my familia Rodríguez—Digna, Leonel, Victor, Nelly, Pio, Michelle, Leo, Iliana, Joaquin, Sammy, Cynthia, Mando, and Monica—for their love and support.

I thank Don Elliott for loving me and teaching me through my formative years. Don was a powerhouse who never stopped working and would stop at any time and in any place to help a person out.

I am grateful to Gord Ogilvie for the warm, free-spirit presence he brings to the family, and for bringing me back to the music. I am thankful to be in family with Leslie and Jonny.

I am grateful for the close connection I have always shared with my father, Rudolph Burch. I admire his glass-half-full, two-feet-on-the-ground, forward-ever approach to life, and his easygoing love is an ongoing source of comfort.

My mother has been a constant source of support and encouragement. In addition to sustaining my somewhat offbeat educational / life path, she has always supported my writing—from typing handwritten grade school essays, to removing passive voice and unnecessary commas in college essays, and line editing my entire dissertation. Above all, she has been a willing sounding board. Many a time I have called her up to drone on about some field observation, writing challenge, or analytic dilemma. She has a knack for listening to all the details and then cutting through them to lift up the essence of what I am trying to say.

My sons, Marcus and Malcolm, are the light of my life. I thank them for the wit, humor, love, aggravation, and perspective they bring to my days.

Finally, there is no one to whom I owe more than the love of my life, Miguel Rodríguez. This book could not have come to fruition without his enthusiastic agreement to uproot our lives in Los Angeles and move to Texas, then to the Inland Empire, back again to Austin, and yet again, to Michigan. Not only did he hold our young family down financially and otherwise through all of this, as you can imagine (or may know), it's not that fun to be the partner of a grad student, much less a person on the tenure track. Through the many hassles, challenges, anxieties, and milestones, Miguel has been my rock.

NOTES

Preface

1. The Los Angeles Reentry Legal Clinic was established as a partnership between A New Way of Life Reentry Project and the University of California at Los Angeles's critical race studies program. For more information, see http://www.reentrylegalclinic.org/.

2. For a creative nonfiction account of this struggle, see Melissa Burch, "To Refuse the Mark: Racial Criminalization and Twenty Years of Struggle to Ban the Box," *Social Justice: A Journal of Crime, Conflict and World Order* 49, no. 1–2 (2023): 177–90.

Introduction

1. Janine and I first met when as a law student, she became a volunteer at the LA Reentry Legal Clinic described in the preface.

2. The Hub's placement rate refers to jobs held for at least one full year. The rate would thus be much higher were it to include those who lose a job and then get another, or leave jobs to take better ones.

3. In directly describing participants in my research, I use the terms they would use to describe themselves. Elsewhere in the text, I sometimes use terms I prefer, but generally embrace the terms of self-identification most commonly used by people in a given setting.

4. Although it was sometimes important to the analysis and I often learned some of the details of peoples' convictions, I found knowing that history problematic for the development of ethical, professional relationships. "Knowing" added to an already dramatic imbalance of power between myself and research participants, who in contrast, did not know about the worst things that I've ever done. There is also a way that once revealed, knowledge of a "criminal" act becomes difficult to forget or set aside. This can sometimes have the effect of reducing whole people to their convictions. For this reason, even in instances in which I am aware of a person's conviction record, I do not include it in the writing unless it is important to the analysis.

5. In the same way that I defer to the identity terms people use to describe themselves, I use "foreman" throughout the text rather than "foreperson" because it is the term that all the people featured in this ethnography would use.

6. The way we talk about crime, policing, prisons, and the people associated with them shapes how we think about them, and what we think can or should happen. Over the past decade, there has been a concerted effort on the part of people impacted by criminalization to reject dehumanizing labels, such as "inmates," "criminals," "prisoners," "convicts," "delinquents,"

"felons," and "offenders," in favor of more person-centered phrases, like "person affected by the justice system" or "person previously incarcerated." This research predates this change, and even today, the shift is not total or universal.

7. The Michelle Montoya School Safety Act of 1999 was passed following the rape and murder of an eighteen-year-old student at Rio Linda high school in California by a substitute janitor who had been previously convicted of armed robbery and was on parole for manslaughter. The first iteration of the act (AB 1610) required an employer to "certify that none of its employees who [would] come in contact with students had been convicted of specified crimes." A later revised bill (AB 2102) aimed to ease the background check requirements for contractors, which (according to numerous letters from contractors included in the bill files) were causing major construction delays. The revised bill clarified that construction contractors would be exempt from mandatory background screening as long as their contact with students was limited by a physical barrier and/or they were continually supervised by a nonconvicted person and/or surveilled by school personnel. See chrome-extension://efaidnbmnnnibpcajpcglclefindmkaj /http://www.ossh.com/fingerprints/forms/cont_req.pdf.

For reasons I was not able to pinpoint, Ronaldo still felt he would be subject to the background check process. It could be that the school district had not yet determined that his contractor met the requirements for exemption. It could also be the case that when you're building fences, it doesn't make sense to also build a barrier between your workers and students, or that as a small business, the company didn't have the personnel to provide "continuous supervision" by someone who has undergone a Department of Justice check as the law requires. Given how many hours I spent trying to untangle the actual requirements and process for establishing exemption, the larger point may be exactly as Ronaldo articulated: regardless of what the law actually requires, the process for figuring it out, and making sure you are not in violation of the contract or in danger of getting sued if something happens, is just too onerous for the average employer to bother with.

8. Michelle Alexander, *The New Jim Crow: Mass Incarceration in the Age of Colorblindness* (New York: New Press, 2010); Marc Mauer, *Race to Incarcerate* (New York: New Press, 2006).

9. What defines a "felony" varies across the United States, but the term is generally used to categorize criminal acts considered serious, and linked to punishments of more than one year imprisonment or death. In 2022, nearly 63 percent of people in prisons and jails were serving a sentence for a conviction classified as "violent." E. Ann Carson and Rich Kluckow, *Prisoners in 2022—Statistical Tables* (Washington, DC: US Department of Justice, Bureau of Justice Statistics, November 2023), https://bjs.ojp.gov/library/publications/prisoners-2022-statistical -tables. Yet this legal distinction does not match common understanding in that a wide range of criminal acts classified as "violent" do not involve any physical harm. For example, in California, burglary is classified as a violent crime even when the dwelling is unoccupied. For a full discussion of contextual and regional nuances, and the consequences of counting behaviors as "violent" or "felonious," see *Defining Violence: Reducing Incarceration by Rethinking America's Approach to Violence* (Washington, DC: Justice Policy Institute, August 23, 2016), https:// justicepolicy.org/research/reports-2016-defining-violence-reducing-incarceration-by -rethinking-americas-approach-to-violence/.

10. An analysis of 2,655 fictitious online job applications showed that employers are 60 percent more likely to call applicants who do not have a felony conviction. Amanda Agan

and Sonja Starr, "The Effect of Criminal Records on Access to Employment," *American Economic Review* 107, no. 5 (2017): 560–64. A survey of over 600 employers in Los Angeles County found that only about 20 percent of employers indicated they would definitely or probably consider an applicant with a criminal history. Harry Holzer, Steven Raphael, and Michael Stoll, "Will Employers Hire Former Offenders?: Employer Preference, Background Checks, and Their Determinants," in *Imprisoning America: The Social Effects of Mass Incarceration*, ed. Mary Patillo, David Weiman, and Bruce Western (New York: Russell Sage Foundation, 2004), 205–44. A study of employers in the Inland Empire found that roughly 75 percent of hiring decision-makers were still unwilling to seriously consider an applicant with a drug or property conviction classified as violent. Ross Oselin, Q. Wang, and Wei Kang, *The CA Fair Chance Act: Summary Findings on Compliance and Efficacy in the Island Empire* (Riverside, CA: UC Riverside Presley Center of Crime & Justice Studies, 2023).

11. Megan Denver, Justin T. Pickett, and Shawn D. Bushway, "Criminal Records and Employment: A Survey of Experiences and Attitudes in the United States," *Justice Quarterly* 35, no. 4 (June 2018): 584–613; Harry J. Holzer, Steven Raphael, and Michael A. Stoll, "Perceived Criminality, Criminal Background Checks, and the Racial Hiring Practices of Employers," *Journal of Law and Economics* 49, no. 2 (2006): 451–80; Mike Vuolo, Sarah Lageson, and Christopher Uggen, "Criminal Record Questions in the Era of 'Ban the Box': Criminal Record Questions," *Criminology & Public Policy* 16, no. 1 (2017): 139–65.

12. *Report of the National Task Force on the Commercial Sale of Criminal Justice Record Information* (Sacramento, CA: National Consortium for Justice Information and Statistics, 2005), 19, https://www.search.org/files/pdf/RNTFCSCJRI.pdf.

13. Christopher Uggen, Mike Vuolo, Sarah Lageson, Ebony Ruhland, and Hilary K. Whitham, "The Edge of Stigma: An Experimental Audit of the Effects of Low-Level Criminal Records on Employment," *Criminology* 52, no. 4 (2014): 627–54.

14. Anne E. Carson, Danielle H. Sandler, Renuka Bhaskar, Leticia Fernandez, and Sonya Porter, *Employment of Persons Released from Federal Prison in 2010* (Washington, DC: US Department of Justice, Bureau of Justice Statistics, December 2021), https://bjs.ojp.gov/library/publications /employment-persons-released-federal-prison-2010. While 67 percent of people returning from prison in the study found work at some point in those four years since leaving prison, the number of people employed at any given time never exceeded 40 percent. See also Keith Finlay, "Great Recession Had Long-Term Economic Impact on People with Felony Convictions, Prison Time," US Census Bureau, February 15, 2022, https://www.census.gov/library/stories/2022/02/dim -job-outlook-for-people-released-from-prison-during-great-recession.html.

15. The National Employment Law Project generated the estimate 80 million by taking the number of individual subjects identified in the most recent *Survey of State Criminal History Information Systems* report (Becki R. Goggins and Dennis A. DeBacco, *Survey of State Criminal History Information Systems, 2020* [Sacramento, CA: SEARCH Group, 2022], table 1, https://bjs .ojp.gov/library/publications/survey-state-criminal-history-information-systems-2020) and reducing that number (114,375,300) by 30 percent to account for possible duplicates (i.e., individuals with criminal records in more than one state or who have died). For a full explanation, see Beth Avery, "Research Supports Fair Chance Policies," National Employment Law Project, April 16, 2024, https://www.nelp.org/insights-research/research-supports-fair -chance-policies/.

16. Today's 1.9 million people are imprisoned or jailed in 1,566 state prisons, 98 federal prisons, 3,116 local jails, 1,323 juvenile correctional facilities, 142 immigration detention facilities, and 80 Indian country jails as well as in military prisons, civil commitment centers, state psychiatric hospitals, and prisons in the US territories. See Wendy Sawyer and Peter Wagner, "Mass Incarceration: The Whole Pie 2024," Prison Policy Initiative, https://www.prisonpolicy.org/reports/pie2024.html. For incarceration rates from 1925 to 2010, see https://commons.wikimedia.org/wiki/File:U.S._incarceration_rates_1925_onwards.png.

17. Gabriel "Jack" Chin, "The New Civil Death: Rethinking Punishment in the Era of Mass Conviction," *University of Pennsylvania Law Review* 160 (April 2012): 1789–833, https://papers.ssrn.com/abstract=2072736; Reuben Jonathan Miller and Forrest Stuart, "Carceral Citizenship: Race, Rights and Responsibility in the Age of Mass Supervision," *Theoretical Criminology* 21, no. 4 (November 2017): 532–48; Michelle S. Phelps, "Mass Probation: Toward a More Robust Theory of State Variation in Punishment," *Punishment & Society* 19, no. 1 (January 2017): 53–73.

18. Jordan T. Camp and Christina Heatherton, "Total Policing and the Global Surveillance Empire Today: An Interview with Arun Kundnani," in *Policing the Planet: Why the Policing Crisis Led to Black Lives Matter*, ed. Jordan T. Camp and Christina Heatherton (London: Verso Books, 2016), 69–77; Dylan Rodríguez, "'Mass Incarceration' as Misnomer: Chattel/Domestic War and the Problem of Narrativity," in *Antiblackness*, ed. João H. Costa Vargas and Moon-Kie Jung (Durham, NC: Duke University Press, 2021), 169–97.

19. Sarah Shannon, Christopher Uggen, Jason Schnittker, Melissa Thompson, Sara Wakefield, and Michael Massoglia, "The Growth, Scope, and Spatial Distribution of People with Felony Records in the United States, 1948–2010," *Demography* 54, no. 5 (2017): 1795–818. These estimates were generated using data collected in 2011; to my knowledge, more recent estimates do not yet exist. California is one of only two states (the other is Indiana) in which an estimated one in four of all adult African Americans has a felony conviction history, and California leads the nation in terms of the percentage of African American adults (12 percent) having served time in prison. Note that at the time of this study, the data needed to develop sound estimates of the rate of felony convictions among Latino/as and other race or ethnic groups were insufficient.

20. Carson and Kluckow, *Prisoners in 2022*.

21. Marie Gottschalk, *Caught: The Prison State and the Lockdown of American Politics* (Princeton, NJ: Princeton University Press, 2015); Wendy Sawyer, "The Gender Divide: Tracking Women's State Prison Growth," Prison Policy Initiative, January 9, 2018, https://www.prisonpolicy.org/reports/women_overtime.html.

22. Bernadette Rabuy and Daniel Kopf, "Prisons of Poverty: Uncovering the Pre-Incarceration Incomes of the Imprisoned," Prison Policy Initiative, July 9, 2015, https://www.prisonpolicy.org/reports/income.html.

23. Lucius Couloute, "Getting Back on Course: Educational Exclusion and Attainment among Formerly Incarcerated People," Prison Policy Initiative, October 2018, https://www.prisonpolicy.org/reports/education.html.

24. Sociologist Devah Pager's groundbreaking study "The Mark of a Criminal Record" (*American Journal of Sociology* 108, no. 5 [2003]: 937–75) sent equally qualified "tester" applicants to apply for jobs in Milwaukee, Wisconsin, documenting who got a callback. Only

5 percent of Black applicants with criminal records got a callback, as compared to 17 percent of white criminalized applicants. A criminal record reduced the likelihood of a callback for Black people by two thirds; for white people, the likelihood of a callback was reduced by 50 percent. In other words, the effect of a criminal record was significantly greater for Black men than for white men, and in fact employers chose white applicants with criminal records over Black applicants without records. For a full analysis, see Devah Pager, *Marked: Race, Crime, and Finding Work in an Era of Mass Incarceration* (Chicago: University of Chicago Press, 2007). See also Harry J. Holzer, Steven Raphael, and Michael A. Stoll, *Employer Demand for Ex-Offenders: Recent Evidence from Los Angeles* (Washington, DC: Urban Institute, 2003), https://www.urban .org/research/publication/employer-demand-ex-offenders.

25. Scott H. Decker, Cassia Spohn, Natalie R. Ortiz, and Eric Hedberg, *Criminal Stigma, Race, Gender, and Employment: An Expanded Assessment of the Consequences of Imprisonment for Employment* (Phoenix: Arizona State University, 2010); Megan Denver, Garima Siwach, and Shawn D. Bushway, "A New Look at the Employment and Recidivism Relationship through the Lens of a Criminal Background Check," *Criminology* 55, no. 1 (2017): 174–204; Nancy G. La Vigne, Lisa E. Brooks, and Tracey L. Lloyd, *Women on the Outside: Understanding the Experiences of Female Prisoners Returning to Houston, Texas* (Washington, DC: Urban Institute, June 11, 2009), https://www.urban.org/research/publication/women-outside-understanding -experiences-female-prisoners-returning-houston-texas.

26. For example, according to the Professional Healthcare Institute ("Home Health Care at a Glance," *Facts* 5, February 2014, https://www.phinational.org/wp-content/uploads/legacy /phi-facts-5.pdf), 91 percent of home care aides are women, 32 percent are Black, 17 percent are Latino/a, 25 percent are immigrants, and one in five is a single mother.

27. Ryan Larson, Sarah Shannon, Aaron Sojourner, and Chris Uggen, "Felon History and Change in U.S. Employment Rates," *Social Science Research*, 2021; David Harding, Jeffrey D. Morenoff, Anh P. Nguyen, and Shawn D. Bushway, "Imprisonment and Labor Market Outcomes: Evidence from a Natural Experiment," *American Journal of Sociology* 124, no. 1 (July 2018): 49–110.

28. Devah Pager, "The Mark of a Criminal Record," *American Journal of Sociology* 108 (2003): 959n37, explains that because white people have greater opportunity in the job market overall, it is fair to say they have more to lose, but in *relative* terms, the effect of a criminal record is greater for Black people. Given grossly different baselines (in her study, only 14 percent of Black people without criminal records received callbacks, relative to 34 percent of white people without criminal records), simply comparing percentage point differences in treatment would be misleading.

29. Lucius Couloute and Daniel Kopf, "Out of Prison & Out of Work: Unemployment among Formerly Incarcerated People," Prison Policy Initiative, 2018, http://www.jstor.org /stable/resrep27307.

30. Alessandro Corda, Martí Rovira, and Andrew Henley, "Collateral Consequences of Criminal Records from the Other Side of the Pond: How Exceptional Is American Penal Exceptionalism?," *Criminology & Criminal Justice* 23, no. 4 (April 18, 2023): 528–48; David Garland, "Penal Controls and Social Controls: Toward a Theory of American Penal Exceptionalism," *Punishment & Society* 22, no. (3 (2020): 321–52.

31. Corda, Rovira, and Henley, "Collateral Consequences of Criminal Records from the Other Side of the Pond"; Alesandro Corda and Sarah Esther Lageson, "Disordered Punishment:

Workaround Technologies of Criminal Records Disclosure and the Rise of a New Penal Entre-preneurialism," *British Journal of Criminology* 60, no. 2 (2020): 245–64; James B. Jacobs, "European Employment Discrimination Based on Criminal Record I—Mandatory Bars," Collateral Consequences Resource Center, January 12, 2015, https://ccresourcecenter.org/2015/01/12/employment-discrimination-based-criminal-record-europe/.

32. The EEOC's *Enforcement Guidance on the Consideration of Arrest and Conviction Records in Employment Decisions* derives its authority from Title VII of the Civil Rights Act of 1964, which prohibits employment discrimination on the basis of race, color, religion, sex, or national origin. Its protection of people with convictions is based on the link between discrimination on the basis of race or national origin and criminal history, and therefore only protects Black and Latino/a people because of their documented overrepresentation in rates of arrest and conviction. To read the latest version of the *Enforcement Guidance on the Consideration of Arrest and Conviction Records in Employment Decisions under Title VII of the Civil Rights Act*, see http://www.eeoc.gov/laws/guidance/arrest_conviction.cfm#sdendnote43sym. See also "The E-RACE Initiative (Eradicating Racism and Colorism from Employment)," US Equal Employment Opportunity Commission, accessed February 8, 2025, https://www.eeoc.gov/initiatives/e-race/e-race-initiativeeradicating-racism-and-colorism-employment.

33. The new guidance was celebrated for going beyond the color-blind notion that racism requires intent and upholding disparate impact theory to insist that it is illegal not only to *treat* applicants differently but also engage in practices that *result* in the disproportionate exclusion of protected classes.

34. Should an employer determine a "nexus" between the conviction record and job duties (e.g., theft conviction / retail clerk), the guidance advises them to conduct individualized assessments considering circumstances surrounding the offense, including any mitigating circumstances, number of prior convictions, a person's age at the time of the conviction or release from prison, length and consistency of employment before and after the conduct (including evidence of having performed the same type of work postconviction without incident), rehabilitation efforts, employment or character references, and whether the individual is bonded under a federal, state, or local program. After taking all of these factors into consideration, discrimination becomes legally permissible through a "business necessity" defense [California Code, Government Code, GOV § 12951; Cal. Code Regs. tit. 2, § 11017.1(f)(4)]; that is, the employer can demonstrate that the conviction(s) being screened for are related to the specific job in question, and reasonably argue that in order to protect the people and/or property of the business, it is "necessary" to exclude people with said conviction(s). For instance, a moving company that screens for theft convictions and argues the safekeeping of customers belongings is a cornerstone of their business operation would easily pass the test. There are a number of problems with these factors. For example, the factor "number of prior convictions" naturalizes the idea that criminal records are the straightforward outcome of "crime" rather than an outcome of *criminalization*, when the guidance itself recognizes that aggressive policing, prosecution, and sentencing are more often directed at poor, Black, Latino/a, American Indian, and Asian Pacific Islander peoples. Similarly, while "nexus between job duties and conviction" may be a progressive move from the previous idea that *all* convictions are relevant, this notion rests on the incorrect assumption that prior offenses indicate crimes to come and past behaviors predict future behaviors; empirical research clearly shows a lack of correlation between the type of conviction

and likelihood of future crime. See Shawn D. Bushway, Brian G. Vegetabile, Nidhi Kalra, Lee Remi, and Greg Baumann, "Providing Another Chance: Resetting Recidivism Risk in Criminal Background Checks," RAND Corporation, January 6, 2022, https://www.rand.org/pubs /research_reports/RRA1360-1.html.

35. When the new guidance was adopted, stringent enforcement parameters made it difficult for plaintiffs to gain any traction. For instance, rather than being taken as a given (as the language of the guidance seemed to suggest), disparate impact had to be proven, case by case, and the standard was nearly impossible to reach given the limited data or resources available for research. Disparate impact had to be demonstrated for a particular industry in a particular geography (e.g., the employer is excluding a greater percentage of Black applicants than applicants from other racial groups in the construction industry in Southern California). Additionally, the plaintiff had to prove that the disproportionate exclusion was a result of the criminal records policy. In contrast, the standard for an employer to demonstrate business necessity was so broadly defined (every business has property and customers to protect) and continually lowered that a defense on this basis was fairly easy to mount. See Candice S. Thomas, "Felony Is the New N-Word: Statistical Evidence to Measure a Disparate Impact Claim for the Use of Criminal Records Checks in Employment Decisions Comments & Casenotes," *University of Cincinnati Law Review* 82, no. 4 (2014): 1295–316. Further, the onus again falls on the plaintiff to prove the business necessity is not legitimate. For an example of the difficulty proving disparate impact, see "Kaplan Defeats EEOC Discrimination Lawsuit. But Why Did Kaplan Win?," Randisi Associates, December 28, 2014, https://www.preemploymentscreen.com/kaplan-defeats -eeoc-discrimination-lawsuit/. See also Meriem Hubbard, Joshua P. Thompson, Anastasia P. Boden, Ilya Shapiro, and Trevor Burrus, "EEOC v. Kaplan Higher Education Corp.," Cato Institute, October 11, 2013, https://www.cato.org/legal-briefs/eeoc-v-kaplan-higher-education -corp. For an example of the broad definition of business necessity, see *Tye v. City of Cincinnati* (1992), which held that the employment practice need not be "absolutely necessary" or "indispensable" to the business but instead only "substantially promote" its efficient operation. For examples of successful lawsuits, see "BMW to Pay $1.6 Million and Offer Jobs to Settle Federal Race Discrimination Lawsuit," US Equal Employment Opportunity Commission, September 8, 2015, https://www.eeoc.gov/newsroom/bmw-pay-16-million-and-offer-jobs-settle-federal-race -discrimination-lawsuit; "Pepsi to Pay $3.13 Million and Made Major Policy Changes to Resolve EEOC Finding of Nationwide Hiring Discrimination against African Americans," US Equal Employment Opportunity Commission, January 11, 2012, https://www.eeoc.gov/newsroom /pepsi-pay-313-million-and-made-major-policy-changes-resolve-eeoc-finding-nationwide -hiring.

36. Beth Avery and Han Lu, "Ban the Box: U.S. Cities, Counties, and States Adopt Fair Hiring Policies," National Employment Law Project, October 2021, https://www.nelp.org /publication/ban-the-box-fair-chance-hiring-state-and-local-guide/.

37. Terry-Ann Craigie, "Ban the Box, Convictions, and Public Employment," *Economic Inquiry* 58, no. 1 (September 2, 2019): 425–45; C. W. Von Bergen and Martin S. Bressler, "'Ban the Box' Gives Ex-Offenders a Fresh Start in Securing Employment," *Labor Law Journal* 67, no. 2 (June 2016): 383–95; Julia Levashina, Jessica A. Peck, and Linda Ficht, "Don't Select until You Check: Expected Background Checking Practices," *Employee Responsibilities and Rights Journal* 29, no. 3 (September 2017): 127–48; Christophe Herring and Sandra Susan Smith, "The Limits

of Ban-the-Box Legislation," Institute for Research on Labor and Employment, University of California at Berkeley, March 2022, https://irle.berkeley.edu/wp-content/uploads/2022/03/The-Limits-of-Ban-the-Box-Legislation-1.pdf.

38. The California Fair Chance Act (AB 1008) requires both public and private sector employers with five or more employees to delay asking about or considering conviction records until after a conditional offer of employment has been made. It establishes a process for employers to follow when making an adverse decision and outlines a formal pathway for appeal. The law further requires employers to follow the EEOC's approach to individualized assessment by taking into consideration the amount of time elapsed since a conviction as well as its nature and job relatedness, and to provide written preliminary notice of intent to rescind a conditional job offer based on conviction record as well as time for the applicant to provide evidence of inaccuracies in the background report, and/or evidence of rehabilitation and mitigating circumstances. For full details, see California Code, Government Code, GOV § 12952; "Fair Chance Act: Guidance for California Employers and Job Applicants," Civil Rights Department, State of California, accessed February 9, 2025, https://calcivilrights.ca.gov/fair-chance-act/. On employers' continued violation of the act, see Sharon S. Oselin, Justine G. M. Ross, Qingfang Wang, and Wei Kang, "Fair Chance Act Failures? Employers' Hiring of People with Criminal Records," *Criminology & Public Policy* 23, no. 2 (November 22, 2023): 361–90.

39. Legal scholar Joseph Fishkin notes that "fifteen states currently prohibit some set of employers from refusing to hire on the basis of a past criminal conviction, with various exceptions." As Fishkin explains, "Most of these laws appear to have been enacted in the late 1970s or early 1980s, in what may have been a previous wave of significant concern about prisoner reentry." Joseph Fishkin, "The Anti-Bottleneck Principle in Employment Discrimination Law," *Washington University Law Review* 91, no. 6 (January 1, 2014): 1459n115.

40. Jennifer Fahey, Cheryl Roberts, and Len Engel, *Employment of Ex-Offenders: Employer Perspectives* (Boston: Crime and Justice Institute, October 31, 2006), http://www.crj.org/assets/2017/07/Employer_Perspectives.pdf; Georgina Heydon and Bronwyn Naylor, "Criminal Record Checking and Employment: The Importance of Policy and Proximity," *Australian & New Zealand Journal of Criminology* 51, no. 3 (September 2018): 372–94; Oluwasegun Obatusin and Debbie Ritter-Williams, "A Phenomenological Study of Employer Perspectives on Hiring Ex-Offenders," ed. Georgios Antonopoulos, *Cogent Social Sciences* 5, no. 1 (January 2019): 1571730; *Workers with Criminal Records: A Survey by the Society for Human Resource Management and the Charles Koch Institute* (Alexandria, VA: SHRM, 2018), https://www.prisonpolicy.org/scans/cki_shrm/report.pdf.

41. Bushway et al., "Providing Another Chance"; Matthew R. Durose and Leonardo Antenangeli, *Recidivism of Prisoners Released in 34 States in 2012: A 5-Year Follow-Up Period (2012–2017)* (Washington, DC: US Department of Justice, Bureau of Justice Statistics, July 2021), https://bjs.ojp.gov/library/publications/recidivism-prisoners-released-34-states-2012-5-year-follow-period-2012-2017; Megan Denver, Justin T. Pickett, and Shawn D. Bushway, "The Language of Stigmatization and the Mark of Violence: Experimental Evidence on the Social Construction and Use of Criminal Record Stigma," *Criminology* 55, no. 3 (2017): 664–90; Harry J. Holzer, Steven Raphael, and Michael Stoll, "The Effect of an Applicant's Criminal History on Employer Hiring Decisions and Screening Practices: New Evidence from Los Angeles," in

Barriers to Reentry? The Labor Market for Released Prisoners in Post-Industrial America, ed. Shawn D. Bushway, Michael Stoll, and David Weiman (New York: Russell Sage Foundation, 2007); Jessica A. Cerda, Douglas M. Stenstrom, and Mathew Curtis, "The Role of Type of Offense and Work Qualifications on Perceived Employability of Former Offenders," *American Journal of Criminal Justice* 40, no. 2 (2015): 317–35; Femina P. Varghese, Erin E. Hardin, Rebecca L. Bauer, and Robert D. Morgan, "Attitudes toward Hiring Offenders: The Roles of Criminal History, Job Qualifications, and Race," *International Journal of Offender Therapy and Comparative Criminology* 54, no. 5 (October 2010): 769–82.

42. Naomi F. Sugie, Noah D. Zatz, and Dallas Augustine, "Employer Aversion to Criminal Records: An Experimental Study of Mechanisms," *Criminology* 58, no. 1 (2020): 5–34.

43. Decker et al., *Criminal Stigma, Race, Gender, and Employment.*

44. Pager, "The Mark of a Criminal Record"; Pager, *Marked*; Holzer et al., "Perceived Criminality, Criminal Background Checks, and the Racial Hiring Practices of Employers."

45. Lori Freedman, *Willing and Unable: Doctors' Constraints in Abortion Care* (Nashville, TN: Vanderbilt University Press, 2010), 4.

46. As I will discuss further in chapter 4, contract terms and insurance policies can be negotiated. The Hub itself, which given its organizational mission *must* employ people with conviction records, provides an excellent case in point. Over the years, the Hub has negotiated with many local governments over background check contract requirements and found that the terms are not immovable. For example, while it is often difficult to entirely remove requirements to *conduct* background checks, few contracts specifically require exclusions or even sharing of the background check results. Additionally, contract language such as "must perform background check to satisfaction" is open to interpretation and does not necessarily mean that approval is needed to hire particular people. Likewise, employers have found that contracts often ask for a certain level or kind of insurance that may be higher or different than the default kind/limit their insurer provides. But companies can negotiate with insurers on coverage amounts and what they'll cover, just like they would with any other aspect of the policy, and/or shop for an alternate insurer. That said, it is also true that in fast-moving business environments, the *perception* that a contract could be canceled, the business could be held liable, or the contractual terms are fixed frequently provides enough of a hiccup to preclude further inquiry. For further discussion of how ambiguity in the law can lead to excessive caution and overcompliance, see chapter 2.

47. https://leginfo.legislature.ca.gov/faces/codes_displaySection.xhtml?lawCode =EDC&sectionNum=45125.#:~:text=If%20a%20school%20district%20is,of%20Justice%20 ascertains%20that%20information.

48. John Jackson, panel discussion, American Anthropological Association meeting, "Was That Racist?," Minneapolis, MN, Thursday, November 17, 2016.

49. My thinking on the role of bias in criminal record discrimination owes much to Petersen. See Amanda M. Petersen, "Beyond Bad Apples, toward Black Life: A Re-Reading of the Implicit Bias Research," *Theoretical Criminology* 23, no. 4 (November 1, 2019): 491–508. On the lack of correlation between bias and behavior, see Patrick S. Forscher, Calvin K. Lai, Jordan R. Axt, and Charles R. Ebersole, "A Meta-Analysis of Procedures to Change Implicit Measures," *Journal of Personality and Social Psychology* 117, no. 3 (2019): 522–59. While the term "implicit bias" was not coined until the mid-1990s by Anthony Greenwald and Mahzarin Banaji, one of the most

famous studies we have illustrating the workings and effects of implicit bias is the "Racial Identification and Preference in Negro Children" study by Kenneth Clark and Mamie Clark. Also known as the "doll study," this research was a significant piece of evidence used in the NAACP's legal case in *Brown v. Board*. See Kenneth P. Clark and Mamie B. Clark, "Emotional Factors in Racial Identification and Preference in Negro Children," *Journal of Negro Education* 19, no. 3 (Summer 1950): 341–50.

50. This section's subtitle is adapted from Peter Ikeler and Calvin John Smiley, "The Racial Economics of Mass Incarceration," *Spectre Journal* 1, no. 2 (Fall 2020), https://spectrejournal .com/the-racial-economics-of-mass-incarceration/. By "racial economics of mass incarceration," the authors signal the theoretical importance of reconstructing the historical relationship between race and class, and how that relationship contributed to the US prison boom. Similarly here, I aim to think about how racialized ideas about risk and criminality became connected to structures for making risk profitable in ways that animated and justified an explosion in the use of criminal background checks.

51. Though it was not possible to inquire directly about the absence of a conviction barrier, my best guess is that it would have had to do with the agency's insurance policy. People with felony convictions may have been excluded from a policy covering workers directly handling merchandise, but not a policy covering workers who only clean facilities. For an explanation of how insurance risk grouping and exclusion from coverage works generally, see chapter 2.

52. In 2024 dollars ($14.48), that first tier would pay less than California's 2024 minimum wage ($16 per hour).

53. Jatin Dua, *Captured at Sea: Piracy and Protection in the Indian Ocean* (Berkeley: University of California Press, 2019); Jonathan Levy, *Freaks of Fortune: The Emerging World of Capitalism and Risk in America* (London: Harvard University Press, 2012); Caley Horan, *Insurance Era: Risk, Governance, and the Privatization of Security in Postwar America* (Chicago: University of Chicago Press, 2021); George S. Rigakos and Richard W. Hadden, "Crime, Capitalism and the 'Risk Society': Towards the Same Olde Modernity?," *Theoretical Criminology* 5, no. 1 (February 1, 2001): 61–84.

To think of risk as "a capital" or commodity is to decenter notions of danger, peril, or objective threat, and instead highlight the processes through which insurers calculate probabilities and sell protection against losses of capital, whether human or property. François Ewald, "Insurance and Risk," in *The Foucault Effect: Studies in Governmentality: With Two Lectures by and an Interview with Michel Foucault*, edited by Michel Foucault, Graham Burchill, Colin Gordon, and Peter M. (Peter Michael) Miller. London: Harvester Wheatsheaf, 1991, 197–210. See also David Garland, "The Rise of Risk," in *Risk and Morality*, edited by Aaron Doyle and Diana Ericson (Toronto: University of Toronto Press, 2003), 48–86.

54. Levy, *Freaks of Fortune*, 37.

55. For an insightful exploration of the linkages between racism, capitalism, and risk, and a discussion of their contemporary expression in prisoner reentry workforce development programs, see Shreya Subramani, "The Entrepreneurial Catch: Toward an Analytic of Racial Responsibilization," *Current Anthropology* 63, no. 4 (June 28, 2022): 367–85.

Scholarship exploring the intertwined relationship between racism and capitalism has built primarily on Cedric Robinson, *Black Marxism: The Making of the Black Radical Tradition* (Chapel Hill: University of North Carolina Press, 1983), in which Robinson demonstrated the simultaneous emergence of capitalism and racism, and how the emergence of capitalism transformed and exaggerated older forms of social difference into racial difference for the purpose of capital accumulation. For a helpful overview of Robinson's intervention and many excellent essays engaging the concept, see Destin Jenkins and Justin Leroy, eds., *Histories of Racial Capitalism* (New York: Columbia University Press, 2021). See also Michael Javen Fortner, "Racial Capitalism and City Politics: Toward a Theoretical Synthesis," *Urban Affairs Review* 59, no. 2 (March 1, 2023): 630–53; Jodi Melamed, "Racial Capitalism," *Critical Ethnic Studies* 1, no. 1 (Spring 2015): 76–85; Laura Pulido, "Flint, Environmental Racism, and Racial Capitalism," *Capitalism Nature Socialism* 27, no. 3 (July 2, 2016): 1–16.

56. Virginia Eubanks, *Automating Inequality: How High-Tech Tools Profile, Police, and Punish the Poor* (New York: St. Martin's Publishing Group, 2018); Price V. Fishback, Jessica LaVoice, Allison Shertzer, and Randall Walsh, "Race, Risk, and the Emergence of Federal Redlining," Working Paper (National Bureau of Economic Research, November 30, 2020); Emily Alexandra Katzenstein, "Race(d) Futures: Race, Risk and the Politics of Prediction" ," (PhD D diss., (University of Chicago, Political Science, 2020); Amanda Tillotson, "Race, Risk and Real Estate: The Federal Housing Administration and Black Homeownership in the Post World War II Home Ownership State," *DePaul Journal for Social Justice* 8, no. 1 (Winter 2014): 25–52; Benjamin Wiggins, *Calculating Race: Racial Discrimination in Risk Assessment* , (New York: Oxford University Press, 2020).

57. Kelly Lytle Hernández, *City of Inmates: Conquest, Rebellion, and the Rise of Human Caging in Los Angeles, 1771–1965* (Chapel Hill: University of North Carolina Press, 2017).

58. Simone Browne, *Dark Matters: On the Surveillance of Blackness* (Durham, NC: Duke University Press, 2015); Frederick Ludwig Hoffman, *Race Traits and Tendencies of the American Negro* (Clark, NJ: American Economic Association, 1896); V. O. Key, *Southern Politics in State and Nation* (Knoxville: University of Tennessee Press, 2012); Khalil Gibran Muhammad, *The Condemnation of Blackness: Race, Crime, and the Making of Modern Urban America* (Cambridge, MA: Harvard University Press, 2010).

59. Ida B. Wells, *Southern Horrors: Lynch Law in All Its Phases* (New York: New York Age Print, 1892); Sarah Haley, *No Mercy Here: Gender, Punishment, and the Making of Jim Crow Modernity* (Chapel Hill: University of North Carolina Press, 2016), 161.

60. On convict laws as a component of the Black Codes restricting Black mobility, see William Cohen, *At Freedom's Edge: Black Mobility and the Southern White Quest for Racial Control, 1861–1915* (Baton Rouge, LA: LSU Press, 1991). On the orientation of the Southern justice system toward the coercion of Black labor, see Douglas A. Blackmon, *Slavery by Another Name: The Re-Enslavement of Black Americans from the Civil War to World War II* (New York: Anchor, 2009). On criminalization as a tool of political disenfranchisement, see Jeff Manza and Christopher Uggen, *Locked Out: Felon Disenfranchisement and American Democracy* (New York: Oxford University Press, 2006); Pippa Holloway, *Living in Infamy: Felon Disfranchisement and the History of American Citizenship* (Oxford: Oxford University Press, 2013).

61. Muhammad, *The Condemnation of Blackness*, 274. For a discussion of the conflation of racism and racial inferiority, see Muhammad, *The Condemnation of Blackness*, 68.

62. Cesare Lombroso, *Criminal Man*, trans. Mary Gibson and Nicole Hahn Rafter (1876; repr., Durham, NC: Duke University Press, 2006). For a masterful critique of Lombroso's work, see Stephen Jay Gould, *The Mismeasure of Man*, rev. and exp. (New York: W. W. Norton, 1996).

63. W. E. B. Du Bois, *The Philadelphia Negro: A Social Study* (Philadelphia: University of Pennsylvania Press, 1899); Wells, *Southern Horrors*; Franz Boas, *The Mind of Primitive Man*, (New York: The Macmillan Company, 1911); Muhammad, *The Condemnation of Blackness.*

64. On the social construction of Black women's criminality, see Kali N. Gross, *Colored Amazons: Crime, Violence, and Black Women in the City of Brotherly Love, 1880–1910* (Durham, NC: Duke University Press, 2006); Cheryl D. Hicks, *Talk with You Like a Woman: African American Women, Justice, and Reform in New York, 1890–1935* (Chapel Hill: University of North Carolina Press, 2010); Haley, *No Mercy Here.* On the social construction of American Indian peoples' criminality, see Luana Ross, *Inventing the Savage: The Social Construction of Native American Criminality* (Austin: University of Texas Press, 1998). For more on how the dynamics of race, gender, and criminality intersect to render Black women vulnerable to male violence and criminalization, see Sharon Angella Allard, "Rethinking Battered Woman Syndrome: A Black Feminist Perspective," in *Domestic Violence at the Margins: Readings on Race, Class, Gender, and Culture*, ed. Natalie J. Sokoloff with Christina Pratt (Piscataway, NJ: Rutgers University Press, 2005), 194–205; Michelle Bograd, "Strengthening Domestic Violence Theories: Intersections of Race, Class, Sexual Orientation, and Gender," in *Domestic Violence at the Margins: Readings on Race, Class, Gender, and Culture*, ed. Natalie J. Sokoloff with Christina Pratt (Piscataway, NJ: Rutgers University Press, 2005), 25–38; Beth E. Richie, *Compelled to Crime: The Gender Entrapment of Battered, Black Women* (New York: Routledge, 1996); Beth Richie, *Arrested Justice: Black Women, Violence, and America's Prison Nation* (New York: NYU Press, 2012).

65. Malcolm Feeley and Jonathan Simon, "The New Penology: Notes on the Emerging Strategy of Corrections and Its Implications," *Criminology* 30, no. 4 (1992): 449–74; Malcolm Feeley and Jonathan Simon, "Actuarial Justice: The Emerging New Criminal Law," in *The Futures of Criminology*, ed. David Nelken (Thousand Oaks, CA: Sage, 1994), 173–201; Bernard E. Harcourt, *Against Prediction: Profiling, Policing, and Punishing in an Actuarial Age* (Chicago: University of Chicago Press, 2007); Kelly Hannah-Moffat, "Punishment and Risk," in *The SAGE Handbook of Punishment and Society*, ed. Jonathan Simon and Richard Sparks (Los Angeles: SAGE Publications Ltd., 2012); Jonathan Simon, "REVERSAL OF FORTUNE: The Resurgence of Individual Risk Assessment in Criminal Justice," *Annual Review of Law and Social Science* 1, no. 1 (December 2005): 397–421.

66. Legal scholar Carol Steiker helpfully named the interweaving of predictive risk regulation with the criminal legal system the "preventative state." Such as state, Steiker wrote, does not only punish to prevent crime but may also "attempt to identify and neutralize dangerous individuals before they commit crimes by restricting their liberty in a variety of ways." Carol S. Streiker, "The Limits of the Preventive State Supreme Court Review—Foreword," *Journal of Criminal Law and Criminology* 88, no. 3 (1998): 774, https://heinonline.org/HOL/P?h=hein.journals/jclc88&i=785. See also Sandra Mayson, "Collateral Consequences and the Preventive State," *Notre Dame Law Review*, January 2015, https://scholarship.law.upenn.edu/faculty_scholarship/2408.

67. Harcourt, *Against Prediction*, 91.

68. Many legal scholars have written about the troubling conflation of systemic racism and economic marginalization with signs of "criminality." See, for example, "Past Imperfect: How Credit Scores and Other Analytics 'Bake In' and Perpetuate Past Discrimination," NCLC Racial Justice and Equal Economic Opportunity, February 2014, https://www.nclc.org/wp-content

/uploads/2016/05/20240227_Issue-Brief_Past-Imperfect.pdf; Harcourt, *Against Prediction*; Bernard E. Harcourt, "Risk as a Proxy for Race," Working Paper No. 323 (University of Chicago Public Law & Legal Theory, 2010), https://chicagounbound.uchicago.edu/cgi/viewcontent.cgi ?article=1265&context=public_law_and_legal_theory; Michael Tonry, "Legal and Ethical Issues in the Prediction of Recidivism," *Federal Sentencing Reporter* 26, no. 3 (2014): 167–76; Kelly Hannah-Moffat, "Actuarial Sentencing: An 'Unsettled' Proposition," *Justice Quarterly* 30, no. 2 (April 2013): 270–96; Sonja B. Starr, "Evidence-Based Sentencing and the Scientific Rationalization of Discrimination," *Stanford Law Review* 66, no. 4 (2014): 803–72.

69. Through online investigation of the payroll services offered by some of the biggest payroll companies in the United States (ADP, ONPay, Patriot, Square, Gusto, Paychex, SurePayroll, IntuitQuickBooks, Rippling, and Paycore), my research assistant Charlotte Smith found that the vast majority offer background checks either with their standard or premium payroll packages, and that the few that do not offer background screening partner with a company that does.

70. Greg Marquis, "Private Security and Surveillance: From the Dossier Society to Database Networks," in *Surveillance as Social Sorting: Privacy, Risk and Automated Discrimination*, ed. David Lyon (London: Routledge, 2002); Micol Seigel, "Violence Work: Policing and Power," *Race & Class* 59, no. 4 (April 1, 2018): 15–33.

71. Charles W. Brackett, "The Rise and Rise of the Criminal Record: Power, Order and Safety in the United States, 1848–1960" (PhD diss., University of Massachusetts at Boston, 2020).

72. Christian Parenti, *Lockdown America: Police and Prisons in the Age of Crisis* (New York: Verso, 1999).

73. Marc Mauer and Meda Chesney-Lind, eds., *Invisible Punishment: The Collateral Consequences of Mass Imprisonment* (New York: New Press, 2002); Kathleen M. Olivares, Velmer S. Burton Jr., and Francis T. Cullen, "Collateral Consequences of a Felony Conviction: A National Study of State Legal Codes 10 Years Later," *Federal Probation* 60, no. 3 (September 1996): 10–17.

74. For a complete inventory of state-sponsored restrictions, see American Bar Association, "National Inventory of Collateral Consequences of Criminal Conviction," accessed March 22, 2025, https://niccc.nationalreentryresourcecenter.org/. See also Beth Avery, Maurice Emsellem, and Phil Hernandez, "Fair Chance Licensing Reform: Opening Pathways for People with Records to Join Licensed Professions," National Employment Law Project, December 18, 2019, https://www.nelp.org/publication/fair-chance-licensing-reform-opening-pathways-for-people-with-records-to-join-licensed-professions/; Margaret Colgate-Love, Patricia M. Harris, and Kimberly S. Keller, "Ex-Offenders Need Not Apply: The Criminal Background Check in Hiring Decisions," *Journal of Contemporary Criminal Justice* 21, no. 1 (February 2005): 6–30.

75. For Hall and collaborators' full definition of moral panic as well as that of Stanley Cohen, on whose definition they built, see Stuart Hall, Chas Critcher, Tony Jefferson, John Clarke, and Brian Roberts, *Policing the Crisis: Mugging, the State and Law and Order* (London: Macmillan, 1993), 20; Stanley Cohen, *Folk Devils and Moral Panics*, 3rd ed. (London: Routledge, 2003).

76. On moral panics driving the use of background checks in the 1980s, see Bill Hebenton and Terry Thomas, *Criminal Records: State, Citizen and the Politics of Protection* (Aldershot, UK: Avebury, 1993), 136–38. On moral panics driving the use of background checks in the 1990s and the rise of state-mandated background checks, see James B. Jacobs and Tamara Crepet, "The Expanding Scope, Use, and Availability of Criminal Records," *New York University Journal of Legislation and Public Policy* 11, no. 2 (2008): 177–214.

77. Sarah Esther Lageson, *Digital Punishment: Privacy, Stigma, and the Harms of Data-Driven Criminal Justice* (New York: Oxford University Press, 2020); Sarah E. Lageson, Elizabeth Webster, and Juan R. Sandoval, "Digitizing and Disclosing Personal Data: The Proliferation of State Criminal Records on the Internet," *Law & Social Inquiry* 46, no. 3 (2021): 1–31.

78. Elbert O. Tiangco and Brian H. Kleiner, "New Developments concerning Negligent Hiring," *Journal of Workplace Learning* 11, no. 1 (January 1, 1999): 16–21; Alonzo Martinez, "From Open Hiring to Negligent Hiring: How to Reduce Risk and Promote Inclusivity," *Forbes*, February 24, 2020, https://www.forbes.com/sites/alonzomartinez/2020/02/24/from-open-hiring -to-negligent-hiring--how-to-reduce-risk-and-promote-inclusivity/?sh=72eb9b9d9f61.

79. Arun Kundnani, *The Muslims Are Coming!: Islamophobia, Extremism, and the Domestic War on Terror* (Brooklyn: Verso Books, 2014); Deepa Kumar, *Islamophobia and the Politics of Empire* (Chicago: Haymarket Books, 2012).

80. It is difficult to precisely quantify a rise in the number of commercial background screening firms over time. Yet many reputable sources mention a notable increase after September 11, 2001. See, for example, *Report of the National Task Force on the Commercial Sale of Criminal Justice Record Information*; Ann Davis, "Firms Dig Deep into Workers' Pasts amid Post-Sept. 11 Security Anxiety, *Wall Street Journal*, March 12, 2002, http://www.wsj.com/articles/SB101 5886922323674160. See also Amy Hurley-Hanson, Cristina Giannantonio, Heidi Carlos, Jessica Harnett, Melanie Jetta, and Madeline Mercier, "The Effects of the Attacks of 9/11 on Organizational Policies, Employee Attitudes and Workers' Psychological States," *Business Faculty Articles and Research* 3 (January 1, 2011): 377–89, which notes that "according to ADP Screening and Selection Services, there has been an increase in background checks between 2001 and 2004 upwards of 65%." Moreover, this article observes, "Pre-screening efforts pre-9/11 were different from the practices in place in a post-9/11 world. According to ChoicePoint, one of the largest employment-screening companies in the country, companies were previously only interested in an applicant's criminal record in their county of residence. Since 9/11, businesses also conduct national criminal-file checks, more detailed background checks into an applicant's history (upwards of ten years) and pre-screening of all applicants for all levels of positions."

81. The term "prison industrial complex" was first used by activist and theorist Mike Davis in "Hell Factories in the Field: A Prison-Industrial Complex," *Nation*, February 20, 1995. The concept is commonly misunderstood as having to do only with economic interests. See, for example, Loïc Wacquant, "Crafting the Neoliberal State: Workfare, Prisonfare, and Social Insecurity," *Sociological Forum* 25, no. 2 (2010): 197–220. Additionally, "economic" is often reductively understood as having to do only with corporations profiting from prison construction and management, the supply of goods to prisons, and the extractive use of imprisoned people's labor. In contrast, activists affiliated with Critical Resistance who first popularized the term have long used it to describe the overlapping and intersecting government and private interests driving the reliance on surveillance, policing, and imprisonment. For elaboration, including how the term differs analytically from phrases such as "carceral state" or "criminal legal system," see, at minute 6:32-9:03, https://www.youtube.com/watch?v=GISJM5HPEDY.

82. Critical Resistance, ed., *Abolition Now!: Ten Years of Strategy and Struggle against the Prison Industrial Complex* (Oakland, CA: AK Press, 2008); Angela Y. Davis, *Are Prisons Obsolete?* (New York: Seven Stories Press, 2003); Eve Goldberg and Linda Evans, *The Prison Industrial Complex and the Global Economy* (Montreal: Kersplebedeb Publishing, May 2003); Julia

Sudbury, *Global Lockdown: Race, Gender, and the Prison-Industrial Complex* (New York: Routledge, 2005); Ruth Wilson Gilmore and Craig Gilmore, "Restating the Obvious," in *Indefensible Space: The Architecture of the National Insecurity State*, ed. Michael Sorkin (New York: Routledge, 2008), 141–61.

83. In *Manufacturing Celebrity: Latino Paparazzi and Women Reporters in Hollywood* (Durham, NC: Duke University Press, 2020), 15, anthropologist Vanessa Díaz similarly adapts the concept military industrial complex to describe how celebrity personas are constantly created and promoted in order to stimulate the consumption of Hollywood media. In this sense, the Hollywood-industrial complex "exists to sustain itself" writes Diaz.

84. David Garland, *The Culture of Control: Crime and Social Order in Contemporary Society* (Chicago: University of Chicago Press, 2001), 26.

85. Critical Resistance (Organization), ed., *Abolition Now!: Ten Years of Strategy and Struggle against the Prison Industrial Complex* (Oakland: AK Press, 2008); Angela Y. Davis, *Are Prisons Obsolete?* (New York: Seven Stories Press, 2003); Rachel Herzing and Justin Piché, *How to Abolish Prisons: Lessons from the Movement Against Imprisonment* (Chicago: Haymarket Books, 2024).

86. Questioning the use of criminal records as a sorting mechanism links this work to critical analyses of classification as a foundational engine of social control. Stanley Cohen, *Visions of Social Control: Crime, Punishment and Classification* (Cambridge, UK: Polity Press, 1985); Michel Foucault, *Discipline and Punish: The Birth of the Prison* (New York: Random House, 1977). More broadly, it connects to studies of classification as a technology with important implications for individual personhood and social relations. See Geoffrey C. Bowker and Susan Leigh Star, *Sorting Things Out: Classification and Its Consequences* (Cambridge, MA: MIT Press, 2000).

87. Edmund T. Gordon, "Cultural Politics of Black Masculinity," *Transforming Anthropology* 6, no. 1–2 (1997): 36–53; Charles R. Hale, *Engaging Contradictions: Theory, Politics, and Methods of Activist Scholarship* (Berkeley: University of California Press, 2008); Edmund T. Gordon, "The Austin School Manifesto: An Approach to the Black or African Diaspora," *Cultural Dynamics* 19, no. 1 (2007): 93–97.

88. This reframing was partly inspired by anthropologist and journalist Cecilia Ballí in her stunning dissertation on the murder of women in Ciudad Juárez, Mexico. Rather than treat the murders as instances of "'true crimes,' where the ultimate goal is an investigation to name the killer," Ballí approaches the murders as "social crimes," shifting the question from "Who killed Esmeralda?" to "Why is it possible that she was killed?" See Cecilia Ballí, "Murdered Women on the Border: Gender, Territory and Power in Ciudad Juárez" (PhD diss., Rice University, 2009), 10.

89. Katherine Beckett, *Making Crime Pay: Law and Order in Contemporary American Politics* (New York: Oxford University Press, 2000).

90. Except for the region's second-largest city, San Bernardino, whose leadership Juan De Lara describes as multiracial and liberal-centrist, the Inland Empire stands apart from the rest of Southern California in terms of political conservatism. At the time of this research (2014–15), the boards of supervisors for both of the Inland Empire's major counties (San Bernardino and Riverside) were—but for one person—made up of all-white, Republican members. See Juan De Lara, *Inland Shift: Race, Space, and Capital in Southern California* (Oakland: University of California Press, 2018), 164–68.

91. For more detail, see Center on Juvenile and Criminal Justice, "California Sentencing Institute: Center on Juvenile and Criminal Justice," accessed January 15, 2024, http://casi.cjcj .org/; United States Census Bureau, "American Community Survey 201," accessed January 15, 2024, https://data.census.gov/table?q=American%20Community%20 Survey%20201.

92. John Husing, "Inland Empire Quarterly Economic Report," Riverside and San Bernadino Counties, October 2016.

93. I never ventured to join the work crew, in part because I felt less comfortable given these were generally all-male crews, compared to work at the office, where most of the staff identified as female. It also seemed, given the outdoor roadside work conditions, that there would be little opportunity to talk in any depth about job seeking or anything else. Given my limited time and energy, I had to prioritize a focus on job market dynamics. Additionally, though, if I am honest, my reluctance had to do with the fact that I had a young child and did not live close by; it would have been a big lift for me to get there by 6:30 a.m. While my decision to forgo this experience thus made sense on multiple levels, in hindsight, I wish I had joined the crew, as it would have been a good way to get to know Hub participants more closely, show solidarity, and more fully understand their experiences.

94. Patricia Hill Collins, *Black Feminist Thought: Knowledge, Consciousness, and the Politics of Empowerment* (New York: Routledge, 2008); Sandra G. Harding, *The Feminist Standpoint Theory Reader: Intellectual and Political Controversies* (New York: Routledge, 2004).

95. Faye V. Harrison, *Outsider Within: Reworking Anthropology in the Global Age* (Urbana: University of Illinois Press, 2008).

96. Beth E Richie, "A Black Feminist Reflection on the Antiviolence Movement," *Signs* 25, no. 4 (2000): 1133–37.

97. Maya J. Berry, Claudia Chávez Argüelles, Shanya Cordis, Sarah Ihmoud, and Elizabeth Velásquez Estrada, "Toward a Fugitive Anthropology: Gender, Race, and Violence in the Field," *Cultural Anthropology* 32, no. 4 (2017): 537–65.

98. Laura Nader, "Up the Anthropologist: Perspectives Gained from Studying Up," in *Reinventing Anthropology*, ed. Dell Hymes (New York: Pantheon Books, 1969), 284–311.

99. Nader, "Up the Anthropologist," 19.

100. For a thoughtful reflection on the political, ethical, and methodological implications of anonymity in ethnographic writing as well as argument for the deliberate rather than default use of pseudonyms, see Carole McGranahan, "The Truths of Anonymity: Ethnographic Credibility and the Problem with Pseudonyms," American Ethnological Society, December 13, 2021.

101. I thank Courtney Morris for this generative insight.

102. In *The Land of Open Graves: Living and Dying on the Migrant Trail* (Oakland: University of California Press, 2015), Jason De Leon helpfully notes that in complex processes involving so many moving and unseeable parts, we can never really know the full story. I also appreciate David Garland's approach to history in *The Culture of Control: Crime and Social Order in Contemporary Society* (Chicago: University of Chicago Press, 2001), 2, in which he explains, "my primary concern is analytical rather than archival."

103. For pointed discussion of the US tendency to attempt to distinguish the worthy from unworthy and emphasize personal responsibility in ways that mask oppressive structural arrangements, see Philippe Bourgois, *In Search of Respect: Selling Crack in El Barrio* (Cambridge: Cambridge University Press, 1995).

1. Looking for Work with a Criminal Record

1. Pierre Bordieu, *Outline of a Theory of Practice*, trans. Richard Nice (Cambridge: Cambridge University Press, 1977).

2. As transformative justice scholar-activist Mimi Kim has observed, our entire society is one in which we "are not given the grace and the space to look in a clear way at the actual consequences of [our] action." See Mimi Kim, *Conversations across Disciplines Panel Discussions | Building Life-Affirming Institutions*, 2022, min. 1:53, https://www.youtube.com/watch?v =wU0VFeYI9vU.

3. Black people constitute 13.7 percent of the US population and only 5 percent of the California population, but 32 percent of prisoners nationally and 28 percent of California prisoners. Latino/as constitute 19.5 percent of the national population and 40 percent of the California population, but 23 percent of those in prison nationally and 45 percent of California prisoners. White people constitute 75 percent of the US population and 36 percent of the California population, but only 31 percent of the national prison population and 20 percent of California prisoners. Nationally, approximately 8 percent of US adults have a felony conviction, but 23 percent of African Americans (and 33 percent of Black men) have a felony conviction. In California, approximately one in five people have a felony conviction, and one in four African Americans. US population data are taken from United States Census Bureau, accessed February 11, 2025, https://www.census.gov/quickfacts/fact/table/US/RHI225223#RHI225223. National estimates of people in prison are taken from Anne E. Carson, *Prisons Report Series: Preliminary Data Release* (Washington, DC: US Department of Justice, Bureau of Justice Statistics, September 2023), https://bjs.ojp.gov/library/publications/prisons-report-series-preliminary-data -release. Estimates of California population and prisoners are taken from Leah Wong, "Updated Data and Charts: Incarceration Stats by Race, Ethnicity, and Gender for All 50 States and D.C.," Prison Policy Initiative, September 27, 2023, https://www.prisonpolicy.org/blog/2023/09/27 /updated_race_data/. Felony conviction data are taken from Sarah Shannon, Christopher Uggen, Jason Schnittker, Melissa Thompson, Sara Wakefield, and Michael Massoglia, "The Growth, Scope, and Spatial Distribution of People with Felony Records in the United States, 1948–2010," *Demography* 54, no. 5 (2017): 1795–818.

4. Prison abolitionist and scholar Ruth Wilson Gilmore has noted that while Black people have been severely and disproportionately affected by mass incarceration, the misperception and misframing of mass incarceration as a phenomenon that has *only* affected Black people impedes our ability to fully grasp the nature of the problem as well as organize broadly for change. See Clément Petitjean, "Prisons and Class Warfare: An Interview with Ruth Wilson Gilmore," Verso, August 2, 2018, https://www.versobooks.com/blogs/3954-prisons-and-class -warfare-an-interview-with-ruth-wilson-gilmore.

5. João H. Costa Vargas, *The Denial of Antiblackness: Multiracial Redemption and Black Suffering* (Minneapolis: University of Minnesota Press, 2018).

6. For a thoughtful discussion of this "spillover" dynamic as well as unchanging antiblackness, see João H. Costa Vargas, *The Denial of Antiblackness: Multiracial Redemption and Black Suffering* (Minneapolis: University of Minnesota Press, 2018), 8–9. For an excellent example of how racialized policies bleed beyond the targeted group, see K-Sue Park's examination of foreclosure in the early United States, showing how racial real estate practices produced general

market and regulatory conditions that detrimentally affected many people. K-Sue Park, "Race, Innovation, and Financial Growth: The Example of Foreclosure," in *Histories of Racial Capitalism*, ed. Destin Jenkins and Justin Leroy (New York: Columbia University Press, 2021), 27–51.

7. Magnus Lofstrom, Joseph Hayes, Brandon Martin, and Deepak Premkumar with research support from Alexandria Gumbs, "Racial Disparities in Law Enforcement Stops," Public Policy Institute of California, October 2021, https://www.ppic.org/publication/racial-disparities-in -law-enforcement-stops/; William J. Sabol and Thaddeus L. Johnson, "Justice System Disparities: Black-White National Imprisonment Trends, 2000 to 2020," Council on Criminal Justice, September 2022, https://counciloncj.foleon.com/reports/racial-disparities/national-trends ?campaign_id=9&emc=edit_nn_20221031&instance_id=76126&nl=the-morning&regi_id =98610377&segment_id=111572&te=1&user_id=83ab454fd8027ba221ecce9932d1636d; Matthew Clair, *Privilege and Punishment: How Race and Class Matter in Criminal Court* (Princeton, NJ: Princeton University Press, 2020); Marie Gottschalk, *Caught: The Prison State and the Lockdown of American Politics* (Princeton, NJ: Princeton University Press, 2015).

8. In this section, I draw heavily on these excellent political economic histories: Ruth Wilson Gilmore, *Golden Gulag: Prisons, Surplus, Crisis, and Opposition in Globalizing California* (Berkeley: University of California Press, 2007); Thomas Patterson, *From Acorns to Warehouses: Historical Political Economy of Southern California's Inland Empire* (Walnut Creek, CA: Routledge, 2014); Juan De Lara, *Inland Shift: Race, Space, and Capital in Southern California* (Oakland: University of California Press, 2018).

9. In addition to Kaiser Steel, so too were shuttered the International Paper plant in Siskiyou County (six hundred workers) and General Motors auto plant in Fremont (sixty-five hundred workers). Michael Bernick, "After Plant Closings: A Labor Day Story," *Forbes*, August 28, 2018, https://www.forbes.com/sites/michaelbernick/2018/08/28/after-plant-closings-a-labor-day -story/.

10. Political economist Thomas Patterson describes how the combined layoffs resulting from the closure of the Norton and March Air Force Bases affected 5 to 7 percent of region's total population, driving unemployment from less than 5 percent in 1990 to almost 15 percent in 1993. Patterson, *From Acorns to Warehouses*, 212.

11. Patterson, *From Acorns to Warehouses*.

12. Thomas Piketty, *Capital in the Twenty-First Century* (Cambridge, MA: Harvard University Press, 2014); João H. Costa Vargas, *Catching Hell in the City of Angels: Life and Meanings of Blackness in South Central Los Angeles* (Minneapolis: University of Minnesota Press, 2006), 36.

13. Passed in 1978, Proposition 13 was touted as protection for homeowners from rising property taxes, but critics say the proposition's major beneficiaries were corporate property owners whose industrial or commercial properties sold less frequently. As Patterson details, the dramatic reduction in county income from property taxes also forced counties to "embark on a continual quest for new revenues," increasing sales taxes and the search for the most profitable land uses. This led to a proliferation of auto malls and big-box retail stores coupled with the disappearance of small businesses, increasing the control of state government and land developers over county finances. Patterson, *From Acorns to Warehouses*, 212–20. As Mike Davis has emphasized, white suburbanites also implicitly understood the measure as a way to stall the encroachment of inner-city populations. See Mike Davis, *City of Quartz: Excavating the Future in Los Angeles*, (London: Verso, 1990), 182–86. For a discussion of the impact on poor communities, see Gilmore, *Golden Gulag*, 42–43.

14. With some variation, the Inland Empire has ranked near the top of foreclosure rates in the country since 2008. Deirdre Pfeiffer, "African Americans' Search for 'More for Less' and 'Peace of Mind' on the Exurban Frontier," *Urban Geography* 33, no. 1 (2012): 64–90; Kfir Mordechay, "Inland Boom and Bust: Race, Place, and the Lasting Consequences of the Southern California Housing Bubble," Othering & Belonging Institute, December 12, 2019, https://belonging.berkeley.edu/inland-boom-and-bust.

15. Patterson, *From Acorns to Warehouses*, 221.

16. De Lara, *Inland Shift*, especially chapter 2.

17. Jason Struna, Kevin Curwin, Edwin Elias, Ellen Reese, Tony Roberts, and Elizabeth Bingle, "Unsafe and Unfair: Labor Conditions in the Warehouse Industry," *Policy Matters* 5, no. 2 (2012), 1–12. For a description of a 390 percent increase in temporary employment between 1990 and 2006, see De Lara, *Inland Shift*, 102–3. Doubly egregious, temporary employment agencies benefit from tax credits meant to assist marginalized workers, even though the jobs they provide often do not convert to permanent employment. See Emily Corwin, "A Tax Credit Was Meant to Help Marginalized Workers Get Permanent Jobs. Instead It's Subsidizing Temp Work," *ProPublica*, August 23, 2022, https://www.propublica.org/article/work-opportunity-tax-credit-temp-permanent-employment.

18. The tremendous pollution to which Inland Empire residents are subject is due in large part to the logistics industry. Black and Latino/a residents situated closest to transportation corridors have disproportionately borne the brunt. In 2008, the South Coast Air Quality Management District found that 50 percent of US residents who breathed unhealthy levels of diesel exhaust particulate matter resided within the Inland Empire basin. De Lara, *Inland Shift*, 56.

19. The Gilmores use "iron-fisted abandonment" to describe the twofold blow of capital, state, and nongovernmental institutional neglect along with targeted criminalization. Ruth Wilson Gilmore and Craig Gilmore, "Restating the Obvious," in *Indefensible Space: The Architecture of the National Insecurity State*, ed. Michael Sorkin (New York: Routledge, 2008), 154. For other helpful elaborations of these concepts, see Ruth Wilson Gilmore and Craig Gilmore, "Beyond Bratton," in *Policing the Planet: Why the Policing Crisis Led to Black Lives Matter*, ed. Jordan T. Camp and Christina Heatherton (London: Verso, 2016), 173–99; Ruth Wilson Gilmore, "Forgotten Places," in *Engaging Contradictions: Theory, Politics, and Methods of Activist Scholarship*, ed. Charles R. Hale (Berkeley: University of California Press, 2008); Laura Pulido, "Flint, Environmental Racism, and Racial Capitalism," *Capitalism Nature Socialism* 27, no. 3 (July 2, 2016): 1–16.

20. Gilmore, *Golden Gulag*; Elizabeth Hinton, *From the War on Poverty to the War on Crime: The Making of Mass Incarceration in America* (Cambridge, MA: Harvard University Press, 2016).

21. The number of California prisoners rose from approximately 35,000 in 1982 to 135,000 in 1995. Cary J. Rudman and John Berthelsen, *An Analysis of the California Department of Corrections' Planning Process: Strategies to Reduce the Cost of Incarcerating State Prisoners* (Sacramento, CA: Assembly Publications Office, 1991), cited in Gilmore, *Golden Gulag*, 5.

22. Kimberle Crenshaw, "Mapping the Margins: Intersectionality, Identity Politics and Violence against Women of Color," *Stanford Law Review* 43, no. 6 (1991): 1241–99; Anna J. Cooper, *A Voice from the South: By a Black Woman of the South* (Chapel Hill: University of North Carolina Press, 2017).

23. Reuben Jonathan Miller and Forrest Stuart, "Carceral Citizenship: Race, Rights and Responsibility in the Age of Mass Supervision," *Theoretical Criminology* 21, no. 4 (November 2017): 532–48.

24. Ellis P. Monk, Michael H. Esposito, and Hedwig Lee, "Beholding Inequality: Race, Gender, and Returns to Physical Attractiveness in the United States," *American Journal of Sociology* 127, no. 1 (July 2021): 194–241; Deborah L. Rhode, *The Beauty Bias: The Injustice of Appearance in Life and Law* (Oxford: Oxford University Press, 2010). See also the interview with criminologist Scott H. Decker on the importance of weight, skin color, height, and smiling versus not smiling for designing effective tester studies. Scott H. Decker, "Consequences of a Prison Record for Employment: How Do Race, Ethnicity & Gender Factor In?," National Institute of Justice, February 1, 2014, https://nij.ojp.gov/media/video/17956.

25. For a provocative discussion of the role of law in manipulating and defining personhood, see Colin Dyan, *The Law Is a White Dog: How Legal Rituals Make and Unmake Persons* (Princeton, NJ: Princeton University Press, 2011).

26. Aliya Saperstein and Andrew M. Penner, "The Race of a Criminal Record: How Incarceration Colors Racial Perceptions," *Social Problems* 57, no. 1 (February 1, 2010): 92–113.

27. Cathy Cohen, "Deviance as Resistance: A New Research Agenda for the Study of Black Politics," *DuBois Review* 1, no. 1 (2004): 27–45.

28. As De Lara notes in *Inland Shift* (167), many Inland Empire cities have supported and passed anti-immigrant laws, including laws requiring all local businesses to check the legal status of new hires through the federal government's E-Verify system.

29. There has long been confusion among employers, advocates, and even lawyers about whether the seven years are counted from the date of arrest, conviction, or final disposition (which would include release from prison), and relatedly, which events job candidates are legally required or advised to disclose. This matter was recently settled: screening firms cannot disclose and employers cannot consider convictions older than seven years from the date of disposition (conviction) for cases that did not result in incarceration in jail or prison, or seven years from the date of release from incarceration for those that did. See *Kemp v. Superior Court* (4th App. Dist., 2022) (86 Cal. App. 5th 981), in which the appellate court clarified that seven years from "parole" runs from the date of parole, explaining in the process that seven years from "release" runs from release from confinement.

30. Shawn D. Bushway, Brian G. Vegetabile, Nidhi Kalra, Lee Remi, and Greg Baumann, "Providing Another Chance: Resetting Recidivism Risk in Criminal Background Checks," RAND Corporation, January 6, 2022, 9, https://www.rand.org/pubs/research_reports /RRA1360-1.html. As the authors explain, "Current Green-based approaches applied by employers are very basic, empirically guided Burgess scales. For example, the type of conviction and the time since conviction can be combined in a matrix to produce a recommendation about whether to hire someone." By "Green-based," the authors refer to the three factors identified by the EEOC in 1987 that employers may use to consider risk: the nature of the job, type of conviction, and time since the last conviction. These factors were based on a 1975 Title VII lawsuit, *Buck Green et al. v. Missouri Pacific Railroad Company*.

31. Originally enacted in 1994, California's Three Strikes law required defendants convicted of any new felony who had previously been convicted of a serious felony to be sentenced to state prison for twice the term otherwise provided for the crime. As long as one of the first two strikes was classified as serious or violent, the third strike, however minor, required a minimum sentence of twenty-five years to life. In 2014, two voter-approved initiatives revised the law to give judges more discretion while reducing penalties for lower-level drug and theft-related crimes.

32. For example, the 1996 Personal Responsibility and Work Opportunity Reconciliation Act repealed the open-ended entitlement to benefits of the Aid to Families with Dependent Children program, replacing it with a time-limited benefit program with mandatory work requirements for most recipients.

33. Under the Gambling Control Act, Legal Code 19859 (https://leginfo.legislature.ca.gov /faces/codes_displaySection.xhtml?lawCode=BPC&sectionNum=19859), the reasons for potential denial of license include (among others):

"(c) (1) Except as provided in paragraph (2), conviction of a felony, including conviction by a federal court or court in another state for a crime that would constitute a felony if committed in California.

"(2) A conviction of a felony for the possession of cannabis, the facts of which would not constitute a felony or misdemeanor under California law on the date the application for a license is submitted, shall not constitute a basis to deny a license pursuant to this section.

"(d) Conviction of the applicant for any misdemeanor involving dishonesty or moral turpitude within the 10-year period immediately preceding the submission of the application, unless the applicant has been granted a relief . . ."

34. Adie Tomer Berube, Elizabeth Kneebone, Robert Puentes, and Alan Berube, "Missed Opportunity: Transit and Jobs in Metropolitan America," Brookings, May 12, 2011. https://www .brookings.edu/research/missed-opportunity-transit-and-jobs-in-metropolitan-america/. A 2024 report notes that 30 percent of Inland Empire workers—approximately four hundred thousand—commute from the Inland Empire to coastal areas. Manfred Keil, Robert Kleinhenz, and Fernando Lozano, *State of the Region: The Inland Empire 2024* (Riverside, CA: Inland Empire Economic Partnership, January 24, 2024, https://ieep.com/state-of-the-region/state-of-the -region-the-inland-empire-2024/.

35. This limit was somewhat flexible, but served as a general benchmark after which special permission had to be granted to continue working on the Hub's transitional work crew.

36. De Lara, *Inland Shift*, 120–26.

37. For further discussion of this in-prison firefighting program and critical analysis of the struggles encountered by its graduates to find work as free-world firefighters, see Melissa Burch, "Fit to Protect: Race, Vulnerability, and the Risk Politics of California Firefighting," *Current Anthropology* 65, no. 4 (August 2024): 724–47. Following the 2025 fires in Los Angeles, a bill (AB 247) was introduced proposing to increase the pay rate for incarcerated hand crew members to $19 per hour while assigned to an active fire incident. https://leginfo.legislature.ca.gov /faces/billTextClient.xhtml?bill_id=202520260AB247.

38. Bernard E. Harcourt, "Risk as a Proxy for Race," Working Paper No. 323 (University of Chicago Public Law & Legal Theory, 2010), https://chicagounbound.uchicago.edu/cgi /viewcontent.cgi?article=1265&context=public_law_and_legal_theory; Harry J. Holzer, Steven Raphael, and Michael A. Stoll, "How Willing Are Employers to Hire Ex-Offenders?," *Focus* 23, no. 2 (Summer 2004): 40–43.

39. Petitjean, "Prisons and Class Warfare."

40. Dierdre A Royster, *Race and the Invisible Hand: How White Networks Exclude Black Men from Blue-Collar Jobs* (Berkeley: University of California Press, 2003).

41. Pager, "The Mark of a Criminal Record, " 39; Devah Pager, *Marked: Race, Crime, and Finding Work in an Era of Mass Incarceration* (Chicago: University of Chicago Press, 2007).

42. Pager, *Marked: Race, Crime, and Finding Work in an Era of Mass Incarceration* (Chicago: University of Chicago Press, 2007): 112–15.

43. Devah Pager, Bart Bonikowski, and Bruce Western, "Discrimination in a Low-Wage Labor Market: A Field Experiment," *American Sociological Review* 74, no. 5 (October 1, 2009): 777–99.

44. Marianne Bertrand and Sendhil Mullainathan, "Are Emily and Greg More Employable Than Lakisha and Jamal? A Field Experiment on Labor Market Discrimination," *American Economic Review* 94, no. 4 (September 2004): 991–1013; Michael Gaddis, "Discrimination in the Credential Society: An Audit Study of Race and College Selectivity in the Labor Market," *Social Forces* 93, no. 4 (2015): 1451–79; Tracy R. Whitaker, "Banging on a Locked Door: The Persistent Role of Racial Discrimination in the Workplace," *Social Work in Public Health* 34, no. 1 (January 2, 2019): 22–27.

45. Valerie Wilson and William Darity Jr., "Understanding Black-White Disparities in Labor Market Outcomes Requires Models That Account for Persistent Discrimination and Unequal Bargaining Power," Economic Policy Institute, March 25, 2022, https://www.epi .org/unequalpower/publications/understanding-black-white-disparities-in-labor-market -outcomes/.

46. Whitaker, "Banging on a Locked Door"; Olugbenga Ajilore, "The Persistent Black-White Unemployment Gap Is Built into the Labor Market," Center for American Progress, September 28, 2020, https://www.americanprogress.org/article/persistent-black-white-unemployment -gap-built-labor-market/; Wilson and Darity, "Understanding Black-White Disparities in Labor Market Outcomes."

47. As described earlier, screening firms in California cannot disclose and employers cannot consider convictions older than seven years from the date of disposition (conviction) for cases that did not result in incarceration in jail or prison, or seven years from the date of release from incarceration for those that did. However, whereas basic third-party background checks that rely entirely on court data reveal only the date of conviction, some screening firms take extra steps to search prison release and parole dates. Meanwhile, employers who choose not to use third-party screeners may conduct their own internet-based searches of publicly available court data, which often reveals the very kinds of events (arrests along with dismissed and older convictions) that third-party screeners are legally barred from reporting and that employers are barred from considering. Thus depending on the method used to collect criminal background information, some job seekers with relatively serious convictions and who are recently released from prison can benefit from the "seven-year rule."

48. My analysis in this section benefited from conversations with Shana Agid and Priya Kandaswamy.

49. Gillian Harkins, *Virtual Pedophilia: Sex Offender Profiling and U.S. Security Culture* (Durham, NC: Duke University Press, 2020); Roger Lancaster, *Sex Panic and the Punitive State* (Berkeley: University of California Press, 2011); Judith Levine and Erica Meiners, *The Feminist and the Sex Offender: Confronting Sexual Harm, Ending State Violence* (New York: Verso, 2020).

50. Amanda Y. Agan, "Sex Offender Registries: Fear without Function?," *Journal of Law & Economics* 54, no. 1 (2011): 207–39; Rose Corrigan, "Making Meaning of Megan's Law," *Law & Social Inquiry* 31, no. 2 (June 1, 2006): 267–312.

51. Until a reform announced in March 2015, all people convicted of sex-related crimes in California were prohibited from living or working within two thousand feet of a park or school under a voter-approved ballot initiative called Jessica's Law.

52. Jonathan Xavier Inda, *Targeting Immigrants: Government, Technology, and Ethics* (Hoboken, NJ: Wiley-Blackwell, 2005).

53. Roger Przybylsi, "Recidivism of Adult Sexual Offenders," US Department of Justice, Office of Justice Programs, July 2015, https://www.ojp.gov/ncjrs/virtual-library/abstracts /recidivism-adult-sexual-offenders.

54. Erica Meiners, "Never Innocent: Feminist Trouble with Sex Offender Registries and Protection in a Prison Nation," *Meridians* 9, no. 2 (2009): 31–62, http://www.jstor.org/stable /40338782; Beth E. Richie, *Arrested Justice: Black Women, Violence, and America's Prison Nation* (New York: NYU Press, 2012); Cassandra Shaylor and Erica Meiners, "Resisting Gendered Carceral Landscapes," in *Women Exiting Prison: Critical Essays on Gender, Post-Release Support and Survival*, ed. Marie Segrave and Carlton Bree (New York: Routledge, 2013), 181–99.

55. Levine and Meiners, *The Feminist and the Sex Offender*.

56. George Yancey, *Who Is White?: Latinos, Asians, and the New Black/Nonblack Divide* (Boulder, CO: Lynne Rienner Publishers, 2003), cited in Costa Vargas, *The Denial of Antiblackness*, 42.

57. Cathy Cohen, "Punks, Bulldraggers, and Welfare Queens: The Radical Potential of Queer Politics?," *GLQ: A Journal of Lesbian and Gay Studies* 3, no. 4 (May 1, 1997): 437–65; Greta R. Krippner and Daniel Hirschman, "The Person of the Category: The Pricing of Risk and the Politics of Classification in Insurance and Credit," *Theory and Society* 51, no. 5 (2022): 685–727.

2. The Making of Common Sense

1. National Advisory Commission on Criminal Justice Standards and Goals, *A National Strategy to Reduce Crime* (Washington, DC: Law Enforcement Assistance Administration, US Department of Justice, 1973), cited in Donald C. Atkinson, Abraham Fenster, and Abraham S. Blumberg, "Employer Attitudes toward Work-Release Programs and the Hiring of Offenders," *Correctional Psychologist* 3, no. 4 (December 1976): 335–44.

2. Afia Bonner, Sarah Flamm, Jacob Lopez, and Charlie Mintz, "Fair-Chance Hiring in Action: A Study of San Francisco's Centralized Conviction History Review Program," Stanford Public Policy Program, March 14, 2016.

3. Jennifer Hickes Lundquist, Devah Pager, and Eiko Strader, "Does a Criminal Past Predict Worker Performance? Evidence from One of America's Largest Employers," *Social Forces* 96, no. 3 (March 1, 2018): 1039–68.

4. *Workers with Criminal Records: A Survey by the Society for Human Resource Management and the Charles Koch Institute* (Alexandria, VA: SHRM, 2018), https://www.prisonpolicy.org /scans/cki_shrm/report.pdf. See also SHRM and Koch Institute, "Getting Talent Back to Work—2021 Report," 2021, https://www.shrm.org/topics-tools/research/getting-talent-back -to-work-2021-report.

5. David F. Greenberg, "Recidivism as Radioactive Decay," *Journal of Research in Crime and Delinquency* 15, no. 1 (1978): 124–25; Carl M. Harris, Ali. R. Kaylan, and Michael D. Maltz, "Advances in Recidivism Measurement," in *Mathematical Frontiers in Criminology*, ed. James A. Fox

(New York: Academic Press, 1981); Pamela Lattimore, Joanna R. Baker, and Ann D. Witte, "The Influence of Probability on Risky Choice," *Journal of Economic Behavior & Organization* 17, no. 3 (1992): 377–400; Michael D. Maltz, *Recidivism* (Chicago: University of Chicago Press, 1984); Peter Schmidt and Ann Dryden Witte, *Predicting Recidivism Using Survival Models* (New York: Springer, 1988); Pamela K. Lattimore, Christy A. Visher, and Richard L. Linster, "Predicting Rearrest for Violence among Serious Youthful Offenders," *Journal of Research in Crime and Delinquency* 32, no. 1 (1995): 54–83; Alfred Blumstein and Kiminori Nakamura, "Redemption in the Presence of Widespread Criminal Background Checks," *Criminology* 47, no. 2 (2009): 327–60; Megan C. Kurlychek, Robert Brame, and Shawn D. Bushway, "Enduring Risk? Old Criminal Records and Predictions of Future Criminal Involvement," *Crime & Delinquency* 53, no. 1 (2007): 64–83; Patricia M. Harris and Kimberly S. Keller, "Ex-Offenders Need Not Apply: The Criminal Background Check in Hiring Decisions," *Journal of Contemporary Criminal Justice* 21, no. 1 (February 1, 2005): 6–30.

6. Neal Shover, *Great Pretenders: Pursuits and Careers of Persistent Thieves* (Boulder, CO: Westview Press, 1996); Christopher Uggen, "Work as a Turning Point in the Life Course of Criminals: A Duration Model of Age, Employment, and Recidivism," *American Sociological Review* 65, no. 4 (August 2000): 529–46.

7. Brent W. Roberts, Peter D. Harms, Avshalom Caspi, and Terri E. Moffitt, "Predicting the Counterproductive Employee in a Child-to-Adult Prospective Study," *Journal of Applied Psychology* 92, no. 5 (2007): 1427–36; Roberto Concepcion Jr., "Need Not Apply: The Racial Disparate Impact of Pre-Employment Criminal Background Checks," *Georgetown Journal on Poverty Law & Policy* 19, no. 2 (2012): 231–53.

8. Karol Lucken and Lucille M. Ponte, "A Just Measure of Forgiveness: Reforming Occupational Licensing Regulations for Ex-Offenders Using BFOQ Analysis," *Law & Policy* 30, no. 1 (2008): 46–72; James A. Merchant and John A. Lundell, "Workplace Violence Intervention Research Workshop, April 5–7, 2000, Washington, DC. Background, Rationale, and Summary," *American Journal of Preventive Medicine* 20, no. 2 (February 2001): 135–40; Erika Harrell, *Black Victims of Violent Crime* (Washington, DC: US Department of Justice, Office of Justice Programs, August 2007), https://www.ojp.gov/ncjrs/virtual-library/abstracts/black-victims-violent-crime.

9. Mark Ames, *Going Postal: Rage, Murder, and Rebellion: From Reagan's Workplaces to Clinton's Columbine and Beyond* (Brooklyn: Soft Skull, 2005); Jeremy Milloy, *Blood, Sweat, and Fear: Violence at Work in the North American Auto Industry, 1960–80* (Champaign: University of Illinois Press, 2017).

10. The Bureau of Labor Statistics published a 1996 paper (chrome-extension://efaidnbmn nnibpcajpcglclefindmkaj/https://www.bls.gov/mlr/1996/11/art4full.pdf) stating, "Firms implementing drug testing programs also can be distinguished by type of industry. The 1989 Conference Board survey showed that three-fourths of the companies with drug testing programs were manufacturers or gas and electric utilities, while nearly half of the companies that reported not having a drug testing program were in banking, insurance, and other financial service industries. The 1988 BLS survey also showed that worksites in mining, communications, public utilities, and transportation were most likely to have testing programs, reaffirming the findings reported by the Conference Board." A 2021 survey by the bureau showed similar results (https://www.bls.gov/brs/2021-results.htm#:~:text=Data%20are%20available%20on%20 how,for%20some%20or%20all%20employees). Evidence also suggests that Black workers are

more likely to work in places that have a drug testing policy, and Black and Latino/a workers are more likely to be fired than white workers if they test positive. Sehun Oh, James Hodges, Christopher Salas-Wright, Brianna Smith, and Trenette Clark Goings, "Ethnoracial Differences in Workplace Drug Testing and Policies on Positive Drug Tests in the United States," *Drug and Alcohol Dependence* 247 (June 1, 2023).

11. Bruce E. May, "The Character Component of Occupational Licensing Laws: A Continuing Barrier to the Ex-Felon's Employment Opportunities," *North Dakota Law Review* 71, no. 1 (1995): 187–210; Deborah L. Rhode, "Virtue and the Law: The Good Moral Character Requirement in Occupational Licensing, Bar Regulation, and Immigration Proceedings," *Law & Social Inquiry* 43, no. 3 (July 2018): 1027–58.

12. SEARCH Group, *Report of the National Task Force on the Criminal Backgrounding of America* (Sacramento, CA: National Consortium for Justice Information and Statistics, 2005), 2, offers nine factors motivating employers, volunteer organizations, and others to conduct background checks, including public safety, compliance with legal requirements, limitation of liability, conditions of doing business, protection of vulnerable populations, customer assurance, avoidance of loss of business, fear of business loss, or public or media backlash over an incident caused by an individual with a past record to regain public or customer trust.

13. Barry W. Nixon and Kim M. Kerr, *Background Screening and Investigations: Managing Hiring Risk from the HR and Security Perspectives* (Oxford, UK: Butterworth-Heinemann, 2008), foreword.

14. "Background Screening—Past, Present and Future," PBSA, December 2004.

15. For a discussion of the impact of advanced computer systems such as the IBM 360 series, see Bill Hebenton and Terry Thomas, *Criminal Records: State, Citizen and the Politics of Protection* (Aldershot, UK: Avebury, 1993), 29.

16. In *Government of Paper: The Materiality of Bureaucracy in Urban Pakistan* (Berkeley: University of California Press, 2012), anthropologist Matthew Hull argues for an understanding of documents as actively mediated by people in ways that influence forms of association and produce social divisions. Additionally, while Hull shows that how documents circulate is likely as important as what they say, he cautions that the rhetoric of technological revolution often overstates the significance of electronic technologies, which supplement and transform (rather than replace) paper-based systems, rest on similar logics, and aim to achieve similar ends.

17. My analysis owes much to legal scholar Alessandro Corda's excellent critical history of criminal record access. I do not quite share Corda's conclusion, however, that "the current wide dissemination of conviction records for non–criminal justice purposes is not the product of deliberate decisions about punishment principles, sentencing policy or crime prevention" but instead "resulted from an unplanned interplay of uncoordinated factors." Alessandro Corda, "More Justice and Less Harm: Reinventing Access to Criminal History Records," *Howard Law Journal* 60, no. 1 (2016), 6.

18. I thank Shana Agid for this apt metaphor as well as for several insightful comments that helped to improve the argumentation in this chapter. According to Allied Market Research, "Employment Screening Services Market Size & Trends 2033," Allied Analytics LLP, October 2024, https://www.alliedmarketresearch.com/employment-screening-services-market, "the global employment screening services market was valued at $4.95 billion in 2020, and is projected to reach $9.92 billion by 2028, growing at a CAGR of 9.2% from 2021 to 2028."

19. Jason De Leon's emphasis on collective agency in *The Land of Open Graves: Living and Dying on the Migrant Trail* (Oakland: University of California Press, 2015) is helpful here. Though my analysis does not share De Leon's emphasis on the role of nonhuman actants, I find productive the idea that in any big phenomenon, the effect of any one actor's activity will depend on how other actors respond, interfere, collaborate, or cooperate.

20. Charles W. Brackett, "The Rise and Rise of the Criminal Record: Power, Order and Safety in the United States, 1848–1960" (PhD diss., University of Massachusetts at Boston, 2020).

21. Greg Marquis, "Private Security and Surveillance: From the Dossier Society to Database Networks," in *Surveillance as Social Sorting: Privacy, Risk and Automated Discrimination*, ed. David Lyon (London: Routledge, 2002). See also David A. Sklansky, "The Private Police," *UCLA Law Review* 46, no. 1165 (1999): 1212–14; Gary Potter, "The History of Policing in the United States," *Eastern Kentucky University Police Studies Online*, 2013, https://www.denvertask force.org/wp-content/uploads/2023/02/the_history_of_policing_in_the_united_states .pdf; Micol Siegel, "Violence Work: Policing and Power," *Race & Class* 59, no. 4 (April 1, 2018): 15–33.

22. Brackett, "The Rise and Rise of the Criminal Record," 197.

23. Corda, "More Justice and Less Harm," 12.

24. Kenneth C. Laudon, *Dossier Society: Value Choices in the Design of National Information Systems* (New York: Columbia University Press, 1986), cited in Corda, "More Justice and Less Harm," 13.

25. Hebenton and Terry, *Criminal Records*, 28.

26. Lee O. Lacy, "Security, Loyalty, and Politics in a Free Society," *American Intelligence Journal* 38, no. 2 (2021): 131–35; S. Sheldon Weinhaus, "The Federal Employee Loyalty-Security Program: A Critique," *Washington University Law Quarterly* 1956, no. 3 (January 1, 1956): 353–72.

27. For an example of a large professional organization that argued for criminal background checks and exclusions, see Homer D. Crotty, "Standards for Bar Examiners: The Time Has Come for Substantial Reform," *Americn Bar Association Journal* 41, no. 2 (February 1955): 120, cited in Brackett, "The Rise and Rise of the Criminal Record," 236.

28. Occupational licensing first surged in the United States from 1890 to 1910 for professions related to health and law, and again following World War II with the emergence of a more service-oriented economy. Since their inception, licensing boards have excluded people with criminal records in their criteria. Critics question licensing's purported aim to standardize the quality of professional services and protect public safety, arguing that licensing negatively impacts consumers and exacerbates overall wage inequality even as it increases wages for those who are licensed. Dick Carpenter, Lisa Knepper, Kyle Sweetland, and Jennifer McDonald, "License to Work: A National Study of Burdens from Occupational Licensing," Institute for Justice, November 2017, https://ij.org/report/license-work-2/; Morris Kleiner, "A License for Protection: Why Are States Regulating More and More Occupations?," CATO Institute, 2006; Daniel J. Smith and Noah J. Trudeau, "The Undertaker's Cut: Challenging the Rational Basis for Casket Licensure," *Journal of Private Enterprise* 34, no. 2 (June 22, 2019): 23–41; Morris M. Kleiner and Evgeny Vorotnikov, "At What Cost? State and National Estimates of the Economic Costs of Occupational Licensing," Institute for Justice, November 2018, https://ij.org/wp

-content/uploads/2018/11/Licensure_Report_WEB.pdf; Department of the Treasury Office of Economic Policy, Department of Labor, and Council of Economic Advisers, "Occupational Licensing: A Framework for Policymakers," White House, 2015, https://obamawhitehouse .archives.gov/sites/default/files/docs/licensing_report_final_nonembargo.pdf.

29. For readers who may not understand how insurance premiums generally work, insurers sort individuals or businesses into classes with others whose propensity to experience an adverse event is roughly shared. These classification systems provide a starting point to identify risks facing a business and its employees, the kinds of coverages needed given the industry, and to determine which people, places, or events should be excluded from coverage. The higher a businesses' risk level and the more events and persons underwritten, the higher the premium. See Kenneth S. Abraham, *Distributing Risk: Insurance, Legal Theory, and Public Policy* (New Haven, CT: Yale University Press, 1986), cited in, Greta R. Krippner and Daniel Hirschman, "The Person of the Category: The Pricing of Risk and the Politics of Classification in Insurance and Credit," *Theory and Society* 51, no. 5 (2022): 685–727.

30. Marcel Frym, "The Treatment of Recidivists," *Journal of Criminal Law, Criminology, and Police Science* 47, no. 1 (1956): 1–7.

31. Frym, "The Treatment of Recidivists," 3.

32. The doctrine governing employer responsibility in the early 1900s was that of *respondeat superior*, which held that employers had a basic responsibility for the actions of their employees as a direct result of, and in the course of their employment. For example, an employee committing a prank on another employee and injuring them in the process wasn't covered because pranking isn't part of the job. Also important was question of whether an employee's dangerous character was or ought to have been known by the employer—whether or not the incident could have been foreseen. For example, in one important case under respondeat superior (*Country Club of Jackson v. Turner*), "The first count is drafted upon the 'theory that the offending servant was of dangerous character and ungovernable temper, which was known or ought to have been known by appellant, and the ground upon which the plaintiff predicated liability was the alleged negligence of defendant in employing and retaining the servant. The second count adopts the theory that the said servant, Cobb, was a vice principal and committed the assault while in the scope of his employment and in furtherance of the business of the club.' As such, it was both *known* that the offender was dangerous, and the actions were taken in the direct scope of their employment—Country Club of Jackson v. Turner, 192 Miss. 510 (Miss. 1941)." See further information in Martin R. Loftus, "Employer's Duty to Know Deficiencies of Employees," 1967, 8.

33. Fleming v. Bronfin, 80 A.2d 915 (D.C. Mun. Ct. App. 1951). Notably, this "duty of care" is also triggered by the government enactment of statutory or licensing requirements, obliging employers within the governed industry. See Harris and Keller, "Ex-Offenders Need Not Apply." See also John C. North, "Responsibility of Employers for the Actions of Their Employees: The Negligent Hiring Theory of Liability," *Chicago-Kent Law Review* 53, no. 3 (January, 1977): 720.

34. Kathleen M. Olivares, Velmer S. Burton Jr., and Francis T. Cullen, "The Collateral Consequences of a Felony Conviction: A National Study of State Legal Codes 10 Years Later," *Federal Probation* 60, no. 3 (September 1996): 10.

35. Margaret Colgate Love, Jenny Roberts, and Wayne Logan, *Collateral Consequences of Criminal Convictions: Law, Policy and Practice* (Washington, DC: Thomas West, 2022), 17. *Collateral Consequences* describes how the loss of status on which these disqualifications depend

derives from the medieval idea of "civil death," through which a person's political and property rights were permanently removed. This idea was embraced as an aspect of English penal practices that utilized severe and socially degrading punishments to separate criminals from society as well as expose them to public shame and ridicule. Although penologists in the United States came to believe in the social reintegration of people convicted of crimes after having served their sentence, "civil death played a significant role in the Colonies and survived in many state systems well into the 20th century as an integral part of criminal punishment." See also Gabriel "Jack" Chin, "The New Civil Death: Rethinking Punishment in the Era of Mass Conviction," *University of Pennsylvania Law Review* 160 (April 2012): 1789–833.

36. Love, Roberts, and Logan, *Collateral Consequences of Criminal Convictions*, 15–16. See also Nora V. Demleitner, "Preventing Internal Exile: The Need for Restrictions on Collateral Sentencing Consequences Symposium: The New Legal Scholarship of Sentencing," *Stanford Law & Policy Review* 11, no. 1 (1999): 155.

37. Love, Roberts, and Logan, *Collateral Consequences of Criminal Convictions*, 18n8; Joseph Fishkin, "The Anti-Bottleneck Principle in Employment Discrimination Law," *Washington University Law Review* 91, no. 6 (January 1, 2014): 1467n139.

38. Elizabeth Hinton, *From the War on Poverty to the War on Crime: The Making of Mass Incarceration in America* (Cambridge, MA: Harvard University Press, 2016); Joy James, ed., *Warfare in the American Homeland* (Durham, NC: Duke University Press, 2007).

39. Jordan T. Camp, *Incarcerating the Crisis: Freedom Struggles and the Rise of the Neoliberal State* (Oakland: University of California Press, 2016); Dylan Rodríguez, *Forced Passages: Imprisoned Radical Intellectuals and the US Prison Regime* (Minneapolis: University of Minnesota Press, 2006).

40. Christian Parenti, *Lockdown America: Police and Prisons in the Age of Crisis* (New York: Verso, 1999), 7.

41. Parenti, *Lockdown America*, chapter 1.

42. Marquis, "Private Security and Surveillance."

43. David Garland, *The Culture of Control: Crime and Social Order in Contemporary Society* (Chicago: University of Chicago Press, 2001); Naomi Murakawa, *The First Civil Right: How Liberals Built Prison America* (New York: Oxford University Press, 2014), chapter 4; Marquis, "Private Security and Surveillance."

44. Parenti, *Lockdown America*, 19.

45. Jack Douglas, "The Challenge of Crime in a Free Society: A Report by the President's Commission on Law and Administration of Justice," *American Sociological Review* 32, no. 4 (1967): 266–67.

46. *National Crime Information Center (NCIC)—The Investigative Tool—A Guide to the Use and Benefits of NCIC*, 1984, https://www.ojp.gov/ncjrs/virtual-library/abstracts/national-crime-information-center-ncic-investigative-tool-guide-use. See also James B. Jacobs, *The Eternal Criminal Record* (Cambridge, MA: Harvard University Press, 2015), 18–21.

47. Whereas in 1930, only nine states had a criminal records repository to which police departments and courts sent all information, today (though with varying degrees of completion) every state has such a repository. Corda, "More Justice and Less Harm"; Jacobs, *The Eternal Criminal Record*, 37.

48. The idea that criminal records should generally be private is rooted in multiple US and California court rulings: *U.S. Department of Justice v. Reporters Committee for Freedom of*

Information, 489 U.S. 749, 780 (1989), finding that "the privacy interest in maintaining the practical obscurity of rap-sheet information will always be high. When the subject of such a rap sheet is a private citizen and when the information is in the Government's control as a compilation, rather than as a record of 'what the Government is up to,' the privacy interest protected by Exemption 7(C) is in fact at its apex while the FOIA-based public interest in disclosure is at its nadir"; *Melvin v. Reid*, 112 Cal.App. 285, 291 (1931), finding that "the use of appellant's true name in connection with the incidents of her former life in the plot and advertisements was unnecessary and indelicate and a willful and wanton disregard of that charity which should actuate us in our social intercourse and which should keep us from unnecessarily holding another up to the scorn and contempt of upright members of society"; *Briscoe v. Reader's Digest Ass'n*, 4 Cal.3d 529, 539–40 (1971), finding that "human forgetfulness over time puts today's 'hot' news in tomorrow's dusty archives. In a nation of 200 million people there is ample opportunity for all but the most infamous to begin a new life."

49. SEARCH Group, *Report of the National Task Force on the Criminal Backgrounding of America*, 45.

50. *Standards for the Security and Privacy of Criminal History Record Information: Third Edition* (1975; repr., Sacramento, CA: SEARCH Group, July 1988),https://www.ojp.gov/ncjrs/virtual-library/abstracts/standards-security-and-privacy-criminal-history-record-information. SEARCH cautioned that while there are some legitimate, noncriminal justice uses of criminal records, such as background checks for positions of trust, criminal records data should not generally be made available to the public. For a full discussion of the debates about disclosure, see Bill Hebenton and Thomas Terry, *Criminal Records: State, Citizen and the Politics of Protection* (Aldershot, UK: Avebury, 1993), 98–117.

51. Privacy scholars have noted the irony: criminal record disclosures were legitimized through the freedom of information laws meant to enable citizens to monitor government institutions or officials, yet the practical effect was to disclose more information about individuals monitored by governments. See Jennifer A. Brobst, "Reverse Sunshine in the Digital Wild Frontier: Protecting Individual Privacy against Public Records Requests for Government Databases," *Northern Kentucky Law Review* 42, no. 2 (April 2015): 191–286; Daniel Solove, *The Digital Person: Technology and Privacy in the Information Age* (New York: NYU Press, 2004), cited in Sarah Esther Lageson, *Digital Punishment: Privacy, Stigma, and the Harms of Data-Driven Criminal Justice* (New York: Oxford University Press, 2020), 22–27.

52. Jacobs, *The Eternal Criminal Record*, 43.

53. Pub. L. 92–544, https://www.fbi.gov/how-we-can-help-you/more-fbi-services-and-information/public-law-92-544; James B. Jacobs and Tamara Crepet, "The Expanding Scope, Use, and Availability of Criminal Records," *New York University Journal of Legislation and Public Policy* 11, no. 2 (2008): 177–214.

54. In *Paul v. Davis*, 424 U.S. 693 (1976) the US Supreme Court decided that the plaintiff had not suffered any violation of his constitutional right to privacy when the local police named him an "active shoplifter," and distributed a flyer that included his name and photograph. See Robert R. Belair and Paul L. Woodard, *Use and Management of Criminal History Record Information: A Comprehensive Report* (Sacramento, CA: SEARCH Group, 1993), https://bjs.ojp.gov/library/publications/use-and-management-criminal-history-record-information-comprehensive-report; Hebenton and Terry, *Criminal Records*, 98–105.

55. Love, Roberts, and Logan, *Collateral Consequences of Criminal Convictions*.

56. Garland, *The Culture of Control*, 12.

57. Demleitner, "Preventing Internal Exile." As explained by Margaret Colgate Love, Jenny Roberts, and Wayne Logan (*Collateral Consequences of Criminal Convictions*, 19), the proposed bill contained a chapter titled "Restriction on Imposition of Civil Disabilities," which prohibited unreasonable restrictions on eligibility for federal benefits and programs, and state or federal employment, based on a federal conviction, and "extended the judicial 'set aside' provisions of the federal Youth Corrections Act to all federal first offenders."

58. Love, Roberts, and Logan, *Collateral Consequences of Criminal Convictions*, 20.

59. Jacobs, *The Eternal Criminal Record*, 41.

60. See, for example, Arrington's Estate v. Fields, 578 S.W.2d 173 (1979); Cramer v. Housing Opportunities Commission, 304 Md. 705, 501 A.2d 35 (1985); Pittard v. Four Seasons Motor Inn, Inc., 101 N.M. 723, 688 P.2d 333 (1984); CK Security Systems, Inc. v. Hartford Accident & Indemnity Company, 137 Ga. App. 159 (1975); Welsh Manufacturing, Division of Textron, Inc. v. Pinkerton's, Inc., 474 A.2d 436 (1984).

61. Joan Clay and Elvis Stephens, "Liability for Negligent Hiring: The Importance of Background Checks," *Cornell Hotel and Restaurant Administration Quarterly* 36, no. 5 (October 1995): 74–81; Julia Levashina and Michael A. Campion, "Expected Practices in Background Checking: Review of the Human Resource Management Literature," *Employee Responsibilities and Rights Journal* 21, no. 3 (September 2009): 231–49.

62. North, "Responsibility of Employers for the Actions of Their Employees," 726; Dermot Sullivan, "Employee Violence, Negligent Hiring, and Criminal Records Checks: New York's Need to Reevaluate Its Priorities to Promote Public Safety," *St. John's Law Review* 72, no. 2 (1998): 27.

63. Ponticas v. KMS Investments, 331 N.W.2d 907 (1983), https://law.justia.com/cases /minnesota/supreme-court/1983/c7-81-1026-2.html.

64. Jacobs and Crepet, "The Expanding Scope, Use, and Availability of Criminal Records."

65. Yunus Piperdy and Scott Rushing, "Past, Present and Future of Risk Factors: The History of Life Insurance Risk Assessment," Research and White Papers, RGA Insurance Company, November 2018, https://www.rgare.com/knowledge-center/article/past-present-and-future-of -risk-factors, notes that by the 1980s and 1990s, "lifestyle" factors used to assess mortality risk included past felony conviction(s) alongside factors such as excessive use of alcohol/and or recreational drugs, foreign travel, and personal aviation.

66. In *Department of Justice v. Reporters Committee for Freedom of the Press*, the Supreme Court held that an individual has a cognizable privacy interest in their criminal history record information, even though all the constituent parts of the record may be public information. The Supreme Court reasoned that the compilation of an entire history of an individual's criminal activity, and in particular, its automation in a format that makes the record easily retrievable, vastly increases the privacy risk to the record subject and makes it appropriate to extend privacy protections to the record. For further discussion, see Belair and Woodard, *Use and Management of Criminal History Record Information*.

67. Later, the 1998 Volunteers for Children Act facilitated access to FBI records for all organizations and businesses dealing with children and vulnerable groups, regardless of state laws granting authorization, and the 2006 Adam Walsh Child Protection Act effectively required states to maintain sex offender registries and the FBI to integrate them in a national database.

68. For deeper treatments of the role of child protection in growing punishment, see Roger N. Lancaster, *Sex Panic and the Punitive State* (Berkeley: University of California Press, 2011); Gillian Harkins, *Virtual Pedophilia: Sex Offender Profiling and U.S. Security Culture* (Durham, NC: Duke University Press, 2020); Erica R. Meiners, *For the Children?: Protecting Innocence in a Carceral State* (Minneapolis: University of Minnesota Press, 2016).

69. Jacobs, *The Eternal Criminal Record.*

70. Jacobs and Crepet, "The Expanding Scope, Use, and Availability of Criminal Records."

71. Love, Roberts, and Logan, *Collateral Consequences of Criminal Convictions;* Olivares, Burton, and Cullen, "Collateral Consequences of a Felony Conviction," 10–17; Joan Petersilia, *When Prisoners Come Home: Parole and Prisoner Reentry* (New York: Oxford University Press, 2003), http://ebookcentral.proquest.com/lib/umichigan/detail.action?docID=431190.

72. For example, *Bryant v. Levigni,* 619 N.E.2d 550 (1993), expanded liability to include the act committed even if the defendant worker is off duty, while *Yonker v. Honeywell,* 496 N.W.2d 419 (1993), found that an employer has the duty to determine whether a candidate will become a threat to a group of coworkers (foreseeability) if they discover that an applicant has previous records.

73. "Healthier Home Care," *University of Chicago Magazine: College Report Alumni Newsmakers,* August 1999, https://magazine.uchicago.edu/9906/CollegeReport/newsmakers3.htm.

74. David McElhattan, "The Exception as the Rule: Negligent Hiring Liability, Structured Uncertainty, and the Rise of Criminal Background Checks in the United States," *Law & Social Inquiry* 47, no. 1 (February 2022): 132–61.

75. In 1991, only eight out of two hundred Massachusetts home care agencies screened potential employees for criminal records. By 2014, forty-one states required home health agencies to conduct criminal background checks for home health care aides, and four other states were planning to implement background checks. See "Healthier Home Care"; Suzanne Murrin, *Home Health Agencies Conducted Background Checks of Varying Types* (Washington, DC: Department of Health and Human Services, Office of Inspector General, May 2015), https://www.aapc .com/codes/webroot/upload/general_pages_docs/document/oei-07-14-00130.pdf.

76. See, for example, Greg Burns, "Low-Cost Criminal Checks Criticized," *Chicago Tribune,* May 2004, https://dealers-insurance.com/data_base_criminal_background_checks.php; Kim M. Kerr, *Workplace Violence Planning for Prevention and Response* (Oxford, UK: Butterworth-Heinemann, 2010), chapter 11.

77. *Report of the National Task Force on Privacy, Technology and Criminal Justice Information* (Sacramento, CA: SEARCH Group, August 2001), https://bjs.ojp.gov/library/publications /report-national-task-force-privacy-technology-and-criminal-justice-information; For a full treatment of the role of digitization, see Lageson, *Digital Punishment.*

78. For a helpful discussion of the dynamics leading courts to sell batches of bulk data, see Lageson, *Digital Punishment,* 77–81.

79. "In the seven-year period 1991–98 the overall rate of crime declined by 22%, violent crime by 25%, and property crime by 21%. . . . During this period the number of state and federal prisoners rose substantially, from 789,610 to 1,252,830—a 59% increase in just seven years." Jenni Gainsborough and Marc Mauer, *Diminishing Returns: Crime and Incarceration in the 1990s* (Washington, DC: Sentencing Project, September 2000), 3.

80. Later, the E-Government Act of 2002 required online access to federal court records.

81. Interview with background screening and security professional on condition of anonymity, January 2021.

82. On the public-private divide and other popular misunderstandings upholding police power, see Siegel, "Violence Work."

83. I borrow here from Gilmore, who made a similar observation with regard to mass incarceration at a public talk. Ruth Wilson Gilmore, "No Easy Victories: Fighting for Abolition: A Conversation with Angela Y. Davis and Ruthie Wilson Gilmore," moderated by Beth Richie, Trinity United Church of Christ, Chicago, November 8, 2017.

84. Matthew Hull, "Corporations and States: A Customer-Service Corporation Inside the Punjab State Police," *Cultural Anthropology* 37, no. 4 (November, 2022): 764–92.

85. *Report of the National Task Force on the Commercial Sale of Criminal Justice Record Information* (Sacramento, CA: National Consortium for Justice Information and Statistics, 2005, https://www.search.org/files/pdf/RNTFCSCJRI.pdf.

86. Maritime Transportation Security Act of 2002, Pub. L. 107–295, 116 Stat. 2064 (2002).

87. Interview with background screening and security professional on condition of anonymity, January 2021.

88. *Market Snapshot: Background Screening Reports: Criminal Background Checks in Employment* (Washington, DC: Consumer Financial Protection Bureau, October 2019), https://files .consumerfinance.gov/f/documents/201909_cfpb_market-snapshot-background-screening _report.pdf. See also Ann Davis, "Firms Dig Deep into Workers' Pasts amid Post-Sept. 11 Security Anxiety," *Wall Street Journal*, March 12, 2002, http://www.wsj.com/articles/ SB1015886922323674160.

89. David Thacher, "The Rise of Criminal Background Screening in Rental Housing— Version A," *Law & Social Inquiry* 33, no. 1 (March 1, 2008): 6. Thacher's case study of the rise of tenant screening reveals how the professionalization of landlording along with the institutional resources it generated in the form of how-to books, expertise, and educational materials were particularly significant in establishing what he describes as the "collective capacity" crucial to the success of tenant background screening. While this infrastructure, as Thacher notes, was not developed *for* background screening per se, it could be strategically leveraged to support screening as it came into vogue.

90. Lageson, *Digital Punishment*, 69. See also Melissa Sorenson, "There's No Such Thing as a National Database for Background Checks," National Association of Professional Background Screeners, April 4, 2013, chrome-extension://efaidnbmnnnibpcajpcglclefindmkaj/https://pubs .thepbsa.org/pub/08D04294-ACC2-75D4-9A68-3749DAE8673B.

91. From inception, accusations of sloppy reporting plagued the background screening industry, resulting in a wave of class action lawsuits relating to the reporting of incomplete and inaccurate information. For example, cases known as "mixed files" in which the criminal record furnished to the employer did not belong to the individual in question as well as other kinds of false positives violated the Fair Credit Reporting Act's maximum possible accuracy provision. Another wave of lawsuits challenged screeners' reporting of arrests, expunged convictions, and old convictions. Courts were also sued for reporting restricted information in the data they were selling to the screeners. Major screening firms were forced to clean up their acts, and much of the industry followed. Though the problem is not entirely resolved, in my view, there is a way in which the continued emphasis on accuracy detracts from deeper questions of access

and use. Moreover, concerns about accuracy have often been used to argue for increased access to criminal record data.

92. Established in 2003, the association is now called the Professional Background Screening Association (PBSA). According to its website, "The organization quickly expanded with members all over the world and the addition of three international councils in the years that followed. The transformation to a global organization and restructuring was completed in 2019 culminating to the rebranding of PBSA." As of 2021, there were approximately two thousand background screening firms in the United States, and of these, roughly four hundred were members of the PBSA. PreemploymentDirectory.com, "Background Screening Industry Resource Guide: 2020–2021," https://preemploymentdirectory.com/wp-content/uploads/2020/12/2020-2021 -Resource-Guide_112920.pdf?utm_source=phpList&utm_medium=email&utm_campaign =2022–23+Background+Screening+Industry+Resource+Guide&utm_content=HTML.

93. The background screening industry cannot grow and maintain the market for background checks without investing time, energy, and money to ensure criminal record data remain readily available. Its efforts thus necessarily include eroding existing protections and/or challenging progressive attempts to protect privacy, due process, and other rights of people with criminal records. Some specifics of how this dynamic manifests in the industry's legislative agenda are discussed in the conclusion.

94. "Home," Professional Background Screening Association, accessed December 1, 2023, https://thepbsa.org/.

95. Gilmore, "No Easy Victories."

96. For a further discussion of how the commercial background screening industry undermined the practical obscurity of court records, see Corda, "More Justice and Less Harm," 38–40.

97. Corda, "More Justice and Less Harm," 1–60.

98. Nixon and Kerr, *Background Screening and Investigations*, xxi.

99. As an example, see Rachel Trindade, "Is Your Background Screening Keeping Up with Today's Hiring Challenges?," *Employment Relations Today* 42, no. 2 (July 1, 2015): 1–7.

100. For a list of HR publications recommending screening, see Levashina and Campion, "Expected Practices in Background Checking," 238.

101. Surveys of employer screening practices are frequently conducted by the screening industry itself, or are commissioned by the industry and conducted by HR organizations. Their own members and clients are often queried. See, for example, *Background Screening Trends & Best Practices Report 2015* (Marietta, GA: Sterling Talent Solutions, 2015), https://www .sterlingcheck.com/wp-content/uploads/2017/05/493-ST-US-RPT-2015-Trends-Practices -Report.pdf (this report notes that only 20 percent of the participants were Employee Screen IQ clients); *National Survey: Employers Universally Using Background Checks to Protect Employees, Customers and the Public* (HR.com, June 2017), https://pubs.thepbsa.org/pub.cfm?id =6E232E17-B749-6287-0E86-95568FA599D1 (survey of 1,528 HR professionals commissioned by the Professional Background Screening Association); *2023 Global Benchmark Report* (Tulsa, OK: HireRight, 2023), https://www.hireright.com/resources/2023-global-benchmark -report?source=thank-you&date=09192024.

102. These seminars or webinars were (and are) hosted by some combination of professional HR associations, employment law firms, and commercial background screening firms. Though

some of these events required a fee, many simply embedded a profit potential in the inference that potential problems could be avoided by contracting with a third-party background screener and consulting with a knowledgeable attorney. While the sheer number of such events and aggressiveness of their messaging struck me as significant, it was difficult as a researcher to gauge their actual influence with little sense of how many or what kinds employers were listening, or how listeners were responding to the information being given.

103. Excerpt from an email invitation to participate in a webinar presented by Hire Right/Fisher & Phillips Attorneys at Law, December 2014.

104. Levashina and Campion, "Expected Practices in Background Checking."

105. McElhattan, "The Exception as the Rule," 133.

106. McElhattan's research also shows how employers' widespread fear of defamation or invasion of privacy lawsuits has eliminated the perceived effectiveness of reference checking along with other plausible—and potentially more substantive—alternatives to criminal background screening.

107. E. Summerson Carr, "Enactments of Expertise," *Annual Review of Anthropology* 39 (2010): 19.

108. For an ethnographically based analysis of how the insurance industry mediates the ways that employers, legislatures, courts, and other institutions understand and comply with antidiscrimination law, see Shauhin Talesh, "Legal Intermediaries: How Insurance Companies Construct the Meaning of Compliance with Antidiscrimination Laws: Law & Policy," *Law & Policy* 37, no. 3 (July 2015): 209–39, https://doi.org/10.1111/lapo.12037.

109. Others have also noted the uncritical adoption of criminal record restrictions in response to public scandals. See, for example, Christel Backman, "Mandatory Criminal Record Checks in Sweden: Scandals and Function Creep," *Surveillance & Society* 10, no. 3/4 (2012): 276–91; Qi Chen, "Exploring the Bottom-Up Reform of Sex Offender Registration in China: Carceral Feminism and Populist Authoritarianism," *Crime, Law and Social Change* 74, no. 3 (2020):273–95, cited in Martí Rovira, "The Global Rise of Criminal Background Checks," *International Criminology* 3, no. 1 (March 1, 2023): 1–11.

110. Charles Ornstein, Tracy Weber, and Maloy Moore, "Problem Nurses Stay on the Job as Patients Suffer," *Los Angeles Times*, July 12, 2009, https://www.latimes.com/local/la-me-nurse12 -2009jul12-story.html.

111. In many cases, reported incidences were either criminal, but entirely unrelated to nursing, or related to nursing ethics, but not criminal, in which case patient harm would not have been detected or prevented by more thorough background screening.

112. For instance, the news reported an instance in which a nurse had been convicted of smuggling rock cocaine to her jailed husband, but not disciplined by the licensing board until nearly ten years later. See Charles Ornstein and Tracy Weber, "Criminal Past Is No Bar to Nursing in California," *ProPublica*, October 4, 2008, https://www.propublica.org/article/criminal -past-is-no-bar-to-nursing-in-california.

113. James W. Hunt, James E. Bowers, and Neal Miller, *Laws, Licenses and other Offender's Right to Work: A Study of State Laws Restricting the Occupational Licensing of Former Offenders* (Washington, DC: National Clearinghouse on Offender Employment Restrictions, 1973). Concerned with the rapid proliferation of collateral consequences and increase in the number of people affected by them, the federal Court Security Improvement Act of 2007 (Pub. L. 110–177

§ 510, 121 Stat. 2534, 2544) directed the National Institute of Justice to collect and analyze the collateral consequences in each US jurisdiction. In 2012, the Criminal Justice Section of the American Bar Association began work on the National Inventory of the Collateral Consequences of Conviction, an online searchable database that identifies and categorizes the statutes and regulations that impose collateral consequences in all fifty states, the federal system, the District of Columbia, US Virgin Islands, and Puerto Rico. See "New Website Launched on Collateral Consequences," American Bar Association, October 1, 2012, https://www.americanbar .org/advocacy/governmental_legislative_work/publications/governmental_affairs _periodicals/washingtonletter/2012/october/collateralconsequences/.

114. Joe Palazzolo, "Criminal Records Haunt Hiring Initiative," *Wall Street Journal*, July 12, 2015, https://www.wsj.com/articles/criminal-records-haunt-hiring-initiative-1436736255.

115. Peter Kochenburger, "Insurers' Use of Criminal History Information" (paper presented at the National Council of Insurance Legislators Special Committee on Race in Insurance Underwriting, Charleston, SC, April 15, 2021), chrome-extension://efaidnbmnnnibpcajpcglclefin dmkaj/https://ncoil.org/wp-content/uploads/2021/04/Peter-Kochenburger-Charleston -Presentation.pdf. To categorize risks and calculate premiums, many insurers rely on the standardized classification and rating systems developed by data analytic or "risk modeling" firms. Kochenburger describes how the wide availability of criminal history data online has led to an increase in these firms' use of these data for their insurance-related products. See, for example, "MIB Signs Agreement with Explore to Make Sherlock® Criminal Record Checks Available to MIB's 400 Life Insurance Members," MIB, April 10, 2019, https://www.mibgroup.com/resources /press-releases/mib-signs-agreement-with-explore.

116. See, for example, "Background Checks Impact Insurance Premiums," ClearStar, July 17, 2018, https://www.clearstar.net/background-checks-impact-insurance-premiums/. ClearStar noting that, "Insurance companies usually look for the level of reference checks, criminal background checks, drug tests, credit checks, and work references. . . . Typically, the more checks performed by the employer, the greater the credit that's usually applied toward the premium. Minimal or no checks usually result in a rating debit and may limit who is willing to undertake the risk."

117. A significant increase in employer's use of criminal background checks since the early 2000s is undeniable. Although as mentioned earlier, the circular methods of many employer surveys make it somewhat difficult to parse an actual bandwagon effect from propaganda, one study asking job seekers themselves showed that 71.1 percent of those who had found employment in the last year had been asked at some point during the hiring process whether they had a criminal record. Megan Denver, Justin T. Pickett, and Shawn D. Bushway, "Criminal Records and Employment: A Survey of Experiences and Attitudes in the United States," *Justice Quarterly* 35, no. 4 (2018): 584–613.

118. Based on a random selection of 544 HR professionals who were members of the organization, the Society for Human Resource Management found that 69 percent of employers conduct criminal background checks on all new hires. "The Use of Background Checks in Hiring Decisions," SHRM, 2012, https://philammann.com/2012/11/16/shrm-report-use-of -background-checks-in-hiring/. See also a national online study of private sector employers conducted by the Harris Poll on behalf of CareerBuilder from August 11 to September 7, 2016, including a sample of 2,379 hiring managers and HR professionals across industries and

company sizes; it found that 72 percent conducted background checks on all new hires. "More than 1 in 4 Employers Do Not Conduct Background Checks of All New Employees, According to CareerBuilder Survey," *Press Room | CareerBuilder* (blog), accessed October 8, 2024, https:// press.careerbuilder.com/2016-11-17-More-than-1-in-4-Employers-Do-Not-Conduct -Background-Checks-of-All-New-Employees-According-to-CareerBuilder-Survey.

119. Elena Pijoan, "Legal Protections against Criminal Background Checks in Europe," *Punishment & Society* 16, no. 1 (2014): 50–73. As Pijoan details, the uptick in criminal background checks in Europe has been largely attributed to legislation relating to employment involving close contact with children or elderly populations. In addition to various country-specific pieces of legislation, EU Directive 2011/92/EU of the European Parliament (on combating the sexual abuse and sexual exploitation of children and child pornography), requires member states to check for potential conviction records among those applying for employment involving close contact with children or elderly populations. See also James Jacobs and Dimitra Blitsa, "US, EU and UK Employment Vetting as Strategy for Preventing Convicted Sex Offenders from Gaining Access to Children," *European Journal on Crime, Criminal Law and Criminal Justice* 20, no. 3 (2012): 265–96; Elena Larrauri and Martí Rovira, "Collateral Consequences of a Conviction in Spain," in *Fundamental Rights and Legal Consequences of Criminal Convictions*, edited by Sonja Meijer, Harry Annison, and Ailbhe O'Loughlin (Oxford: Hart Publishing, 2019), 27–44.

120. Rovira, "The Global Rise of Criminal Background Checks." Rovira's original dataset analyzes the rate of requests for official criminal record certificates for nonjudicial purposes per one hundred inhabitants for fifty-two countries between 2002 and 2019. Importantly, an increasing global use of criminal background checks does not necessarily point to unifying policy trends in terms of allowable use or access. For a thoughtful discussion of underlying needs and debates that may drive regional and country-specific policy variations, see Leandro Gastón and Carlos Carnevale, "Criminal Records and Employment Restrictions in Argentina: Between Post-Sentence Discrimination and Resistance Strategies," *Criminology & Criminal Justice* 23, no. 4 (April 18, 2023).

3. Criminal Stigma and the Politics of Helping

1. Donald Braman, *Doing Time on the Outside: Incarceration and Family Life in Urban America* (Ann Arbor: University of Michigan Press, 2004); Jock Young, *The Exclusive Society: Social Exclusion, Crime and Difference in Late Modernity* (London: SAGE Publications Ltd., 1999).

2. John E. Baur, Alison V. Hall, Shanna R. Daniels, M. Ronald Buckley, and Heather J. Anderson, "Beyond Banning the Box: A Conceptual Model of the Stigmatization of Ex-Offenders in the Workplace," *Human Resource Management Review* 28, no. 2 (June, 2018): 204–19; Barnard Weiner, *Judgments of Responsibility: A Foundation for a Theory of Social Conduct* (New York: Guilford Press, 1995).

3. Parts of this chapter were first published in Melissa Burch, "Scripting the Conviction: Power and Resistance in the Management of Criminal Stigma," *American Anthropologist* 123, no. 3 (2021): 645–57.

4. Erving Goffman, *Stigma: Notes on the Management of Spoiled Identity* (Englewood Cliffs, NJ: Spectrum Books, 1963).

5. Eden B. King, Jennifer L. Knight, and Michelle R. Hebl, "The Influence of Economic Conditions on Aspects of Stigmatization," *Journal of Social Issues* 66, no. 3 (2010): 446–60; Crystal Paul and Sarah Becker, "'People Are Enemies to What They Don't Know': Managing Stigma and Anti-Muslim Stereotypes in a Turkish Community Center," *Journal of Contemporary Ethnography* 46, no. 2 (2017): 135–72; Bruce G. Link and Jo C. Phelan, "Conceptualizing Stigma," *Annual Review of Sociology* 27 (2001): 363–85; Catherine Kohler Reissman, "Stigma and Everyday Resistance Practices: Childless Women in South India," *Gender & Society* 14, no. 1 (2000): 111–35.

6. Manuela Barreto and Naomi Ellemers, "Current Issues in the Study of Social Stigma: Some Controversies and Unresolved Issues," *Journal of Social Issues* 66, no. 3 (September 2010): 431–45; Graham Scrambler, "Health-Related Stigma," *Sociology of Health & Illness* 31, no. 3 (2009): 441–55.

7. Seminar offered by Robbin and Associates, San Bernardino, CA, December 17, 2014.

8. Reuben Jonathan Miller, "Devolving the Carceral State: Race, Prisoner Reentry, and the Micro-Politics of Urban Poverty Management," *Punishment & Society* 16, no. 3 (July, 2014): 305–35.

9. Marie Gottschalk, *Caught: The Prison State and the Lockdown of American Politics* (Princeton, NJ: Princeton University Press, 2015), 81, building on Magnus Hörnquist, "The Imaginary Constitution of Wage Labourers," in *Imaginary Penalties*, ed. Pat Carlen (Devon, UK: Willan, 2008), 181.

10. Gordon Lafer, *The Job Training Charade* (Ithaca, NY: Cornell University Press, 2004), cited in Gottschalk, *Caught*.

11. Melissa Burch, "(Re)Entry from the Bottom Up: Case Study of a Critical Approach to Assisting Women Coming Home from Prison," *Critical Criminology* 25 (2017): 357–74.

12. Deirdre A. Royster, *Race and the Invisible Hand: How White Networks Exclude Black Men from Blue-Collar Jobs* (Berkeley: University of California Press, 2003).

13. Paul Willis, *Learning to Labor: How Working-Class Kids Get Working-Class Jobs* (New York: Columbia University Press, 2017), 129.

14. Lehn M. Benjamin and David C. Campbell, "Programs Aren't Everything (SSIR)," *Stanford Social Innovation Review* (Spring 2014): 42–47.

15. Erving Goffman, *The Presentation of Self in Everyday Life* (New York: Anchor, 1959), 205.

16. CT Turney, "The Candor Trap," New Orleans, LA, 2016.

17. Kristen P. Jones and Eden B. King, "Managing Concealable Stigmas at Work: A Review and Multilevel Model," *Journal of Management* 40, no. 5 (July 1, 2014): 1466–94; Turney, "The Candor Trap"; Terri A. Winnick and Mark Bodkin, "Anticipated Stigma and Stigma Management among Those to Be Labeled 'Ex-Con,'" *Deviant Behavior* 29, no. 4 (2008): 295–333.

18. What happened to Ché took place before the widespread implementation of Ban the Box policies, but even after Ban the Box policies were implemented, a candor trap remained in that some employers were troubled when candidates did not proactively offer information about their criminal records. While no longer asking directly for the information, many employers felt it appropriate for someone with red flags on their record to preemptively reveal and explain them. As of this writing, employers continue to verbally ask job candidates if they "can pass" a background check.

19. Johanna Shih, "'. . . Yeah, I Could Hire This One, but I Know It's Gonna Be a Problem': How Race, Nativity and Gender Affect Employers' Perceptions of the Manageability of Job Seekers," *Ethnic and Racial Studies* 25, no. 1 (2002): 99–119.

20. Burch, "Scripting the Conviction."

21. Summerson E. Carr, *Scripting Addiction: The Politics of Therapeutic Talk and American Sobriety* (Princeton, NJ: Princeton University Press, 2010), 16.

22. As discussed in the introduction, the lines between categories such as violent and non-violent, or misdemeanor and felony, are much less clear-cut or fixed than one might think, and these labels often do not match common understanding. For further discussion, see Gottschalk, *Caught*, 168–69.

23. Unequivocal personal responsibility is central to a range of criminal justice contexts, including parole board hearings along with applications for expungement, certificates of reha-bilitation, and pardons. While circumstantial factors that explain the reasons for an unlawful act are encouraged, they must be introduced in a way that does not detract from the framework of individual choice.

24. Goffman, *Stigma*, 217.

25. Goffman, *Stigma*, 35.

26. Anthropologist Edmund T. Gordon argues that young Black who engage in "reputational practices of masculinity"—such as reproductive prowess, material consumption, or dominating other males through violence—are not simply rebelling or mechanically responding to oppres-sion but instead are actively choosing accommodation or resistance. Through these reputational practices, they reject the social norms of Anglo civil society. Though Brian is not Black, I saw him as engaging in a similar politics. Edmund T. Gordon, "Anthropology and Liberation," in *Decolonizing Anthropology: Moving Further toward an Anthropology of Liberation*, ed. Faye V. Harrison (Arlington, VA: Association of Black Anthropologists, 1997), 150–69.

27. A more extended version of Linda's experience of rejection was first published in Melissa Burch, "Captive Afterlives in the Age of Mass Conviction," *History and Anthropology* 5 (July 10, 2019): 515–20.

28. Barreto and Ellemers, "Current Issues in the Study of Social Stigma"; Scrambler, "Health-Related Stigma"; Stuart Hall, "Introduction: Who Needs 'Identity'?," in *Questions of Cultural Identity*, ed. Stuart Hall and Paul du Gay (London: Sage, 1996), 1–17.

29. Paul and Becker, "People Are Enemies to What They Don't Know."

30. Ruth Wilson Gilmore, "The Worrying State of the Anti-Prison Movement," *Social Justice*, February 23, 2015.

31. Lisa Marie Cacho, *Social Death: Racialized Rightlessness and the Criminalization of the Unprotected* (New York: NYU Press, 2012); Gottschalk, *Caught*.

32. Sarah Glenn-Leisitkow, personal communication, March 2022. Glenn-Leisitkow's analy-sis is further supported by research demonstrating that even when employers have positive experiences with racialized individuals, these experiences do not tend to alter their attitudes about the group as a whole. See Devah Pager and Diana Karafin, "Bayesian Bigot? Statistical Discrimination, Stereotypes, and Employer Decision Making," *ANNALS of the American Acad-emy of Political and Social Science* 621, no. 1 (January 1, 2009): 70–93.

33. Link and Phelan, "Conceptualizing Stigma," 367.

34. Paul and Becker, "People Are Enemies to What They Don't Know."

4. Good Sense Hiring in Small and Midsize Business

1. The US Small Business Administration classifies businesses as "small" using a combination of factors including ownership structure, number of employees, and earnings; the thresholds for these factors vary by type of industry. The Internal Revenue Service classifies small businesses as those holding less than $10 million in assets. For the purposes of this study, I uncritically accepted business owners' self-classifications.

2. Communication scholar Angèle Christin and sociologist Sarah Brayne make a similar observation with regard to judges and law enforcement, noting that these and other legal professionals tend to see algorithmic tools as unnecessary, untrustworthy, and an infringement on their expertise. See Sarah Brayne and Angèle Christin, "Technologies of Crime Prediction: The Reception of Algorithms in Policing and Criminal Courts," *Social Problems* 68, no. 3 (August 1, 2021): 608–24.

3. Right On Crime, already a few years underway, may have influenced Inland Empire employers' perspectives in ways I did not detect. It is a national campaign of the Texas Public Policy Foundation that supports conservative solutions for reducing crime, restoring victims, reforming offenders, and lowering taxpayer costs. The movement was born in Texas in 2007 and has led the way in implementing conservative criminal justice reforms across the nation. See RightonCrime.com. See also Deborah Small, "Cause for Trepidation: Libertarians' Newfound Concern for Prison Reform," *Salon*, March 22, 2014, https://www.salon.com/2014/03/22/cause_for_trepidation_libertarians_newfound_concern_for_prison_reform/.

4. During the research and writing, I thought often of the job market discriminations faced by both of my parents. My mother battled deep sexism in a male-dominated business world where she was regularly mistaken for a secretary, told by her male employees that they didn't feel "comfortable" having a female boss, and made to deliver talks on the shop floor with nude pinups in the backdrop! The pervasive antiblackness my father endured in the Toronto job market, coupled with a lack of education and formal training, made it impossible for him to get a foothold and build a life in Canada.

5. Laura Giuliano, David I. Levine, and Jonathan Leonard, "Manager Race and the Race of New Hires," *Journal of Labor Economics* 27, no. 4 (October 2009): 589–631; Michael Stoll, Steven Raphael, and Harry Holzer, "Why Are Black Employers More Likely than White Employers to Hire Blacks?," Institute for Research on Poverty Discussion Paper No. 1236-01, August, 2001, https://www.irp.wisc.edu/publications/dps/pdfs/dp123601.pdf.

6. Lawrence Grossberg, "On Postmodernism and Articulation: An Interview with Stuart Hall," in *Stuart Hall: Critical Dialogues in Cultural Studies*, ed. David Morley and Kuan-Hsing Chen (London: Routledge, 1996), 131–50; Jennifer Daryl Slack, "The Theory and Method of Articulation," in *Stuart Hall: Critical Dialogues in Cultural Studies*, ed. David Morley and Kuan-Hsing Chen (London: Routledge, 1996), 112–30.

7. California voters approved the sale of $9 billion in state bonds in 2008 in hopes that the line from Los Angeles to San Francisco would be running by 2020, but as of 2022, had failed to lay a single track.

8. Another major source of stress for the trucking industry had been generated by freight rate deregulation the 1980s and 1990s. As Karen Levy describes, deregulation "created a race to the bottom that depressed truckers' wages, made their work significantly more difficult, and led

many truckers to feel like 'throwaway people.'" Karen Levy, *Data Driven: Truckers, Technology, and the New Workplace Surveillance* (Princeton, NJ: Princeton University Press, 2022), 11. The effort to lower freight rates for consumers rendered business models like Weber Trucking—in which the trucks are owned by the company, and the drivers are employees with decent wages, health insurance, and paid vacation—cost ineffective. Instead, the industry began to see a proliferation of "owner-operators," a business model in which individual subcontractors own and maintain their own trucks and get paid by the load. Without overhead, newly trained drivers could mortgage a truck and start hauling with little effort, driving haul prices below their actual costs and easily underbidding companies with higher operation costs. In failing to account for traffic and wait times, or the cost of repairs, health insurance, licensing, and permits, however, owner-operators often end up making fifteen dollars per hour or less, causing drivers to churn through employment options quickly in search of stable and decent wages. Thus one of Paul's running jokes was, "Behind every successful owner-operator is a wife with a very good job!"

9. Toyota denied the move was driven by California regulation, instead citing proximity to its main manufacturing plants, the lower cost of living and housing, a lower corporate tax burden, and a $40 million incentive package from the State of Texas, while Elon Musk said Nevada was chosen because the state had proved it "can do things quickly" and "get things done." "Nevada Chosen for High-Tech Tesla Car Battery Factory," *BBC News*, September 5, 2014, sec. US & Canada, https://www.bbc.com/news/world-us-canada-29073329. On the dismantling of Kaiser Steel and China's growing favor among foreign investors, see Juan D. De Lara, *Inland Shift: Race, Space, and Capital in Southern California*, (Oakland: University of California Press, 2018), 17–21.

10. In a study of employers in midsize Northeastern US cities, political scientist Kristen Bumiller describes a similar situation: employers struggling "to find workers that could meet even the minimal demands of their jobs." Bumiller reasons that their positioning at the bottom of tight labor markets (i.e., requiring hard work at low pay) leads them "to approach new employees with fairmindedness, allowing them to prove their worth despite their criminal records." See Kristin Bumiller, "Bad Jobs and Good Workers: The Hiring of Ex-Prisoners in a Segmented Economy," *Theoretical Criminology* 19, no. 3 (August 1, 2015): 336–54.

11. John Lukies, Joseph Graffam, and Alison J. Shinkfield, "The Effect of Organisational Context Variables on Employer Attitudes toward Employability of Ex-Offenders," *International Journal of Offender Therapy and Comparative Criminology* 55, no. 3 (May 2011): 460–75.

12. After this happened, they had changed their policy to exclude applicants with DUIs in the past seven years. While close attention to problems with alcohol or other drugs is obviously important in truck driving, fixed look-back periods are generally unreasoned. Shawn D. Bushway, Brian G. Vegetabile, Nidhi Kalra, Lee Remi, and Greg Baumann, "Providing Another Chance: Resetting Recidivism Risk in Criminal Background Checks," RAND Corporation, January 6, 2022, https://www.rand.org/pubs/research_reports/RRA1360-1.html.

13. Pub. L. 107–295, 116 Stat. 2064 (2002). See also Jacobs, *The Eternal Criminal Record*, 44; Jacobs and Crepet, "The Expanding Scope, Use, and Availability of Criminal Records."

14. According to company statistics, most of the turnover is concentrated among the newest drivers, who Paul characterized as "not old enough to appreciate the benefits of being an employee," which include job security, health benefits, and the option to sleep at home most nights. Still, only 40 or so of the 120 drivers left within the first or second year, usually during seasonal slowdowns.

15. The Transportation Security Administration conducts a background check to determine eligibility for the card. There are twelve permanently disqualifying offenses as well as sixteen convictions that disqualify applicants for seven years from the date of conviction or five years after release from prison.

16. Note that a question about criminal history was still on Weber Trucking's application prior to the enactment of California's statewide Ban the Box law in 2013. Yet as I will discuss in the conclusion, it was my observation that little changed in terms of its tendency to hire or not hire people with convictions when the question was removed from the application; the change had little effect on how the business conducted background checks or who was disqualified as a result of the checks.

17. Though liability insurers have of course always been concerned about accidents, ticket history, and driving experience, insurance companies increasingly may play a larger role in hiring decisions. For an explanation of how this works, see "D. Actions against Insurers for Negligent Hiring" (https://www.friedgoldberg.com/request-trucking-claims-book/theories-of-liability/): "The trucking company obtains the necessary information from the new applicant and then submits the information to the insurance company. The insurance company reviews the information and then determines if the insurer will provide coverage for the new applicant. The trucking company's decision to hire the driver is thus based entirely on the 'insurability' of the driver."

18. According to 2024 statistics from the US Department of Labor (https://www.bls.gov/cps/cpsaat39.htm), 76 percent of HR managers are women. In addition to a gendered pay gap, however, one 2010 survey of chief HR officers at US Fortune 200 companies found that male chief HR officers spend significantly more time than their female counterparts performing "strategic" advising and counseling activities, whereas female chief HR officers spend more time performing functional activities. Karra Barron, "The Gender Divide in HR," Visier, accessed October 13, 2024, https://www.visier.com/blog/gender-divide-part-1/.

19. Ilana Gershon, *Down and Out in the New Economy: How People Find (or Don't Find) Work Today* (Chicago: University of Chicago Press, 2017), 185–206.

20. American Trucking Associations, "Relative Contribution/Fault in Car-Truck Crashes," February 2013, https://s3-us-west-2.amazonaws.com/corpweb-static/pdf/20190218+Samsara+Safety+Bank/ATA+-+FINAL+2013+Car-Truck+Fault+Paper.pdf.

21. Some of the biggest problems with the rating system (consistency, accuracy, transparency, how violations were weighted, and the ability to account for context and overall practices) have since been addressed through a variety of changes, though I do not know to what extent carriers feel satisfied with the changes. Interestingly, one of the industry's biggest concerns was that the scores were made available to the public. Legislation enacted in 2015 (the Fast Act) restricted some parts of the score from the public's view.

22. Levy, *Data Driven*.

23. In "The Rise of Risk," in *Risk and Morality*, ed. Aaron Doyle and Diana Ericson (Toronto: University of Toronto Press, 2003), 73, David Garland points to the work of prominent risk scholars who have studied the effects of actuarial risk management on decision-making in mental health and criminal justice settings, including Robert Castel, "From Dangerousness to Risk," in *The Foucault Effect: Studies in Governmentality*, ed. Graham Burchell, Colin Gordon, and Peter Miller (Chicago: University of Chicago Press, 1991), 281–98; Nikolas Rose, "At Risk

of Madness," in *Embracing Risk: The Changing Culture of Insurance and Responsibility*, ed. Tom Baker and Jonathan Simon (Chicago: University of Chicago Press, 2001), 209–37; Pat O'Malley, ed., *Crime and the Risk Society* (Aldershot, UK: Dartmouth, 1998); Malcolm Feeley and Jonathan Simon, "The New Penology: Notes on the Emerging Strategy of Corrections and Its Implications," *Criminology* 30, no. 4 (1992): 449–74.

24. Ronald Smothers, "Ceta Cutbacks Leaving Thousands Unemployed; The Budget Targets Last of Eight Articles on Key Programs the President Wants to Cut," *New York Times*, April 11, 1981, sec. U.S., https://www.nytimes.com/1981/04/11/us/ceta-cutbacks-leaving -thousands-unemployed-budget-targets-last-eight-articles.html.

25. An increase in systematic monitoring in modern organizations and economic sectors are yet another expression of the larger shift toward formalized risk management. On the rise of systems of auditing, inspection, and verification, see Michael Power, *The Audit Society: Rituals of Verification*, subsequent ed. (Oxford: Oxford University Press, 1997).

26. Automation and a lack of funding for apprenticeships had shifted the employment landscape in similar ways for mechanics. Moses talked about how when he had been shop foreman many years ago, he had thought of himself as less of a boss and more of a teacher, deriving great satisfaction from watching his trainees' skills and confidence increase incrementally. Now the shop foreman required that new hires have some previous experience, with exceptions made only for graduates from the twenty-month program at the local technical institute. One reason for this was the new fleet of clean-air trucks, which are computerized rather than mechanical. The tools and know-how required to fix them was so different that even some of the best mechanics, the guys known to be able to outwrench anybody, were unable to fix—or even learn to fix—the new trucks. Modern-trained mechanics who *did* have the skills to diagnose and fix the new trucks wanted to earn significantly more money than Weber Trucking could pay. Additionally, drivers as well as mechanics owning their own tools were now required by state law to be paid two times the minimum wage for training. It was thus both a financial risk and investment to hire someone inexperienced who may get some experience by working for the company and then leave, not allowing the company to recoup its investment in their training. Recalling a guy and his brother who started out their careers lubing trucks and changing oil at Weber Trucking back in the day, Paul remarked, "If I would have had to have paid them two times the minimum wage, they never would have gotten that shot. . . . We don't have the deep pockets to pay people to learn."

27. Political scientist Marie Gottschalk has observed there is not really such a thing as "penal policy" because actors make decisions about punitive measures within broad political-economic contexts. See Marie Gottschalk, *Caught: The Prison State and the Lockdown of American Politics* (Princeton, NJ: Princeton University Press, 2015), 20.

28. It is my best guess the change in employment law affecting Weber Trucking's pay structure related to piecework, which affects many industries, including trucking. In piecework, employees are paid by the "piece," which in trucking could translate to either being paid by the load or mile. As a result of a class action lawsuit, the California legislature changed the pay calculations for piecework in 2013 so that employees had to be paid for things like mandated rest time. In 2015, the legislature wrote these changes into law (AB 1513). Useful explainers on this law can also be found at https://tbowleslaw.com/new-california-laws-2016/; https://www .littler.com/publication-press/publication/california-governor-signs-ab-1513-severely-limiting -piece-rate.

Conclusion: Limits and Possibilities in the Struggle to End Criminal Record Discrimination

1. The Seattle ordinance went much further than most Ban the Box laws. With only a few exceptions, it banned background checks and adverse action based on background checks except as required by law. "The Ordinance prohibits landlords from requiring disclosure or inquiring about any arrest record, conviction record, or criminal history of current or prospective tenants, and from taking adverse action against them based on that information." The courts ruled that not allowing landlords to ask about criminal history or conduct background checks was a violation of their First Amendment rights. US Ninth Circuit Court, Chong Yim v. City of Seattle, vol. 21-35567, 2023, https://cdn.ca9.uscourts.gov/datastore/opinions/2023/03/21/21-35567.pdf.

2. Naomi Murakawa, *The First Civil Right: How Liberals Built Prison America* (New York: Oxford University Press, 2014).

3. Alex Vitale, panel presentation, Centering the Margins: A Critical Criminology Conference, Eastern Michigan University, Ypsilanti, April 12–13, 2019.

4. Lisa Marie Cacho, *Social Death: Racialized Rightlessness and the Criminalization of the Unprotected* (New York: NYU Press, 2012), 18.

5. Cathy J. Cohen, "Punks, Bulldaggers, and Welfare Queens: The Radical Potential of Queer Politics?," *GLQ: A Journal of Lesbian and Gay Studies* 3, no. 4 (May 1, 1997): 443.

6. For example, California's widely supported Proposition 47, which allowed for the reduction of certain low-level felony convictions to misdemeanors, leading to the reclassification, resentencing, and release of tens of thousands of people, wrote into its "purpose and intent" language the necessity to "ensure that people convicted of murder, rape, and child molestation will not benefit from this Act." This language is repeated throughout, cementing people with "violent" felony convictions as unworthy of sentencing reforms. See chrome-extension://efaid nbmnnnibpcajpcglclefindmkaj/https://oag.ca.gov/system/files/initiatives/pdfs/13-0060%20 %2813-0060%20%28Neighborhood%20and%20School%20Funding%29%29.pdf.

7. Joseph Fishkin, "The Anti-Bottleneck Principle in Employment Discrimination Law," *Washington University Law Review* 91, no. 6 (January 1, 2014), 1429–519.

8. Here, Fishkin builds on Lani Gunier and Gerald Torres, *The Miner's Canary: Enlisting Race, Resisting Power, Transforming Democracy* (Cambridge, MA: Harvard University Press, 2003) whose core observation that structural problems affecting racial minorities often also affect or preview effects on others. Fishkin writes of the famous Griggs case, that "though the pool of those excluded by the diploma requirement was disproportionately black, it is likely that in absolute numbers, of the future job applicants who benefited from the removal of this unnecessary bottleneck, the majority were white." Racial disparity serves as a prompt, but then others benefit.

9. Robin D. G. Kelley, "Why Black Marxism, Why Now?," in *Black Marxism, Revised and Updated Third Edition: The Making of the Black Radical Tradition* (Chapel Hill: University of North Carolina Press, 2021), xv.

10. On how whites benefit most from lenient criminal justice policies, see Marie Gottschalk, *Caught: The Prison State and the Lockdown of American Politics* (Princeton, NJ: Princeton University Press, 2015), 132–34. On how meeting a hiring manager in person doesn't increase Black

job seeker's prospects, see Devah Pager, *Marked: Race, Crime, and Finding Work in an Era of Mass Incarceration* (Chicago: University of Chicago Press, 2007); Devah Pager, Bruce Western, and Naomi Sugie, "Sequencing Disadvantage: Barriers to Employment Facing Young Black and White Men with Criminal Records," *Annals of the American Academy of Political and Social Science* 623 (2009): 195–213. On the possibility that denying employers' access to criminal records may lead to statistical discrimination against Black people (one of the first studies to suggest a categorical discrimination thesis), see Harry J. Holzer, Steven Raphael, and Michael A. Stoll, "How Willing Are Employers to Hire Ex-Offenders?," *Focus* 23, no. 2 (Summer 2004): 40–43. Using a similar methodology as Pager (measuring employer "callbacks" to fictitious applicants), economist Amanda Agan found a dramatic increase in the Black-white gap in employer callbacks after Ban the Box policies went into effect in the cities of New Jersey and New York in 2015. Amanda Agan, "Increasing Employment of People with Records," *Criminology & Public Policy* 16, no. 1 (February 1, 2017): 177–85. Similarly, economists Jennifer Doleac and Benjamin Hansen analyzed individual-level data from the 2004–14 Current Population Survey to predict the probability of employment for young Black and Hispanic men before and after Ban the Box policies took effect, concluding that restricting access to criminal records produced categorical discrimination. Jennifer Doleac and Benjamin Hansen, "Does 'Ban the Box' Help or Hurt Low-Skilled Workers? Statistical Discrimination and Employment Outcomes When Criminal Histories Are Hidden," Working Paper (National Bureau of Economic Research, 2016).

11. Allison Dwyer Emory, "Protective State Policies and the Employment of Fathers with Criminal Records," *Social Problems* (November 2, 2021): 17.

12. Jens Steffek, "The Limits of Proceduralism: Critical Remarks on the Rise of 'Throughput Legitimacy,'" *Public Administration* 97, no. 4 (2019): 784–96.

13. Murakawa, *The First Civil Right*. See also Melissa Burch, "To Refuse the Mark: Racial Criminalization and Twenty Years of Struggle to Ban the Box," *Social Justice: A Journal of Crime, Conflict and World Order* 49, 1–2 (2023): 177–90.

14. For example, in response to a groundswell of criticism of California's policy of relying on the labor of incarcerated people to fight wildfires, and then later denying them employment in all but the lowest-ranking firefighting jobs, a September 2020 Bill (AB 2147) established a "discretionary dismissal" process for those who had participated in conservation fire camps while in prison and created a pathway to employment. While a welcome reform, it excluded people with certain violent and sex-related felony convictions, and did nothing to address the obstacles to employment for the many people with criminal records who have not been incarcerated, or did not get the opportunity to work in conservation camps while incarcerated. Now, with the impression that the issue has been addressed, it will be more difficult to circle back to push for a change that would include a wider group of people.

15. Margaret Colgate Love, Jenny Roberts, and Wayne Logan, *Collateral Consequences of Criminal Convictions: Law, Policy and Practice* (Washington, DC: Thomas West, 2022). The Model Penal Code was introduced in 1962 to offer a comprehensive criminal code that would allow for standardized laws to exist throughout the country. This code is seen as the basis for much of criminal law doctrine and principles such as liability. A model code was thought to be needed because before its inception, the penal codes of the states were all very different and highly inconsistent.

16. The Comite d'action des prisonniers (Prisoners Action Committee) was the successor to Le Groupe d'information sur les prisons. Among those arrested was the famous French

philosopher Michel Foucault, for whom, as scholar Liam Martin describes, exclusion from work was a central theme in theorizing the consequences of criminal branding. Liam Martin, "Reentry within the Carceral: Foucault, Race and Prisoner Reentry," *Critical Criminology* 21, no. 4 (May 28, 2013): 503. See also Michael Hames-García, "Are Prisons Tolerable?," in *Challenging the Punitive Society: Carceral Notebooks Volume 12, 2016,* ed. Bernard Harcourt, Perry Zurn, and Andrew Dilts (New York: Publishing Data Management, 2017), 150–86; Brady Thomas Heiner, "Foucault and the Black Panthers," *City* 11, no. 3 (December 1, 2007): 313–56.

17. Hames-García, "Are Prisons Tolerable?," 170.

18. Los Angeles County's recent Fair Chance Ordinance requires employers to provide applicants with a "good cause" justification for the review. This is an important step forward in that it interrupts knee-jerk checking and forces employers to actually think about why they want to conduct a background check. See https://dcba.lacounty.gov/fairchance/. In December 2023, the California Civil Rights Department filed a first-of-its-kind lawsuit against Ralphs Grocery for violations of the Fair Chance Act. The department accused the grocer of "ignor[ing] the law's requirements, including by screening out otherwise qualified applicants on the basis of criminal histories that do not have any adverse relationship with the duties of the job for which they were applying." See https://calcivilrights.ca.gov/2023/12/21/civil-rights-department-files -first-of-its-kind-lawsuit-against-ralphs-over-alleged-violations-of-californias-fair-chance-act/. For an example of protected class legislation, see https://www.11alive.com/article/news /politics/formerly-incarcerated-persons-protected-class-atlanta/85-ebff5ab3-2506-4bf0-9da8 -cbcb19cfd419. On certificates of rehabilitation that also provide immunity to employers in the event of a negligence claim, see Benjamin Levin, "Criminal Records, Employment Discrimination, and the Limits of Back-End Solutions," *OnLabor,* January 20, 2022.

19. The *Hamrick* case (https://caselaw.findlaw.com/court/ca-court-of-appeal/2129152 .html) leveraged the gap between the 1976 decision in *Paul v. Davis* (finding that an individual record was not considered private) and the 1989 decision *Department of Justice v. Reporters Committee for Freedom of the Press* (finding that a compiled record matched to an individual *is* considered private). It also built on a 1994 Superior Court of Los Angeles County ruling that disallowed the dissemination of compiled court records. See *Westbrook v. Cty. of Los Angeles,* 27 Cal. App. 4th 157, 165 (1994), in which the court observed that there is a difference between obtaining information on a specific individual and obtaining "a compilation of data from a data base maintained by the Municipal Courts of Los Angeles County, including the name, birth date and zip code of every person against whom criminal charges are pending in those courts, together with the case number, date of offense, charges filed, pending court dates, and disposition." Such a compilation, the court found, "is protected from dissemination except as authorized by Penal Code sections 13200 through 13300."

20. The vague and potentially infinite concept of "compelling need or reason" has always represented a weak spot. As we saw in chapter 2, while 1970s' logic said that criminal records were private unless one had a compelling need, before long, many entities seemed to have argued their need was compelling.

21. "SB 809 California Fair Employment and Housing Act: Fair Chance Act: Conviction History," https://leginfo.legislature.ca.gov/faces/billNavClient.xhtml?bill_id=202320 240SB809. A similar Bill, SB 460 proposed to prohibit housing providers from inquiring about an applicant's criminal history, requiring an applicant to disclose their criminal history, or requiring an applicant to authorize the release of their criminal history, and from basing any

adverse action on information contained in an applicant's criminal history unless to comply with federal law. https://leginfo.legislature.ca.gov/faces/billTextClient.xhtml?bill_id =202320240SB460#99INT

22. Ross Chambers, *Room for Maneuver: Reading (the) Oppositional (in) Narrative* (Chicago: University of Chicago Press, 1991).

23. Antonio Gramsci, *Selections from the Prison Notebooks*, ed. Quintin Hoare and Geoffrey Nowell Smith (1971; repr., London: International Publishers Co., 1989).

24. W. Barry Nixon, "Wake Up Call for the Background Screening Industry," *Background Buzz*, August 2020; Checkr editor, "Fair Background Checks Mean a Better Future," July 30, 2021, https://checkr.com/blog/fair-background-checks-mean-better-future.

25. The California Court of Appeal's decision in *All of Us or None v. Hamrick* was met with considerable backlash from the background screening industry. With the support of the Consumer Data Industry Association, the Professional Background Screening Association (PBSA) quickly introduced a bill aiming to overturn or scale back the ruling. Introduced by Senator Steven Bradford of the California State Senate (D-Inglewood), SB 1262 (https://leginfo .legislature.ca.gov/faces/billTextClient.xhtml?bill_id=202120220SB1262) would have reallowed the searching and filtering of results based on a defendant's driver's license number or date of birth, or both. For more information on this effort, see "The California Legislature Must Protect the Public by Allowing Background Checks for Employers, Nonprofits, and Landlords," CDIA, accessed February 26, 2025, https://www.cdiaonline.org/california-court-system/. Governor Gavin Newsom vetoed the bill, writing, "While this bill may provide for a more convenient process for companies conducting commercial background checks, it would also allow any member of the public to easily access individuals' sensitive personal information online." With the help of a firm specializing in voter initiatives, the PBSA tried again in 2023 with the introduction of SB 647. For more information, see Rod Fliegel and Garrick Chan, "Bill Seeks to Alleviate the Slowdown of Criminal Background Checks in California," Littler, March 21, 2022, https://www.littler.com/publication-press/publication/bill-seeks-alleviate-slowdown -criminal-background-checks-california; Roy Mauer, "California's Background Check Limits Are Impeding Hiring," *SHRM* (blog), November 18, 2024, https://www.shrm.org/topics-tools /news/talent-acquisition/california-background-check-limits-hamrick. On the PBSA's fight against SB 460, a similar bill relating to housing, see "The California Legislature Must Protect the Public."

26. Among the Uber cases most sensationalized were the following: a driver charged with sexually assaulting a teenage passenger in Hawaii who was not reported to have a criminal record (Chelsea Davis, "Uber Driver Arrested for Sexually Assaulting Teenage Passenger," *Hawaii News Now*, April 20, 2016 [https://www.hawaiinewsnow.com/story/31769822/uber-driver-arrested -and-charged-with-sex-assault]); a driver in Delaware charged with assaulting a passenger who was not reported to have a criminal record (Josh Shannon, "Police: UD Student Attacked by Rideshare Driver," *Newark Post*, May 18, 2016 [https://www.newarkpostonline.com/news /police-ud-student-attacked-by-rideshare-driver/article_6bdc4b31-1ba4-5cf0-b2cb -2cf1f20d5084.html]); a driver in South Carolina charged with kidnapping and raping a passenger who was not reported to have a criminal record (Jauregui, Andres, "Uber Driver Accused of Kidnapping and Raping Female Passenger," *HuffPost*, August 12, 2015 [https://www.huffpost .com/entry/uber-driver-kidnap-raping-female-passenger_n_55cb354de4b0923c12beac92]);

a driver in Boston convicted of raping a passenger, and whose background check had come up clear despite the fact that he had no license, insurance, or registration, and had been charged with other sexual assaults (Sebastian Murdock, "Uber Driver's Rape Sentencing Is Just the Latest Controversy for Company," *HuffPost*, October 20, 2015 [https://www.huffpost.com/entry/uber-driver-sentenced-rape-female-passenger_n_56264dffe4b0bce347022d25]); and a driver in Maryland who shot at police from his vehicle and was discovered to have a lengthy criminal record (Kevin Lewis, "Police: Uber Driver Arrested after Attempting to Murder Police Officers," *ABC7 News*, May 25, 2016 [https://wjla.com/news/crime/police-uber-driver-arrested-after-attempting-to-murder-police-officers]).

27. https://leginfo.legislature.ca.gov/faces/billTextClient.xhtml?bill_id=201520160AB1289.

28. Lyft confirmed that he had indeed worked for its company at some point. He does not appear to ever have worked for Uber.

29. Prop 22, which added a section on app-based drivers to the California Code (chap. 10.5. sec. 7458), details the criminal background check legislation/regulation around Uber/Lyft drivers.

30. Journalist Mark Ames demonstrates how insecure, stressful, and hostile workplace conditions that became commonplace in the 1980s and 1990s led to a dramatic rise in workplace murder and massacres. Mark Ames, *Going Postal: Rage, Murder, and Rebellion: From Reagan's Workplaces to Clinton's Columbine and Beyond* (Brooklyn: Soft Skull, 2005). Scholar Jeremy Milloy traces changes in the economy, racial dynamics, and labor processes since World War II to show how a phenomenon once understood as having to do with race and class conflict was transformed into a health and safety concern to be managed by workplace violence experts. Jeremy Milloy, *Blood, Sweat, and Fear: Violence at Work in the North American Auto Industry, 1960–80* (Champaign: University of Illinois Press, 2017).

31. Gramsci, *Selections from the Prison Notebooks*; Stuart Hall, Bob Lumley, and Gregor McLennan, "Politics and Ideology: Gramsci," in *On Ideology* (London: Hutchinson, 1977); Stuart Hall, "The Problem of Ideology—Marxism without Guarantees," *Journal of Communication Inquiry* 10, no. 2 (June 1, 1986): 28–44.

32. "Selections from the Prison Notebooks Excerpts," *Dig* (podcast), January 14, 2023, the-digradio.com/gramscinotebooks.

33. Raymond Williams, *The Long Revolution* (1961; repr., Peterborough, Ontario: Broadview Press, 2009); Raymond Williams, *Marxism and Literature* (1977; repr., Oxford: Oxford University Press, 2009).

34. Edmund T. Gordon, "Anthropology and Liberation," in *Decolonizing Anthropology: Moving Further toward an Anthropology of Liberation*, ed. Faye V. Harrison (Arlington, VA: Association of Black Anthropologists, 997), 150–69.

INDEX